Innovation in Marketing

The Chartered Institute of Marketing/Butterworth-Heinemann Marketing Series is the most comprehensive, widely used and important collection of books in marketing and sales currently available worldwide.

As the CIM's official publisher, Butterworth-Heinemann develops, produces and publishes the complete series in association with the CIM. We aim to provide definitive marketing books for students and practitioners that promote excellence in marketing education and practice.

The series titles are written by CIM senior examiners and leading marketing educators for professionals, students and those studying the CIM's Certificate, Advanced Certificate and Postgraduate Diploma courses. Now firmly established, these titles provide practical study support to CIM and other marketing students and to practitioners at all levels.

 The Chartered
Institute of Marketing

Formed in 1911, The Chartered Institute of Marketing is now the largest professional marketing management body in the world with over 60,000 members located worldwide. Its primary objectives are focused on the development of awareness and understanding of marketing throughout UK industry and commerce and in the raising of standards of professionalism in the education, training and practice of this key business discipline.

Books in the series

Forthcoming

Innovation in Marketing

Edited by
Peter Doyle and Susan Bridgewater
Warwick Business School

Published in association with The Chartered Institute of Marketing

OXFORD   BOSTON   JOHANNESBURG   MELBOURNE   NEW DELHI   SINGAPORE

To Sylvia, Ben and Hugo, with love Peter
To Andrew, James and Samuel, with love Sue

Butterworth-Heinemann
Linacre House, Jordan Hill, Oxford OX2 8DP
225 Wildwood Avenue, Woburn, MA 01801-2041
A division of Reed Educational and Professional Publishing Ltd

Ɛ A member of the Reed Elsevier plc group

First published 1998

British Library Cataloguing in Publication Data
A catalogue record for this book is available from the British Library

ISBN 0 7506 4121 5

Composition by Genesis Typesetting, Rochester, Kent
Printed and bound in Great Britain by Biddles Ltd, Guildford and King's Lynn

Contents

Foreword

The Marketing Council has been pleased to support the research on which this book is based. Peter Drucker wrote 'the business has two – and only these two – basic functions: marketing and innovation. Marketing and innovation produce results; all the rest are costs.'

This quotation expresses the central role of marketing and innovation in creating competitive companies and indeed competitive national economies. These fourteen case studies show examples of best practice in achieving innovation in Britain. They provide insights into world class marketing and innovation performance.

As the researchers show, neither marketing nor innovation is a simple process. It depends upon leadership from top management, the creation of the right culture and the focus on markets, which offer the potential to generate growth and profits. The case studies also emphasize the importance of marketing. Successful innovation is about more successfully meeting the needs of customers. It is impossible to be continually innovative without creating a market-led orientation in the business.

The authors demonstrate that marketing is more than just a functional job – it is getting the entire business focused on creating and satisfying customers. Successful marketing depends upon building effective cross-functional teams, which work as a unit in creating value for customers. Innovation, too, is about forging partnerships with other organizations, which co-operate in building effective innovation processes.

John Stubbs
The Marketing Council

Introduction

The purpose of this book is to help readers understand how successful market-led innovation is achieved. The research was substantially funded by a generous grant from The Marketing Council. Most of the cases have been written by members of the Faculty of the Warwick Business School. They would like to acknowledge the wholehearted support of the companies whose work is described in these fourteen case studies.

The case studies can be read as illustrations of successful market-led innovation. But they have also been written as case studies suitable for teaching on courses on marketing or innovation run by business schools and other professional bodies. Teachers familiar with the case study method will find these cases excellent vehicles for classroom discussion. They allow students to explore the innovation process, obstacles to innovation, and the role of marketing in building successful new products and services.

The case studies show that innovation is the result of a complex set of processes. As the model shows, it depends upon the organization's marketing ability, its strategy, the resources, networks and processes it builds, together with the culture and leadership in the firm.

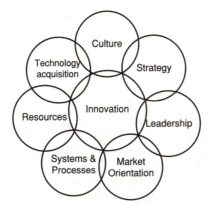

Innovation performance

All the case studies focus on how the companies sought to achieve innovation performance. The way in which this was achieved relates to the competitive situation of the firm, its size and stage of development. For example, First Direct, SBCH Dr. Best Flex and Schweppes' Oasis are classic cases of innovation within large organizations in mature industry sectors. Virgin Atlantic and Virgin Direct centre upon creation of small, flexible units within a larger organization to extend a successful brand into a new market. By contrast, Psion and LINX Printing Technologies are based on the introduction of new-to-market, high-technology products.

Strategy

At the heart of innovation lies a strategy, which identifies clearly defined goals or target markets. Clear statements of innovative strategy can be seen in all of the cases. For example, Virgin's aim to 'find the big, bad wolf then slay it' and Schweppes' aim to be 'the fastest growing non-cola soft drinks company in Europe'.

Market orientation

In all of these cases, the strategy is based on market orientation and offering added value to customers. This involves identification of the benefits and analysis of the ways in which the firm can better serve customers' needs and wants. First Direct, Virgin Direct and Virgin Atlantic are cases in which innovation means going back to the basic benefit sought and redesigning the marketing strategy and mix through which this is provided. In the cases of Land Rover Discovery, First Direct, Schweppes' Oasis and Orange, sophisticated market research reveals weaknesses in competitive offerings. For LINX, Rank Xerox and Psion market focus leads to development of new products and technologies.

Leadership

Top management support of 'best practice' in the innovation process is of vital importance. Leadership may be based on a charismatic or visionary leader, as in the cases of Psion, LINX, Virgin and BAA, or a product or market champion as in the cases of British Steel and Schweppes' Oasis. Top management are also key to creation and support of values which permeate the organization through the more formal benchmarking and mission statements seen in SBCH, Schweppes and Rank Xerox. The absence of good leadership may mean that good marketing is insufficient to bring about innovation, as can be seen in the Le BonBon sweets case.

Culture

An innovative organizational culture is one in which creativity and entrepreneurial spirit can be achieved and fostered. At its core are organizational attitudes and basic beliefs regarding the role of innovation and improvements to business competitiveness. Such attitudes may underpin the brand values, as in the case of Virgin.

They may allow a risk-taking approach to business, as in the cases of SBCH, Rank Xerox or First Direct. An innovative culture may also result in the creation of organizational structures, which promote innovation. These include the creation of cross-functional teams, as in the case of First Direct, or flat structures, which allow the firm to remain close to the customer as in the LINX and NIS Invotec cases.

People

At the core of an innovative organizational culture is respect for the contribution which people make. Cross-functional teams, such as those used in First Direct and Land Rover Discovery, are designed to build on complementary capabilities. Cultural values of openness and trust allow the value of people as a resource to be harnessed by the organization. For example, in Virgin Direct, there is emphasis on what 'we' can do, whilst Schweppes' Oasis and First Direct place value on the unique contribution of the individuals within the organization. Rank Xerox and BAA emphasize the importance of training to bring out these contributions.

Resources

Innovation has additional resource implications. Investment may be required in Research and Development to support technological advances such as those of Rank Xerox, Psion and LINX, or in market research to identify new opportunities, as in the cases of Schweppes and Land Rover. Investments may be long-term in nature. For example, the launch of Orange mobile phones required an ongoing process of investment in infrastructure. In the case of First Direct, success has required profits to be ploughed back into growth.

Technology strategy and acquisition

Investment in technology is central to the success of some innovations. Technological advances may be developed in house, as with the computer systems for Virgin Direct, or else technology may be acquired, as in the NIS Invotec case. As can be seen in the cases of Rank Xerox and Psion, innovation is not based on technology alone, but technology can play a role in developing applications of value to customers.

Systems and processes

Technological advances may be valuable not only in developing innovative end products and services, but in improving the process of innovation within the organization. Thus, NIS Invotec uses CAD/CAM to increase the speed to market, whilst both First Direct and Virgin Direct have developed database services which improve customer service.

Chapter 1

Marketing and innovation

Peter Doyle

In most businesses innovation is regarded as the key to corporate success. In today's rapidly changing environment a company cannot long maintain its market share or profits unless it is innovative. If a company's products or services are not continually improved, competitive pressures invariably lead to falling prices, declining margins and the commoditization of its offer. Innovation is the path to achieving growth in sales and profitability.

Innovation can mean new products (e.g. the Psion case study, Chapter 12), but it can also mean new markets (e.g. British Steel, Chapter 7), new marketing channels (e.g. First Direct, Chapter 10), new processes (e.g. Rank Xerox, Chapter 6) or new marketing concepts (e.g. Cadbury Schweppes, Chapter 2). Innovation can mean major breakthroughs or it can mean a stream of incremental changes. Research shows that a strong market focus and an effective marketing department are important correlates of powerful innovation performance. But marketing does not take place in a vacuum. If the organization lacks leadership and has ineffective core processes and capabilities, good marketing will be insufficient (for example see the Le BonBon case, Chapter 13). Further, if marketing personnel do not interface effectively with other functions in operating across the firm's core processes, marketing will not add value.

In this introductory chapter we review the essential determinants of business success today, the meaning of innovation and the types of innovation strategies that appear to work most effectively.

Success – today's strategic requirements

The essence of business in a competitive world is developing a strategy and organization that can meet customer needs more effectively than competitors. Companies that can create customer preference grow and prosper; those that can not simply wither away. But customer needs are not static, they change with tastes, fashion, competitive offers and new technological possibilities. What is regarded as a good product by customers today will not be so regarded tomorrow. In computers, electronics, pharmaceuticals, cars – indeed in virtually all industries – products and services are rapidly rendered obsolete by innovative solutions. Figure 1.1 shows the essential Darwinian nature of business. Businesses survive when they maintain a continuous fit to the changing market environment.

Figure 1.1 The basic challenge

Successful business starts with an appreciation of the environment – what are the emerging needs of customers and what are the emerging possibilities for developing effective solutions to these needs?

Today's key challenges

Many of the environmental challenges facing today's businesses can be grouped under three dimensions.

Collapse of boundaries

The boundaries which used to create barriers to new entrants and to limit competition in individual markets are eroding. First, globalization has meant buyers and competitors no longer recognize geographic country limits. Large customers now search professionally for suppliers from around the globe. Advances in information technology, fewer trade restrictions and lower transportation costs mean that more and more companies now face global competition. Second, the boundaries between industries are crumbling. For example, high street banks no longer face competition just from one another, but now face competitors in supermarkets, IT businesses like Microsoft, and players from quite different sectors diversifying into financial services. Third, the technological separation of industries is disappearing. For example, cars, once considered to be a mechanical engineering sector, now contain more and more electronics. In fact all industries are now becoming hi-tech, if not in their products, then certainly in their delivery systems. For example, the fastest growing company on the Internet is Amazon.com – a bookshop.

Rising customer expectations

Increasing competition and global over-supply in many industries has resulted in consumers expecting more. Customers now expect greater value from suppliers in terms of lower prices and higher quality. Customers too now want solutions tailored to their individual needs, not imperfectly fitting mass-market answers. Initially this has resulted in an expansion of variety – manufacturers offer more and more variants of a product, each tailored to specific micro segments of the market. But such variety leads to rising working capital requirements and pressures on cash flow. As a result, more and more manufacturers are switching to make-to-order systems whereby fast manu-facturing and delivery techniques are employed to produce rapid response to customer orders.

Speed of change

These changes in customer expectations, technologies and management practices have led to an acceleration in the speed of change across all industries. More and more markets are becoming like the fashion industry, with customers expecting and companies delivering, a continual series of new models. Unless a new car, toothpaste, computer or machine tool is perceived to be 'new' and 'the latest thing' customers lose interest. Continual, incremental innovation has become essential to preserve market share and profit margins. Change affects not only the products but also the distribution channels and communications media companies employ. IT and electronic marketing are creating opportun-ities for new entrants to transform distribution channels and communications, finding new, cheaper and more effective means of delivering value to customers.

The success criteria

The criteria for maintaining success in today's rapidly changing global environment can be summarized under five headings.

Strategy must fit the environment

Companies like Cadbury Schweppes, Virgin, Psion and First Direct succeed because they give today's customers what they want. They have the brands and distribution channels which offer up-to-date solutions for customers. But in a rapidly changing environment this match between the firm's offer and the customer's need is only a temporary one. Without continued innovation, the business will soon drift into decline and obsolescence. This leads to the next principle.

Successful strategies erode

History suggests that nothing fails like success. Today's market leaders are generally tomorrow's basket cases. Once, Britain's Alfred Herbert was the world's largest machine-tool company – now it has disappeared. Little more than a decade ago IBM had 80 per cent of the computer market – today it has 8 per cent. Almost invariably, new competitors, innovative technology, new distribution channels or changes in customer tastes soon undermine market dominance. Hanging on to market leadership is an immensely difficult business, requiring enormous investment, high rates of innovation and great flexibility on the part of managers.

Effectiveness is more important than efficiency

Peter Drucker made the famous distinction between efficiency – doing things right – and effectiveness – doing the right things. It is a crucial distinction. Efficiency is essentially about cost reduction; effectiveness is about innovation. Faced with a changing environment, where competitors are developing innovative new products or services, managers cannot build viable strategies based upon lowering costs. Innovations first offer customers superior benefits, but in the longer run they also offer lower costs too. Innovation must be matched with innovation if the firm is to hold onto its markets.

Speed and decisiveness

Today's pace of change puts a greater premium on firms moving rapidly. Companies that are fast innovators normally find it easier to establish competitive advantage than those that come later to market. Often too they get premium prices, which mean a faster pay back on their earlier investments. Companies that are slow at developing new products incur greater development costs and often have to launch at discounted prices to catch up in the battle for market share.

Organization is more vital than strategy

In a world of rapid change any strategy can only be temporarily successful. Continued success depends upon adapting strategy to develop new products, new channels and new markets. The real task then is to build an organization and a culture, which is change – or innovation – orientated. That is, a business where management create the systems, structures and attitudes which stimulate people to be customer-focused and creative in continually developing new solutions to customer needs. Such businesses recognize that success is about continued learning and permanent change.

Symptoms and causes of decline

Companies go into decline when they suffer inertia – when their strategies and organizations no longer fit the requirements of the new market conditions. In this situation the products and services are no longer effectively meeting the wants of customers. When a crisis arises management need to distinguish between the symptoms and causes of failure (Figure 1.2).

The symptoms, which normally trigger boardroom alarm, are declining profitability. The common reaction is to focus on this symptom and to try to reverse the decline by cutting costs and investment. The problem is seen to be a financial one and the solution is seen to be rationalization. Generally, it is quite easy to produce an improvement in profits and at least temporarily

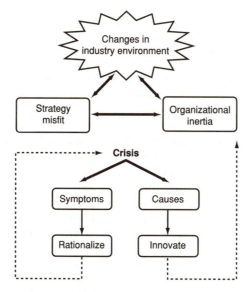

Figure 1.2 Symptoms and causes of failure

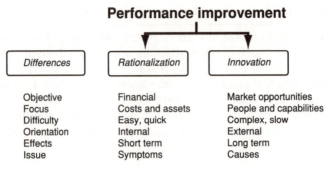

Figure 1.3 Alternative strategies for performance improvement

demonstrate the appearance of a 'turnaround'. All that is required are hard decisions to cut costs, discretionary expenditures and to dispose of saleable assets.

However, this internal focus never provides a lasting solution because it deals with the symptoms rather than the causes of the problem. The decline in performance is rarely caused by a lack of cost control but rather by a failure at innovation. (Figure 1.3). Solving the fundamental problem requires developing new products and services which improves the firm's competitiveness in the market. It requires a longer term, more complex change programme of transforming the firm's capabilities and competitiveness. It is about developing offers which customers will prefer to those of the company's competitors.

The innovation process

People often confuse invention and innovation. Invention is about new products but innovation is about new solutions, which offer value to customers. An innovation may, or may not, involve new technology. Its central characteristic is that it enables customer's needs to be met more effectively. Opportunities for innovation are created by environmental change. Over time people develop new wants and new knowledge enables new solutions to be developed. Again, Peter Drucker summarized this neatly when he defined innovation as 'exploiting change as an opportunity'.

Innovation is most commonly thought of as a new product. But it is not the only, or probably the most common, form of innovation. New channels of distribution such as First Direct telephone banking or the Amazon.com Internet bookstore, can revolutionize markets. New marketing concepts such as Cadbury Schweppes' Oasis drink or Diet Coke can also generate huge markets. New markets or new market segments can also provide a great boost for growth. Xerox is finding big growth opportunities in China; British Steel found growth opportunities in the construction segment, which balanced its maturing engineering market. Finally, new processes such as Pilkington's float glass process can create new opportunities by enabling firms to offer cheaper or higher quality products.

Criteria for successful innovation

Not all innovations are successful. In fact, most surveys suggest the failure rate of new products and ideas is overwhelming. To be successful an innovation needs to meet the test of four challenging criteria.

It must offer customer value

A new product might have breathtaking technology but unless customers see it as offering them superior benefits they will not buy it. For example, an atomic wristwatch with an accuracy of within one second in a hundred years might be a great technical feat, but it is questionable whether many customers would see much value in the breakthrough. They would ask themselves – how would it help me? What could I do better with such a product? It is important for innovators to undertake consumer research very early in the development process to identify whether there is a potential competitive advantage and market segment for the product.

It must be perceived as unique

A product might have unique technology but unless the benefits appear to be unique, it is unlikely to have much appeal to customers. Scientists impressed by the originality of their technology will often over-estimate the potential of their invention. For customers it is the uniqueness of the results not the uniqueness of the technology that counts.

It must be marketable

To be of value to the firm, the innovation must find enough customers willing to pay prices sufficient to cover costs and to generate an economic surplus. Concorde, the world's first and still the only supersonic passenger aircraft, was again a marvellous engineering accomplishment. Unfortunately the economics never added up. The plane was too small and the operating costs were too high to make it attractive to airlines. They could see no way of making a fleet of Concordes into a profitable venture.

It must be sustainable

An innovation, which can be easily and quickly copied, will not add much value to the company. It is important for the innovator to think about creating barriers to new entrants. Sometimes patents can provide such a barrier. Decisiveness in capturing market share is also important to shut out the market to competition. In many markets building a brand to enhance the product's uniqueness is the best approach. Competitors can usually make a drink taste like Coca Cola or make a cigarette that is similar to Marlboro. But what is virtually impossible to emulate is the Coca Cola or Marlboro brand values, and it is these which over the longer run drive customer preference.

Innovation strategies

Looking at how companies try to innovate, it is possible to identify four types of strategy: marketing department, acquisition, invention and market-led. Only the last appears to offer a successful path to sustainable growth and continued innovation.

Marketing department-led innovation

In successful companies marketing is seen as a total approach to business. Everyone's job, whether they are in the purchasing department, engineering, R&D, human resources or the marketing department, is to focus on developing activities which satisfy customers. A customer focus is the orientation which co-ordinates all the functions of the firm. However, in some companies marketing has wrongly become associated solely with the work of the marketing department.

Where marketing departments become too powerful they sometimes usurp the innovation role. Innovation becomes the task of the marketing department. This rarely works well because the marketing director does not control many of the activities crucial to innovation. Innovation then focuses on those activities which fall within the marketing department's authority – normally advertising, promotions and line extensions.

In these circumstances innovation is seen to be about developing a new advertising campaign or new promotional technique. Another favourite marketing department approach is segmenting the market, developing differentially priced brands and seeking to trade-up customers. For example, United Distillers added new line extensions to their original Johnny Walker Red Label Scotch whisky – Black, Blue, Gold, etc. – at ever increasing prices. The idea being that customers would move-up over time to more prestigious, higher margin brands.

The problem with marketing department-led innovation strategy is that it fails to harness the skills and creativity of the whole organization. As a result the innovations tend to be trivial and not offering genuine value to customers. They are often gimmicks, highly vulnerable to real value creation by more effective competitors.

Acquisition-led innovation

British companies have often sought to find growth and innovation by acquisition. Rather than painstakingly building an organizational capability to develop innovation inside, they buy companies with interesting new products and services. This has apparent advantages. First, it is much faster. Shifting a production-oriented culture to an innovative, market-led one is a long-term complex change process. By contrast an acquisition can be made very quickly. Acquisitions do not appear to require a cultural transformation or the development of hard-won capabilities.

Unfortunately, research convincingly shows that acquisitions rarely provide the answer for companies lacking innovation skills. Up to four out of every five acquisitions fail to generate shareholder value for the acquiring company. One reason is that the acquirer's and the acquiree's culture do not mesh. The acquirer's management lacks the background and orientation to get the best out of creative people and the enthusiasm for innovation drains away in the new hostile environment. Genuine sustained growth and innovation are based upon the capabilities and attitudes of people within the organization. Such capabilities are not quickly built, rather they are the result of generations of investment and inculcation. There are no short cuts to organizational renewal.

Invention-led strategies

Some companies, especially science-based ones, seek genuine inventions. These are products which are technically superior to those currently on the market. If successful these inventions may offer genuine value to customers and be highly desirable. A problem with inventions however, is that the value may not be sustainable.

Inventions can apply to services as well as products. For example, Direct Line revolutionized the car insurance market in the UK in the early 1990s. Before Direct Line, car insurance was sold by thousands of brokers who acted as intermediaries between the insurance company and the customer. Direct Line used new information technology, advertising and direct telephone response to cut out the brokers. The company was able to offer much lower insurance rates and provide faster and more effective service to customers. Direct Line quickly became market leader.

Unfortunately, like many products and service inventions, while it offered genuinely superior value to customers, it proved to be a non-sustainable invention. It had two problems. First, Direct Line's offer appealed to price-sensitive customers attracted by the discounts the company offered. Price-sensitive customers tend not to be loyal and to switch when other companies offer even lower prices. Second, the Direct Line invention was easy to copy. Competitors were forced to quickly emulate the telephone sales approach pioneered by Direct Line. Within two years, every insurance company was offering a service comparable to Direct Line.

Market-led innovation

The fourth and most effective way to build sustainable innovation is through a comprehensive market orientation. This focuses on building value-generating relationships with customers, system partners and staff within the organization. There are three pillars to the market-led approach to innovation.

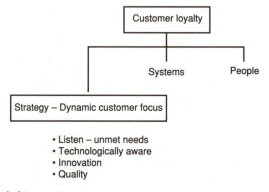

Figure 1.4 Market-led innovation: strategy

Strategy – a dynamic customer focus

Innovation is about meeting customer needs more effectively than competitors. Strategy therefore has to be geared to customers. But since customer's needs change and new opportunities appear which enable needs to be more effectively met, this means strategy has to be dynamic, recognizing that no solution that the company has will last. The first key aspect of a market-led strategy is listening to customers. It is important to research customers, to understand their problems and objectives, and how they operate. Customers want suppliers to provide solutions not products. To do this, companies need to have expert knowledge of the customer's activities.

Second, the company needs an orientation to pursue innovative solutions. Its people should be geared to look for new and better ways to solve the customer's problems and generate better results for them. Change rather than stability should be the accepted norm.

Third, market-led organizations have the highest quality aspirations. They want to satisfy customers 100 per cent of the time, not 80 or even 90 per cent of the time. They understand that ultimately the organization's reputation is built on its commitment to quality. Finally, market-led businesses take a long-term prospective. They expect their organizations to be around for an indefinite future and do not expect all investments to have a quick pay-off.

Systems – an effective organization

Without the systems to deliver high quality products and services, a market orientation is nothing more than an aspiration. Marketing effectiveness depends upon means as much as goals. The company needs to build up the core processes – innovation, operations and customer service and support, which enable the firm to provide fast, high quality solutions for the customer's emerging problems.

This requires the organization to build effective internal and external networks or partnerships. The internal networks are the partnerships between the functional specialists in the organization. Today effectiveness is increasingly about teams – different specialists working together as partners to solve customer problems. External networks are the alliances the organization makes with other businesses to build its core processes. Today no firm can build up sufficient expertise in the multiple technologies and diverse markets in which it operates. Increasingly they look for partners who will provide specialist inputs in IT, manufacturing or sales skills. The organization's ability to put together this constellation of internal and external networks determines the effectiveness of its supply chain or value delivery system.

Figure 1.5 Market-led innovation: systems

Finally, management has to control the brand interface. Increasingly competition is not between individual firms but between networks of partnered organizations. Virgin, Cadbury Schweppes and Marks and Spencer all depend upon complex networks of partnering suppliers and distributors. Normally, however, it is one company in the network that controls the brand. It is the brand that customers buy and it is the company whose name is on the brand, which has the power in the network and usually appropriates the majority of the value created. If a company does not have a brand recognizable to end-users it is in a vulnerable situation.

People – commitment and capabilities

Ultimately the effectiveness of the organisation in developing its systems and implementing its strategy depends upon the commitment and skills of its staff (Figure 1.6). Creating these capabilities depends first upon the ability of the organization's leaders to communicate an inspiring vision of innovation and commitment to customers. It also puts a premium on selecting staff who will share this vision and be committed to implementing it. Training and development to build the skills required must also become top priority. Management then have to empower staff to use their skills and commitment to delivering results.

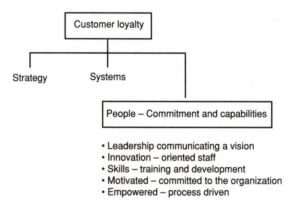

Figure 1.6 Market-led innovation: people

The role of marketing

In the last thirty years marketing has become more and more important in management. In a large part this is due to the increasingly competitive nature of business. Until the late 1950s, the world was characterized by excess demand. People had to queue or wait to buy new cars, telephones and products of all kinds. Quality and service standards were often appallingly low. In normal periods, companies with modern manufacturing facilities had little trouble selling their products. But during the 1960s this began to change; countries had recovered from the ravages of World War II and the South East Asian manufacturing miracle began to take up speed. Gradually manufacturing capacity began to exceed normal demand. Excess capacity began to characterize more and more industries – cars, steel, wine, electronics and many others.

In this new era, marketing rather than manufacturing became the basis for competitive advantage. The issue became how to create consumer preference rather than having the ability to produce products and services. Finding manufacturing capacity was much easier than creating unique brands.

As the discipline of marketing evolved, its meaning changed (Figure 1.7). During the early period, the 1950s and '60s, marketing was synonymous with selling. The task of marketing was seen as getting customers to buy what the company produced. The key techniques were viewed as advertising and sales promotion. In the late 1960s and early '70s, however, there was a fundamental change. Marketing was transformed from a concept based on selling to one based on understanding the needs of customers. The new idea of marketing was employing market research to understand customer wants and expectations and then designing and delivering products and services that matched these wants. Rather than sell what the company produced, a more effective way to compete was seen as having the company offer what the customer wanted. In an era of growing competition for customer preference, this was a very rational change.

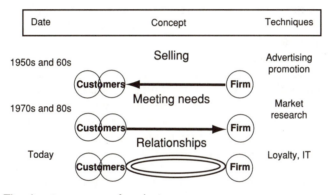

Figure 1.7 The changing concept of marketing

During the 1990s the concept of marketing changed for a third time. Implicitly or explicitly both the two earlier ideas of marketing focused on winning new customers. But today's concept of marketing emphasizes keeping existing customers. Various studies by researchers and consultants showed convincingly that, for most firms, profit and growth depended upon the company's ability to create long-term loyalty among its customers. If it could keep its existing customers loyal, then it would be easier to grow and it would have a lower cost base. In general, the longer a customer stays with a company, the more the customer spends, the less price-sensitive he becomes and the easier he is to service. By contrast, new customers are costly to recruit and spend less than established customers. The new emphasis in marketing became measuring customer satisfaction, developing loyalty programmes and forging close links with customers to service them better.

In defining marketing it is important to distinguish two different ideas. Marketing is first a total business philosophy, a primary focus for everyone in the organization. Second, marketing is a discrete set of activities, which are often the function of the marketing department. Such specialist activities often include market research and developing advertising and promotions. It is this first idea of marketing which is the most important one in creating a competitive and innovative business. The marketing philosophy says that the successful organization depends upon its ability to create long-term relationships with customers, which satisfy their needs more effectively than competitors.

Forty or more years ago companies were not market-led; the marketing philosophy did not permeate the business. They were generally product-led. The central focus of the firm was on the problems of making products, not on understanding customers. During the 1950s and '60s, increasing competition led to more firms hiring marketing experts and with this came the growth of the marketing department. The function of these marketing departments, however, was generally selling and promotion. They had little influence on the strategy of the firm, their job was seen as promoting what the firm did. Firms had a marketing function but not a marketing philosophy.

It was another decade before top companies accepted that being market-led was the central dimension of the entire business. Today few companies are unconvinced that marketing and innovation are the key requirements for success. Paradoxically, while the marketing philosophy is accepted as the core of the business, marketing departments are waning in many firms. Many organizations are seeking to become more market oriented without growing their marketing departments. This paradox is not difficult to explain.

Companies increasingly appreciate that marketing is primarily not a function within the business, but rather the task of everyone in the organization. A firm's competitiveness depends upon the effectiveness with which it organizes its three core value-generating processes – innovation, operations and customer service and support (Figure 1.8). To work effectively each of these processes needs a cross-disciplinary approach. None are the

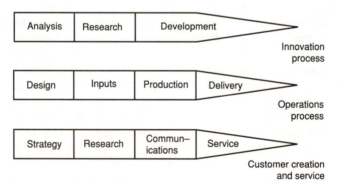

Figure 1.8 The firm's core processes

task of a single department. Innovation, operations and satisfying customers depend upon the commitment of everyone in the firm.

Not only is effective co-operation and teamwork required within the firm, but as we noted above, these processes increasingly depend upon partnerships with other firms – the external network partners (Figure 1.9). Today marketing and innovation are too complex and important to be regarded as the task of only one department. The shrinking of marketing departments is paradoxically often associated with the growing primacy given to marketing and innovation. By clarifying that the tasks are not the function of the marketing department, they raise the status of innovation and marketing within the business.

Figure 1.9 The network organization

We can summarize the key tasks of management in today's organization as three. The first task of management is to identify opportunities created by change. The long-term survival of the firm depends upon adapting to a changing environment. Environmental change creates both threats and opportunities. The threat is that the failure to anticipate and adapt will render obsolete the firm's market offer and destroy shareholder value. The opportunities are created when management see how these changes are creating the space for new products, services and distribution channels which will enable it to capture new markets and build new sources of wealth.

The second task of management is to build the networks or delivery processes, which can realize these opportunities. This means creating the project teams within the firm and the partnerships with other organizations to deliver the innovations, efficient products and services, and customer service and support.

The third task of management is to build the brands, which make competitive emulation difficult and form an enduring focus for customer loyalty. In the long run these brands depend on the ability of management to create organizations which are focused on understanding customers and developing the new solutions they will expect in the future.

Chapter 2

Cadbury Schweppes: the launch of 'Oasis' into the adult soft drinks market

Susan Bridgewater

Background

Soft drinks consumption in the UK is increasing steadily. Total sales of soft drinks increased by 10.3 per cent in 1995 to £6.4 billion and by 5 per cent in 1996 to £6.75 billion. A growing proportion of this growing soft drinks market is comprised of fruit juices and health drinks (see Figure 2.1). One of the factors contributing to the growth in this sector is the development of the adult soft drinks market, which cuts across fruit juices, juice drinks and health drinks. Changing eating habits have been the major driving force behind the growth of the adult soft drinks market, as many adults are trying to reduce their consumption of tea and coffee and alcohol. Consequently, a new and fast growing segment of the adult soft drinks market is for non-alcoholic adult, or 'New Age' drinks. These are aimed at 20 to 35 year olds who 'don't want alcohol, but consider themselves too old for traditional pop' (Matthews, 1995). 'New Age' drinks include iced tea and coffee, herbal drinks, flavoured waters and sparkling juices.

> 'While many of these additive-free products are marketed as 'healthy' it is also price – around $1 plus for a single serving – that sets them apart from standard pop.'
>
> Matthews, 1995

By 1995, this segment of the US drinks market had grown to $6 billion (£3.7 billion). Two of the leading brands, Snapple, an adult fruit juice, owned by Quaker Oats, and Coca Cola's Fruitopia, had launched into the UK targeted at the parallel segment of the UK market. They joined a range of waters and sparkling fruit juices already aimed at this growing adult market:

> 'since the beginning of this decade, the market has witnessed an upsurge in products targeted specifically at the adult market. Adult consumers can now choose from a range of fruit juices, still and sparkling juice drinks, flavoured waters, herbal drinks, carbonates, sports and energy drinks and iced teas, suitable for many occasions, with or without a meal. A high proportion of these drinks tend to be marketed on a premium platform. They are more likely to include natural ingredients, containing less sugar, with more subtle and sophisticated flavours.'
>
> Matthews, 1995

The launch of Schweppes 'Oasis', a still fruit juice and water drink, in June 1995, took the market by storm. This adult still drink was researched and specifically targeted at the tastes of UK customers. Within eighteen months of its launch it had gained 70 per cent of the market. Such was its success that Fruitopia, its major competitor, is in the process of withdrawing from the UK. This case study looks at the reasons for the success of this new product.

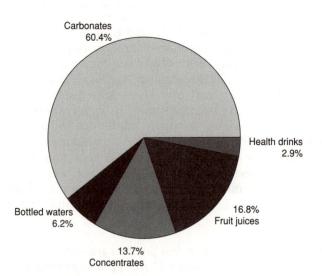

Figure 2.1 The adult soft drinks market. Source: Key Note Report, Fruit Juices and Health Drinks, January 1997

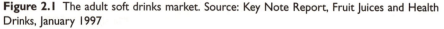

The idea

The marketing manager responsible for the launch of Oasis, Andrew Mann, summed up the generation of the idea for Oasis as follows:

> 'There were three main sources of information which created the idea for Oasis. Firstly, we were monitoring international trends. It was clear that 'New Age' drinks was a growing segment in the US market which might possibly succeed in the UK. Secondly, we were looking at demographic trends in the UK. There is an ageing population. Also, the adults of today have grown up with a soft drinks culture. We felt that they might continue to drink soft drinks as adults. However, their tastes are for something less sweet and fizzy. Finally, we had seen the growth in the premium area of other segments in the UK, for example premium crisps, like Doritos and Phileas Fogg, and premium ice creams such as Haagen Daaz. These trends made us believe that there was an opportunity in the adult, premium drinks market.'

The soft drinks culture identified by Andrew Mann was bringing significant changes to the soft drinks market in 1995. No longer were adults necessarily switching to tea and coffee drinking. Kevin White, commercial director of Coca Cola Schweppes Beverages, cites statistics that:

> 'as recently as 20 years ago, tea sales outstripped soft drinks by 500 per cent . . .'
>
> Matthews, 1995

Indeed, soft drinks consumption by adults had increased from a per capita figure of 800 ready-to-drink litres (RTDL) per annum in 1981 to 2300 RTDL in 1996. This is projected to increase to 5900 by 2011 (see Figure 2.2).

The percentage of soft drinks consumed by adults has also increased from 50 per cent to 60 per cent in the period from 1987 to 1995 (see Figure 2.3). Thirty per cent of all soft drinks are consumed by adults in the 20 to 35 age group (NDM, 1993/4).

In the United States, New Age beverages represent 4 per cent of the total soft drinks market. The current UK soft drinks market is 9 billion litres in volume. If adult juice drinks reached this proportion of the total market, the segment would be 360 million litres. The size of the target market must be set in context with the sales by volume of the leading carbonated soft drinks in the UK. Brands such as Lucozade and Lilt have sales of around 100 million litres, while Coca Cola is a massive 1.4 billion litres by volume.

The total UK soft drinks market is split 50:50 sparkling to still. However, out-of-home, impulse purchase of drinks is still split 80:20 in favour of sparkling products (NDM, 1993/4).

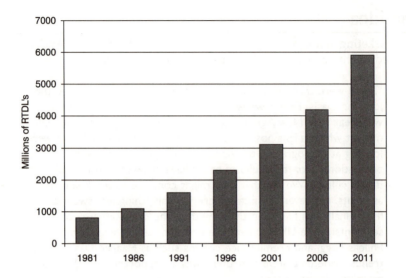

Figure 2.2 Soft drinks consumption by the 25+ age group. Source: NDM/CCSB estimates

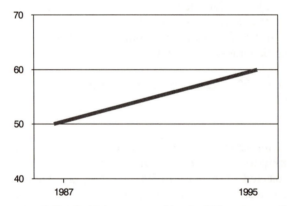

Figure 2.3 Percentage of all soft drinks consumed by the 21+ age group. Source: NDM

One reason for Andrew Mann's belief in the potential of still drinks is that adults' tastes alter as they get older. They tend to prefer something more natural and less sweet:

> 'No one's saying that Coke or Pepsi drinking will die out ... But it is undoubtedly true that we are seeing a certain amount of cola fatigue among the 20–35 age group ... I believe that 1995 could be a decisive year in adult drinks marketing.'
>
> Matthews, 1995

The non-alcoholic adult drinks segment of the UK market differs from its US equivalent in that it contains few iced tea or coffee products. Marketing manager Joy Lester, now responsible for this part of Schweppes' portfolio, explained:

> 'Adult drinks are split into waters, mixers and what we call still juice drinks. This differs somewhat from 'New Age' drinks in the USA, which also includes herbal drinks. There are some of these products in the UK, such as our own Shezan, and some iced teas. However, the major remaining part of the adult drinks market in the UK is juice drinks.'

Adult soft drinks consumers wanted to be seen drinking a product with more 'street cred' as they reached their twenties. The stereotypical image of the target consumer was that of someone in the 21–35 age group, high disposable income, probably a city boy or girl in their second job.

Concept testing

Having identified a new product idea, the next stage for Schweppes was to test the concept. Qualitative market research was undertaken both within and outside of London. This took the form of approaching likely prospects in the street and asking them if they would be prepared to participate in a focus group in a nearby church hall.

The qualitative research phase looked at two existing products in the adult still juice drinks market to see what consumers thought of them. Snapple, owned by Quaker Oats, is a US juice drink launched into the UK in June 1994. Fruitopia, owned by Coca Cola Beverages, entered the UK market shortly afterwards. Both are US products transferred with relatively little modification into the UK. Fruitopia's flavour range included Passion Fruit Lemon Affinity, Banana Vanilla Rapture and Citrus Bliss. The positioning of these products was summarized by Andrew Mann as follows:

> 'Snapple had a US 'hokey' homespun image. Fruitopia, on the other, has a 'hippie' New Age feel. UK respondents felt that Snapple was 'boring' whilst the Fruitopia flavours were too weird. The advertising was also considered bizarre and psychedelic.'

Consumers' reservations about the two competitive brands suggested a gap in the market for a product which lay between these two extremes (see Figure 2.4).

The areas covered by the focus groups were the product, packaging and the advertising concept. It was decided to simplify the product range by focusing on three flavours at launch. The three main areas of soft drinks sales in the UK

Psychedelic	**Gap in the market for a drink**	Homespun
weird flavours	**which is sophisticated with**	traditional flavours
e.g.: Fruitopia	**interesting but not wierd flavours**	e.g. Snapple

← ─────────────────────────────────────── →

Figure 2.4 Consumer perceptions of adult still juice drinks market

market are lemon drinks, orange drinks and red fruit drinks. However, recent years have also seen:

> 'An explosion in the flavours available. Consumer tastes are changing, becoming more sophisticated and adventurous, reflecting the increased adult interest in the market. While tropical flavours such as mango, passion fruit and guava juice are gaining popularity, manufacturers are increasingly introducing new tastes, using fruits which have not traditionally been combined together.'
>
> Key Note Report, 1997

Accordingly, the main product offer comprised Oasis product for consumers with each of the three main taste preferences, but added a twist to the flavours: Classic lemon, Citrus punch (a mix of orange, tangerine and lemon flavours) and Summer fruits (a mix of apple, redcurrant, strawberry and cherry). The full product range comprised ten flavours.

After the focus group, respondents were given product samples for an in-house trial. They were asked to comment on the colour, flavour and sweetness of the Oasis product, as well as their propensity to buy the product before and after trial. The trial results were established by a telephone follow-up of all respondents.

A significant difference between the UK and US markets was also found in the area of packaging. Whilst a 500 ml format was standard in the USA and might be appropriate in hot weather, this confused UK customers, who were not sure whether it should be one or two servings. Therefore it was decided that Oasis should be packaged in 375 ml bottles. This was the correct amount for a single serving. It had the additional benefit of being offered at a more attractive price when sold alongside the rival brands.

The results of the qualitative research were tested by a quantitative research phase carried out by the in-house market research department. In this, respondents were asked to rank order four cells representing two different pack designs and two price points.

The Oasis brand

In parallel to the development of the Oasis product and packaging, market research tested the concept at the heart of the Oasis brand. Positioned between homespun Snapple and wacky Fruitopia, an identity was needed for Schweppes' still fruit juice drink, which established it as a refreshing premium adult drink. Schweppes developed the concept of a product which 'rejuvenates you and restores you to your old self' in conjunction with advertising agency M&C Saatchi.

The Oasis name is based on the idea of the belief that everyone has a personal 'mirage', something which they associate with feeling good. This 'feel good' mirage is experienced at an Oasis. The name promises a rejuvenation, which will be delivered by the product. This brand image is built upon in the advertising for Oasis and in the packaging of the product. The advertising message is that someone begins by not being themselves, drinks an Oasis, sees a mirage and then resumes their expected behaviour. The strapline for the product is: 'Open, pour, be yourself once more.'

The launch adverts centre on stereotypical figures such as a taxi driver, being nice to his customers until an Oasis restores him to his standard level of unhelpfulness. Later adverts conveyed the same message using personalities such as East Enders' character Frank Butcher recovering from unusual good cheer and Mystic Meg from unprecedented accuracy in her predictions! The voice over by alternative comedian Lily Savage is designed to identify with the target age group. The tone of the advertising is down to earth, a deliberate contrast to the Fruitopia image. This image is created by use of adverts capitalizing on British humour.

The bottle in which Oasis is packaged reinforces the brand identity. In the soft drinks market, a proprietary bottle can be an asset. The distinctive shape of the Coca Cola bottle is a design icon, strongly associated with the brand, and is legally protected from duplication by any other firm. Schweppes opted for a proprietary bottle, which would become associated with Oasis. This is of particular importance as it is intended that the product is drunk from the bottle. The chosen bottle has a ripple effect at the top to represent a mirage in the oasis (see Figure 2.5).

Marketing mix

Product

The Oasis product is made of still spring water and 10 per cent real fruit juice. It has a healthy image based on use of only natural colours and flavourings and on its freedom from preservatives and additives. Focus on a core range of three flavours was preferred as these fitted with the main flavour categories in the UK market. In addition, a narrower product range was more likely to be listed by outlets as a total package would improve launch impact.

The proprietary bottle is made of glass to suit the adult target market and to reinforce the premium image of the product. It is a 375 ml wide-mouth bottle,

Figure 2.5

which can be resealed for ease. No large 'family size' bottles of Oasis are available as this was felt to conflict with the premium positioning. The trade pack configuration is a case of twelve units. Again, this differs from US competitor products, which favour larger 24 bottle packs. The logic underlying this choice is that Schweppes does not wish the pack to be prohibitively expensive for independent buyers who may be price sensitive.

Price

The premium positioning of Oasis is reflected in its price. The consumer is typically not price-sensitive as they tend to buy the product on impulse or socially outside the home. The unit price is attractive compared to rival products because of the single serving pack size. Price to retail and independent stockists is moderated by smaller case size. Schweppes stress that a high cash margin can be achieved on the Oasis product.

Place

Oasis is strongest in the 'impulse' purchase sector of the market. Joy Lester describes the adult soft drinks market as being split between grocery, impulse and leisure. Sixty per cent of the sales of Oasis are via impulse outlets. These include garage forecourts and newsagents. These stockists are likely to be price sensitive, hence the decisions on cash and carry pack size.

Drinks cooler cabinets are available to retail outlets from Coca-Cola Schweppes Beverages, the bottling firm used by Schweppes in the UK. The firm cannot legally dictate that such a cooler cabinet should only stock its products, as the percentage of each firm's products displayed has to be a reflection of true market share. However, this entitles Schweppes to two thirds of the display space available. A plan-o-gram is provided to the retailer to encourage them to stock at least the core Oasis range and to display it to best advantage (see Figure 2.6).

Merchandising

- Oasis is a premium soft drink for adults
- Oasis should be displayed in chillers as a range, or on ambient display
- Oasis should be sited between waters and carbonated soft drinks
- Chiller and shelf P.O.S. is available to encourage rate of sale

---

Figure 2.6 Merchandising

Promotion

One of the major challenges which the predominance of sales via impulse purchase poses is that of how to keep Oasis at the front of consumers' minds. One of the strengths of Coca Cola Schweppes Beverages (CCSB) is that it has a large sales force who 'sell in' products and are also responsible for merchandising.

For maximum impact in the impulse outlets, however, Schweppes also employs over 500 students every summer at sub-sales force level. This seasonal sales support comprises young, enthusiastic individuals who target corner shops and garages and make product drops to ensure that these remain fully stocked. It is an additional benefit that these educated and vibrant sales staff fit with the image of Oasis.

The promotional support for the launch of Oasis was designed to build awareness of the product. A budget of £2.5 million was spent on television and poster advertising. Oasis has a very high level of unprompted recall amongst the target market. Research carried out for Schweppes by agency Millward Brown shows the effectiveness of the advertising (see Figure 2.7).

The unprompted recall of the Oasis adverts is higher than that for competitors Fruitopia and Snapple. Prompted recall figures show up to 80 per cent awareness of its advertising, higher than for Fruitopia at 75 per cent and Snapple at 20 per cent (see Figure 2.8).

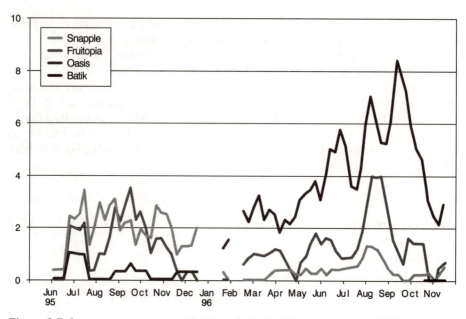

Figure 2.7 Spontaneous awareness of adult soft drinks brands, based on 16–35 age group

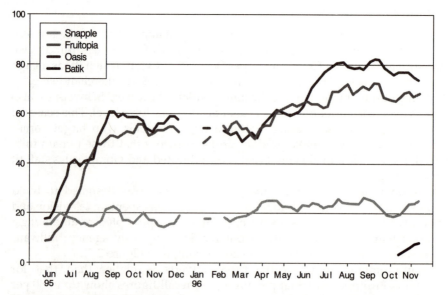

Figure 2.8 Prompted awareness of adult soft drinks brands, based on 16–35 age group.
© Millwood Brown International 1995

Launch support

Oasis: Natural refreshment and better still it's better still

■ **Awareness**
- National media
  - £2.5 million
  - National TV
  - Posters
- National P.R.
- 70% of target will see it 4+ times
- 2 bursts
  - June/July
  - September

■ **Trial**
- "Refreshment Guarantee" across all packs at launch

Figure 2.9 Launch support

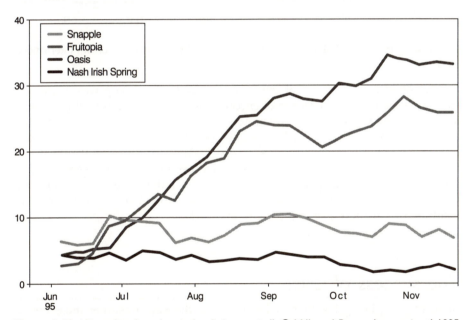

Figure 2.10 How often brands are drunk: 'ever tried'. © Millward Brown International 1995

In addition to television adverts, Oasis has been advertised on Capital Radio and in magazines aimed at its target age group such as Mizz, She and Cosmopolitan. Promotional support also includes sponsorship of the Capital Radio chart-show 'Hall of Fame'. Launch support for Oasis is summarized in Figure 2.9.

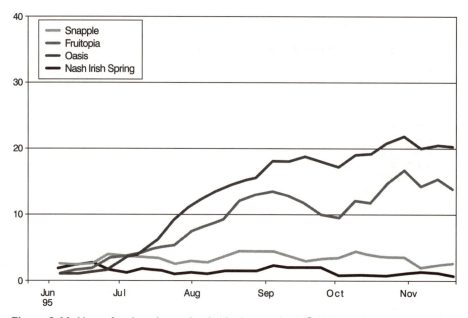

Figure 2.11 How often brands are drunk: 'drink nowadays'. © Millward Brown International 1995

After building awareness of the Oasis brand, the next step was to prompt trial of the product. As a means of encouraging initial purchase, all packs had a 'Refreshment Guarantee'. If consumers bought the product and then did not like it, there was a money back guarantee (see Figure 2.9). This was designed to take the risk out of trying a new product. Millward Brown research shows that Schweppes achieved high levels of success in building awareness and achieving trial of Oasis. In the six months after its launch, Oasis had been tried by over 30 per cent of its target market and more than 20 per cent had continued to drink it (see Figures 2.10 and 2.11).

The success of Oasis

In addition to being the market leader using the key consumer measures of spontaneous awareness, 'ever tried' and 'drink nowadays', Oasis has the highest market share. Indeed, the sales volume of Oasis has been much higher than originally anticipated. This high margin product was expected to occupy a market niche, but has achieved a mass-market level of distribution intensity. Oasis has been adopted by a broader age group than originally expected and has, consequently, achieved a higher than anticipated volume of sales. Whilst Oasis was targeted at the over 20 age group, with sufficient disposable income to be attracted by a premium product, the brand has actually achieved a high level of sales among 16 to 20 year olds. The explanation for this seems to be that teenagers aspire to more sophisticated adult premium drinks.

Oasis has achieved a 70 per cent share of its target market and outsells its nearest competitor, Fruitopia, by 3 to 1. This leadership position has been achieved across grocery, impulse and leisure sectors of the market. Sales volume was 13 million ready-to-drink litres (RTDL) in 1995, the year of its launch. This increased to 19 million RTDL in 1996. So great is the success of Oasis in this market that Coca-Cola withdrew Fruitopia from the UK market at the end of 1996. Despite achieving the number two position in its sector, rewards did not match investment for the company (Key Note Report, 1997).

Creating sustainable advantage

One of the most significant challenges for Oasis, as it enters its third year, is to keep the momentum going. The success of Oasis has prompted competitors to revise their marketing strategies. The withdrawal of Fruitopia from the UK market seems, at first sight, to be a major success for Oasis. However, it may challenge Oasis. Andrew Mann believes that the drive to keep one step ahead of Fruitopia was a positive force, which drove Schweppes to keep on being innovative. However, the remaining competitors are in better shape now than previously. Snapple has now been launched in a 375 ml bottle, which enables it to compete on price. Such competitive responses have resulted in further innovations for Oasis. The lower selling Oasis flavours have been replaced by new ones identified by consumer research. A three-bottled multi-pack, containing one bottle of each of the core flavours, has been launched to build sales from 30 per cent in the grocery market.

In addition, two brand extensions have been launched. There is now Oasis Light, to cater for the calorie conscious segment of the adult market, and Oasis Revitaliser, targeted at the energy drinks segment of the market. Revitaliser contains 20 per cent fruit juice and added extras such as guarana, ginseng and vitamins to give a three-hour boost.

There is strong above- and below-the-line promotional support for these new developments. Nonetheless, the major challenge for Schweppes is to build on the dominance of the Oasis brand.

References

Matthews, V. (1995) Management (Marketing and Advertising): Fizzing with confidence – US 'New Age' soft drinks for adults are increasingly popular in the UK, *Financial Times*, p. 17.

Key Note Report (1997) *Fruit Juices and Health Drinks*.

Nestlé, (1994) *National Drinks Survey (1993/4)*, Nestlé UK.

Chapter 3

SmithKline Beecham Consumer Healthcare (SBCH): Dr. Best Flex Toothbrush

Dr Veronica Wong

Background

SBCH is part of SmithKline Beecham (SB) which was established in 1989 through the merger of SmithKline Beckman and the Beecham Group.

SB is today a major global enterprise and the world's fifth largest healthcare company, with approximately £7 billion in sales. It is organized into three divisions – Pharmaceuticals, Consumer Healthcare and Healthcare Services. SB's overall business is to discover, develop, manufacture and market pharmaceutical products, vaccines, over-the-counter (OTC) medicines and health-related consumer products, and to provide healthcare services including clinical laboratory testing, disease-management and pharmaceutical benefit management.

In 1995, SB's sales from continuing operations increased 16 per cent to £7 billion, while trading profit grew to £1.47 billion, a 19 per cent growth over 1994. Pre-tax profit rose 7 per cent to £1.36 billion from the previous year. Overall the corporation has seen growth in sales and market capitalization of 45 per cent and 150 per cent respectively since 1990. Continual investment in product development and strong strategic positioning in the marketplace have primarily fuelled its growth.

For the consumer healthcare division, SBCH, worldwide sales in 1995 were £2.01 billion, an increase of 35 per cent over 1994, while profits grew by 59 per cent to £333 million. Globally, it is the third largest consumer healthcare company, with approximately 5500 employees worldwide, Europe is its biggest market (44 per cent of sales), followed by North America which accounts for 28 per cent of sales and the rest of the world with a further 28 per cent. Main product categories are OTC medicines which include analgesics, respiratory tract, gastrointestinal, dermatological and vitamins, oral care products, nutritional drinks/healthcare and (in the US) CNS/feminine hygiene products.

Focal benchmark case

This case highlights an oral care product – the Dr. Best Flex toothbrush – which was launched by Lingner & Fischer, the German subsidiary of SBCH in 1988. SBCH had no toothbrush business, except in Germany, in 1988. However, the Dr. Best Flex product very quickly transformed the seemingly static German toothbrush market and provided SBCH the impetus to grow its international toothbrush business. Systematic and continuous product innovation, backed by good marketing practice, revolutionized SBCH's fortunes in the global toothbrush market.

The toothbrush business

Lingner & Fischer's toothbrush was first produced in 1953 and Dr. Best became a familiar name to the German consumer. For years, however, Dr. Best had been losing market share to Blendax, the number one brand produced by the US competitor, Procter & Gamble. At the beginning of 1987, Lingner & Fischer faced tough decisions concerning what it should do with its Dr. Best brand. Blendax, by this time, had established an enormous lead, with just under 60 per cent share (in value terms) of the German toothbrush market. Dr. Best's 6 per cent share of the market placed the survival of the brand in serious doubt. Lingner & Fischer's general manager, Manfred Scheske, then marketing director, recalled that Dr. Best nearly faced extinction:

> 'We've identified some strengths, namely the brand name, and the awareness, but, also, quite a number of weaknesses, and we really had a hot debate on selling or building the brand.'

Manfred Hansen, marketing manager at that time, expressed that he was 'rather upset about that', because he 'felt that Dr. Best was a good brand, with a very high brand awareness figure, and there was no need to sell that.' Its aided brand awareness figure was, in reality, equal to the market leader, a level that is extremely expensive to build!

After considering the strengths and weaknesses of the brand, the German marketing team decided that they would attempt a major re-launch of the brand. There was clearly a lack of innovation and initiative in the industry, with few competitors coming up with really good ideas for decades. The general attitude was that a toothbrush is a toothbrush – absolutely and utterly generic! The team, however, felt that there might be a chance to salvage the brand if they tried hard enough.

The Dr. Best (Aquafresh) Flex toothbrush

The starting point for the Dr. Best team was to commission market research to gain more a detailed understanding of consumers' attitudes to toothbrush performance. Although these were largely predictable, one response, in particular, drew the attention of the team. Consumers were interested not only in physically cleaning the teeth, but also ensuring that they did not hurt their gums. This would be achieved with a toothbrush that behaved with a degree of gentleness.

The team acknowledged that consumers are not gullible – words extolling the benefits of the brand alone were not sufficient. Very early in the process they involved a design studio, Halm, with which they had prior experience, to exchange ideas about potential concepts for the product. SBCH needed a revolutionary concept, which embraced the benefit – gentle on the gums – consumers wanted, and were willing to pay a premium for. Halm responded with a design that would yield that benefit – a distinctive, attractive, expensive-looking toothbrush, with a flexible neck and a dual component grip that could be clearly visualized (the 'snake' in the flexible neck) for the consumer.

The Dr. Best Flex: the 'snake' in the flexible neck

The flexible neck bends to absorb excess pressure, reducing the risk of damage to gums, while the non-slip grip gives better brush control. Until then, the flexible two-component grip technology was only used in expensive products like electric razors. The innovative feature in a toothbrush would, however, allow them to charge a premium price. At the concept development stage, R&D and Technical Operations (TO) assisted the brand team in developing the flexible grip concept into a 'prototype' that could be used to explain and test the concept properly.

The team then approached two different manufacturers to develop pilot moulds and samples from these moulds were sent for three weeks of quantitative in-home consumer tests. These trials confirmed that the tooth-brush's performance-in-use exceeded the 'action standards' the group had agreed for the toothbrush. The team realized they had to proceed with their potential winner as fast as they could. By this time – November 1987 – Dr. Best's trade position was so weak that it faced de-listing. The pressure was on for Lingner & Fischer to launch the new toothbrush by summer 1988, that is, in six months' time.

Detailed launch plans were developed, with budgets for product development, production supply and advertising defined and released. Meanwhile, after the encouraging product test results, advertising development had already commenced, with Lingner & Fischer working very closely with their agency – Grey. The advertising brief emphasized the unique 'gentle on the gums' strategy. The entire team was, by that stage, full of enthusiasm, for they believed they had a great product, brand and positioning that was unbeatable in the market place.

Lindsay Cullen and her team at the agency wanted to inject a degree of 'personality' into the brand. They found their personality in Chicago – a dentist by the name of Professor Dr. Best. The real Dr. Best carried a great deal of conviction and increased the believability of the advertising. According to Lindsay Cullen 'The fact that we had a real visible benefit in the product itself was of enormous importance to us. It's an advertiser's dream.' The next task was to develop a demonstration to show how gentle the toothbrush really was. The agency played around with the toothbrush to see if they could brush something as delicate as a raw egg without damaging it. Eventually they hit upon a tomato, which turned out to be the perfect vehicle for demonstrating the 'gentle to the gums' benefit in the ad. Accompanying this was the advertising claim that built on an expression 'Die klugere gibt nach' – or 'The more intelligent yields'. In this case 'The more intelligent toothbrush yields'. Alternative advertisements, using Dr. Best as the presenter, were tested with consumers. The tests confirmed the superiority of the tomato demonstration, with results showing a shift in buying intention of 33 points.

Meanwhile, problems with the production and supply of the new toothbrush surfaced. Traditionally, an outside manufacturer supplied Dr. Best toothbrushes. The team's preferred supplier, Schiffer, announced that it required nine months lead time to produce the new toothbrushes. There was a lot of risk involved and it was impossible to shorten time to market given the new technology. Lingner & Fischer commissioned a second manufacturer to produce the new toothbrush. When Schiffer was shown what the alternative supplier could produce, the scenario changed. Within 48 hours Schiffer joined the team and moved at the speed of the team.

By the launch date, all the marketing factors had been individually tested. However, there just was not the time for the complete mix to be put into a simulated test market, which was normally done. On the basis of the excellent test results for individual marketing factors, the group justified their decision to launch without full testing.

The Dr. Best Flex toothbrush was launched as the Plus Flex on 2 May 1988. The innovation became one of the most outstanding oral care products ever seen. The SBCH German subsidiary took toothbrushes into a new phase

through its innovative TV advertising, featuring the 'tomato' idea and a
dramatic product differentiation with a flexible neck and two-component grip.
The new toothbrush triggered a radical change in consumer buying habits and
revolutionized the whole nature, size and value of the toothbrush market.
Within 12 months, it achieved 12 per cent market share and broke through
new price ceilings. The brand's market share continued to increase steadily
(see Figure 3.1).

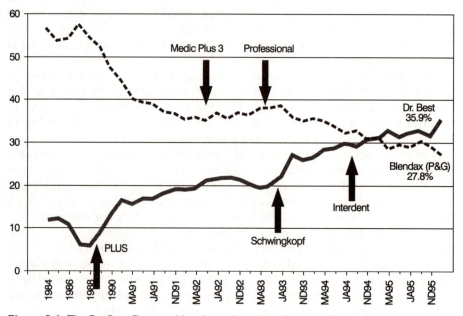

Figure 3.1 The Dr. Best Flex toothbrush: market share (JA = July/August; MA =
March/April; ND = November/December). Source: Nielsen

By 1990, it was the number 2 brand and Procter & Gamble's once
unassailable position in this market was under threat. P&G responded with the
introduction of me-too products (Medic Plus 3 launched in 1992 and
Professional in 1993). Dr. Best's recovery continued despite this, and the brand
stayed ahead of competition. By 1995, the brand finally overtook Blendax. In
1996, Dr. Best secured a 35.9 per cent share (value) of the German toothbrush
market, compared with Blendax's 27.8 per cent.

This turnaround was very much attributed to strategic new product
planning and effective execution. SBCH brand group expected competitors
would respond vigorously and rapidly. To protect its innovation, Lingner &
Fischer started development work on a series of line extensions and new
concepts for the successor to the Dr. Best Flex almost immediately. The group
also filed patents and design registrations covering the product and related
product concepts. In the early years of launch, the Flex and its attractive line

extensions – the Compact, Sensitive, Junior and Design variants – enabled the brand to make a significant impact on the German market. Usage and attitude studies revealed that consumers wanted 'better cleaning and plaque removal'. In July 1993, SmithKline Beecham relaunched the Dr. Best Flex as Dr. Best Schwingkopf, the toothbrush with both a flexible grip and 'directable' floating head. This provided an additional visible benefit that achieved the benefit of 'getting access into cavities' and cleaning the 'difficult to reach' areas of the mouth that conventional brushes miss. It rapidly took SBCH's market share to 30 per cent. Within a year of launch, the new Flex toothbrush was rolled out across Europe, the USA and Canada. In late 1994, SBCH introduced the new, improved Interdent, which contained all the benefits of a directable head, flexible neck and inter-dental filaments to give even better cleaning in-between teeth.

The Interdent

Today SBCH's Lingner & Fischer are among Germany's most successful marketers. The numbers speak for themselves. Dr. Best toothbrush sales grew from 4 million in 1988, when the original Dr. Best Flex was launched, to 40 million in 1996. SBCH expects to sell about 80 million toothbrushes in 1996 outside Germany under the 'Aquafresh' brand, of which 20 million will be in Europe and 60 million in North America, Asia and other parts of the world. Globally, SBCH are no longer the minnow, but the drivers of this market.

To fully appreciate how the SBCH German subsidiary achieved this spectacular success, we examine the guiding principles of innovation at SBCH.

SBCH innovation and marketing practices

SBCH recognizes that innovation and sound marketing practices are the key to building and maintaining leadership in the consumer healthcare market. SBCH's wider (corporate) attitude and approach to new product development and competitive marketing is manifested throughout the Dr. Best Flex project.

Performance, leadership and strategy

The impetus for continued investment in innovation and marketing comes from the corporation's strategic intent, which explicitly challenges its staff to strive to be the 'Simply Better Healthcare Company'. This 'charter' is clearly communicated throughout SmithKline Beecham. Accordingly, SBCH strategic intent is to be the world leader in science-based consumer healthcare. The goal is 'to attain OTC leadership in every market in which it competes'. To reach that goal, management stresses that the firm must outperform its competitors at every level. SBCH chairman, Harry Groome, acknowledges that at the heart of their 'Simply Better' strategy is 'doing the best for consumers', and the way to gain a truly competitive edge is to combine marketing skills and scientific knowledge and understanding to create a world-class, customer-driven company.

To realize their vision, SBCH has established a global Marketing Leadership Programme (MLP) which essentially endorses the role that marketing and science skills play in achieving corporate goals. The MLP is seen as an 'organizational innovation', which involves two co-ordinated streams of activity. One is concerned with identifying world-class marketing practices and sharing this knowledge throughout the company. The other involves increasing marketing's understanding of the scientific element of the company's products so that they can better influence development work, product enhancements, clinical trials, regulatory authorities and life cycle planning, as well as sell and market more effectively to healthcare professionals. Essentially, the MLP focuses on training, learning and communication for all, particularly market-ing, people in the corporation. With a better understanding of working in a regulated environment, they can evaluate sufficiently their own products and new product opportunities. Not only does this lead to new product/product development efforts that have synergies with current marketing and scientific and technical capabilities of the firm, it ensures that innovation and product improvement are backed by sound customer and market understanding and good marketing practices. The innovation focus is to make the most use of prescription drug (Rx) in OTC to create opportunities, identify and develop new products and to position products with the best possible claims. The key is to lead the industry by responding first to the fast changing healthcare environment. As in the Dr. Best Flex project, the innovation orientation is long-term, and continuous to sustain a brand's competitiveness.

Culture

Compared to world class competitors, SBCH is flexible and instinctive. However, SBCH acknowledges that it has sometimes been reluctant to take risks, which can impede serious innovation. As such, management is placing more emphasis on encouraging risk-taking and rewarding entrepreneurship to promote an innovative culture. Additionally, as in the development of the Dr. Best Flex toothbrush, the firm knows it must stay in tune with markets and know its consumers well. Market research therefore plays a key role, as it did in highlighting the latent need that existed for a toothbrush that is gentle on the gums and driving the creativity for idea generation. Innovation rarely occurs in isolation from financial, market or technical risks. Ongoing research is crucial in helping to reduce uncertainty and innovation risks. An emphasis on rapid early consumer testing precisely generated the insights that the Dr. Best Flex team needed to manage the risks and to justify the decision to accelerate time to market. Team effort and the early involvement of external suppliers is also a critical facet of the project. Furthermore, the openness to ideas whether internally or externally generated (thus avoiding the 'not-invented-here syndrome'), together with the willingness to test and experiment with these, facilitates project success and helps to foster the culture for innovation.

Organizational learning, resourcing and developing world-class practices

A significant feature of SBCH's culture is its emphasis on learning and emulating world class practices. The company's Marketing Leadership Programme started as a result of two studies. One study benchmarked best practices within SBCH in the USA, UK and Germany against practices in world class corporations including Procter & Gamble, Mars and Unilever. The other initiative determined how best to develop science skills for selling and marketing consumer healthcare products. The best practices uncovered in the study were widely researched, tested and improved in collaboration with marketing, market research and R&D/Technical Operations (OP) people in over fifteen countries. The results were reviewed extensively by people at all management levels. The aim was to secure agreement on global standards to demonstrate best practices. The rationale was that, through sharing best practice and learning from each other, including some of the best and sharpest minds in the business, the organization will gain a distinct advantage over competition.

To institutionalize corporate-wide learning and implementation of best practices, top management created the MLP, which initially covered three modules – Market Research, Advertising, New Product Development. Later, more modules, ranging from 'Opportunity Identification' and 'Advertising Execution' to 'Pricing' and 'Product Delivery Systems' were introduced. Each module, delivered in hard-copy and on-line formats, resembles a learning/tool kit structured in a consistent way. The module establishes the key principles which apply to the designated process. It identifies the process checklists, key actions to take and staff to involve, with illustrative benchmark cases. It also provides diskette-based forms, which are standardized for global use, but have sufficient detail to allow adaptation to specific product/local practice, when working on the process. Managers and their teams can run through the processes and checks in an interactive way, enabling them to keep track of all their projects. The modules, aimed at improving science skills for marketing consumer healthcare products, are also presented as self-learning formats, with local 'coaches' to provide application support. The standardized formats permit activities to be compared and offer feedback to facilitate continuous learning. Importantly, the leadership programme complements SBCH's Category Management System, with modules covering all key processes in all categories in which SBCH operates.

The MLP, with the support of top management, is an on-going competence development programme intended to benefit marketing, sales, R&D and commercial staff. It is maintained by a permanent structure, with a support team at headquarters and leadership project teams in the countries. These teams ensure that everyone, including new staff, gets the right training and feedback to ensure the programme is working. The enabling modules are assessed and updated regularly in line with market environmental changes, and improved based on staff's feedback. In terms of resourcing knowledge acquisition and developing individuals' talent for effective marketing and new product development, the MLP is instrumental. However, standardization of practices in the company is seen as a step towards continuous improvement, not to stifle creativity and restrict practices. Top management asserts that the general guidelines should not limit the creative flair that each individual 'genius' is encouraged to express, but that global 'rules' inspired by individual genius will create the best possible results.

Principles and processes for innovation

SBCH has articulated a set of new product development principles, which are described from a marketing standpoint. Essentially, as in the Dr. Best Flex toothbrush project, the task is to get an idea to market once it has been identified, with due consideration for continuity of planning, testing and development. The detailed elements of the NPD process, hence, the intricacy of plans, will vary depending on the type of project – a completely new product, a product improvement, roll-out of an existing product to new geographic markets, etc. But, as a rule, the activities are planned, not left to chance. SBCH has developed nine general principles to guide NPD.

The first principle is to conduct research for the long-term to gain understanding of markets and consumers. This was a strong feature in the Dr. Best Flex case and activity in this area continued to support the Dr. Best Flex team. The second principle is to invest in regular research to understand SBCH competitive strengths and product advantages over competition. Market research was instrumental in uncovering fresh leads and innovation opportunities for the Dr. Best brand subsequent to the re-launch in 1988.

The third rule is to evaluate and learn through systematic, global evaluation of competitors' products. This does not always mean imitating competitors' product strategies. Interestingly, the Dr. Best Flex team had responded to the general lack of innovation in the 'generic' toothbrush market and challenged the status quo by turning to consumers to see what they had to say. In this case, consumers, not competition, provided the inspiration for innovation.

The fourth principle for innovation at SBCH is to strive for product superiority based on key benefits sought by the consumer. In 1988, the Dr. Best Flex Plus was launched on a highly successful 'gentle on the gums' platform; the next toothbrush achieved 'better cleaning and plaque removal';

the follow-up Dr. Best Schwingkopf had a 'flexible neck and directable head' realizing the benefit of cleaning those 'difficult to reach' places. A later variant, the Interdent, was re-launched with a flexible handle and head.

The fifth principle is to evaluate new products and concepts thoroughly and systematically. The sixth rule calls for investment in continual product improvement and updating and rejuvenation to stay ahead of competition. SBCH increased its share of a substantially increased overall market through a relentless focus on line extensions, such as packaging variations, compact and junior designs and bristles for sensitive teeth. Similarly subsequent re-launches aimed at adding value or benefits that mattered to consumers.

The seventh principle – to use discretion when determining which steps in the NPD process are needed – means that the new product team should aim to launch products as quickly as possible whilst avoiding taking unnecessary risks. Generally, a 'fast track' approach, taking short-cuts, is appropriate for incremental, lower risk, familiar products and markets; Marketing has to justify any short-cuts. The Dr. Best Flex team did just that – they judged that, given the pressure on them to accelerate new product launch, they would not test the entire marketing mix in a simulated test market. To a great extent the marketing department could justify the short-cut because of proven test results for individual marketing factors. And they had done their 'homework'.

The next principle is to always act to patent and protect SBCH new products against competition. The Dr. Best Flex team began, almost immediately, a programme of continuous improvement, with follow-up usage and attitude studies used to investigate new concepts for the successor to the Dr. Best Flex. However, they were convinced that despite their patent-protected design, competition would copy their innovation in the shortest time possible.

Last, but not least, as a matter of principle, new product teams must have access to R&D/Technical Operations (TO) resources for new initiatives. This is achieved via the Category Management System and ensures R&D/TO resources are focused on projects with the greatest – invariably global – potential. For local brands with a significant potential, it is still possible, with the approval of Category Management, to get R&D/TO to resource the local initiative. In the Flex toothbrush project, the marketing department was able to get limited R&D/TO resources directly at the concept development stage to help the team develop a concept into a form that could be tested with consumers. Such access was important because a prototype was required to explain the concept properly (that is, the 'snake' in the flexible neck and dual component grip in the Flex toothbrush).

Looking more specifically at the NPD process, SBCH views this as a continuous process, with a new project starting as soon as the previous one is completed, although, in practice, new projects can be initiated before other ones are finished. This is particularly important in products with long development lead times where it is appropriate to develop future product generations in parallel. Management are aware of six steps taken in developing new products:

I Review, develop and screen new product concepts

In the Flex toothbrush projects, this step helped the team to get ideas based on a sound knowledge of market segments, consumer needs, usage/habits and attitudes as well as competitive activity. The idea originator or the brand group must discuss the new product idea with local and category management, R&D/TO, purchasing, market research and the advertising agency. Local brands will rely on local management; for global brands, early involvement of category management assists learning and could save development time and money. The product concept should be defined and, subsequently, be refined and evaluated by use of qualitative and quantitative research. In the case of global brands, the category team should be briefed.

2 Create and evaluate the project brief

Once research shows an idea is worth developing, it is important to request R&D/TO resource, to prepare and propose the brief with local marketing management and the category management team. There should be a formal evaluation of the technical, manufacturing and financial feasibility of the project by a project evaluation team. A project group should be developed if there is agreement to proceed.

3 Project management phase

This phase can vary from a few weeks to years depending on the complexity of the project, requirement of clinical trials, regulatory requirements and so forth. R&D/TO and market research are mainly involved at this stage. Category managers play a key role in sharing information, and the idea originator is kept informed of progress throughout. During this phase, the firm will need to develop the detailed project plan (costing, operations, production and marketing plans, regulatory submissions, training, etc.). It will need to confirm the product performance standards for the product with R&D/TO, define suitable research methods and the role for market research in undertaking quantitative product tests. Then it will need to do the necessary research and analyse the results quickly.

4 Develop and recommend launch plan

At this stage a superior and/or differentiated product is developed and the main feasibility issues resolved. Critically, all key functions – finance, purchasing, manufacturing, sales, market research and the advertising agency – in addition to local or category management are involved. Actions include developing the launch plan in parallel with product testing, involving and fully informing other departments, assessing the need to test launch plans prior to a broad-scale launch (the decision not to test must be justified, as we saw in the Dr. Best Flex case). The launch plans and recommendations should be checked when product test results are known.

5 Test launch plans

This step considers the type and suitability of simulated/pre-test marketing and test marketing to be conducted. In addition to sales, marketing and manufacturing input, R&D/TO are also involved to manage the product details of the test. Throughout, local or category management's agreement is sought. The test method for the launch plans must be agreed with market research, 'action standards' or success criteria to be measured and how to carry out the test launch. Test results should be used to modify launch plans if necessary. If the success criteria are met, then the product should be launched.

6 Launch

The launch phase details actions to ensure the launch occurs on time. Local or category management and all key functions are involved, including, where appropriate, the legal department. Specifically the team must confirm monitoring and tracking methods with market research, monitor and review launch results, revising the plan, if necessary, to improve results, assess competitors' responses and consider product defences. Then the team must begin to plan the next project, as product development is a continuous process.

The phenomenal success of the Dr. Best Flex toothbrush has reaffirmed SCBH management's belief in the critical role that product innovation plays in achieving market success. As senior management distils the lessons to be gained from the revitalization of the Dr. Best Flex brand, it recognizes that SCBH must now continue to run the treadmill of innovation to maintain its lead in terms of market share. It is no longer 'David', but 'Goliath' in this revitalized sector.

Chapter 4

Virgin Atlantic Airways: ten years after[1]

Jean-Claude Larréché

June 1994. Virgin Atlantic Airways celebrated the tenth anniversary of its inaugural flight to New York. Richard Branson, the airline's chairman and founder, reminisced about its tremendous growth. In ten short years, he had established Virgin Atlantic as Britain's second largest long-haul airline, with a reputation for quality and innovative product development. Richard Branson turned his thoughts to the challenges that lay ahead.

The origins of the Virgin Group

'Branson, I predict you will either go to prison, or become a millionaire.' These were the last words that the 17-year-old Richard Branson heard from his headmaster as he left school. Twenty-five years later, Richard Branson ruled over a business empire whose 1993 sales exceeded £1.5 billion.[2] He had started his first entrepreneurial business at the age of twelve, selling Christmas trees. Soon after leaving school, he set up *Student*, a national magazine, as 'a platform for all shades of opinion, all beliefs and ideas . . . a vehicle for intelligent

[1] This case was written by Jean-Claude Larréché, the Alfred H. Heineken Professor of Marketing at INSEAD. The case is intended to be used as a basis for class discussion rather than to illustrate either effective or ineffective handling of an administrative situation. Reprinted with permission of INSEAD. Copyright © 1995 INSEAD, Fontainbleau, France.

[2] In June 1994, £1 sterling = US$1.51.

comment and protest'. The magazine, whose editorial staff had an average age of 16, featured interviews by Richard Branson with celebrities and articles on controversial issues.

In 1970, Richard Branson founded a mail-order record business – called Virgin to emphasize his own commercial innocence. The first Virgin record shop was opened in London's Oxford Street in 1971, soon followed by a recording studio and a label which produced records for performers such as Phil Collins, Genesis and Boy George. The Venue nightclub opened in 1978. In 1980, Virgin Records began expanding overseas, initially on a licensing basis; it later set up its own subsidiaries. Virgin Vision was created in 1983, followed by Virgin Atlantic Airways and Virgin Cargo in 1984, and Virgin Holidays in 1985.

In November 1986, the Virgin Group, which included the music, communication, and retail divisions, was floated on the London Stock Exchange. The airline, clubs and holidays activities remained part of the privately-owned Voyager Group Ltd. In its first public year, Virgin Group plc had profit of £13 million on £250 million turnover – far beyond expectations. Its public status, however, was short lived: Richard Branson believed he could not be an entrepreneur while chairing a public company. In October 1988, he regained full control by buying back all outstanding shares. The constraints that he had struggled with during the company's public life were replaced by an overwhelming sense of relief and freedom. A partnership with Seibu Saison International, one of Japan's largest retail and travel groups, was equally brief. In 1990, Richard Branson sold 10 per cent of the equity of Voyager Travel Holdings, the holding company for Virgin Atlantic, to the Japanese group in return for an injection of £36 million of equity and convertible loan capital – only to buy out his Japanese partner for £45 million in 1991.

In 1992, Richard Branson sold Virgin Music (by then the world's sixth largest record company) to Thorn EMI for £560 million. By 1994, the Virgin Group consisted of three holding companies: Virgin Retail Group, Virgin Communication, and Virgin Investments which controlled over 100 entities in 12 countries. Figure 4.1 summarizes the group's activities.

The creation of Virgin Atlantic Airways

In 1984, Richard Branson was approached by Randolph Fields, a 31-year-old lawyer who wanted to start a transatlantic airline. Fields' plan was to operate a business-class-only B747 service to New York. Richard Branson quickly made up his mind. He announced that the new airline, to be named Virgin Atlantic Airways, would be operational within three months. Needless to say, his decision struck Virgin's senior management as completely insane.

Richard Branson, who knew nothing about the airline business, set out to learn from the downfall of Laker Air, an airline launched in 1970 by Freddie Laker with six planes and 120 employees. Laker Air was originally designed as

Virgin Retail Group	Virgin Communication	Virgin Group	Voyager Investments	
			Voyager Group	Virgin Travel Group
Operates a chain of megastores in the UK, continental Europe, Australia and Pacific selling music, video and other entertainment products. Operates game stores in the UK. Wholesale record exports and imports	Publishing of computer entertainment software	Investments: joint-ventures	Clubs and Hotels	UK's second largest long-haul international airline: Virgin Atlantic Airways
	Management of investments in broadcasting including Music Box. Investments in related publishing and entertainment activities, television post production services	Property developments	Airship and balloon operations	Freight handling and packaging
		Magnetic media distribution	Storm model agency	Inclusive tour operations: Virgin Holidays
Note:	Book publishing	Management and corporate finance services to the Virgin organization		
Marui of Japan own 50% of Virgin Megastores Japan	Virgin Radio, Britain's first national commercial contemporary music station			
WH Smith own 50% of Virgin Retail UK				

Figure 4.1 The Virgin Group of companies. Virgin consists of three wholly owned separate holding companies involved in distinct business areas, from media and publishing to retail, travel and leisure. There are over 100 operating companies across the three holding companies in 12 countries worldwide. Source: Virgin Atlantic

a low-risk business, flying under contract for package-holiday firms. In 1971 however it introduced a low-budget, no-frills service between London and New York. Laker's over-confidence led to several mistakes, including purchasing three DC-10s before the US government had approved his London–New York line, and generally ordering more aircraft than he could afford. He accumulated a £350 million debt while the big transatlantic carriers slashed prices. This eventually led to Laker Airways' demise in 1981.

Richard Branson hired two former Laker executives, Roy Gardner (who later became Virgin Atlantic's co-managing director) and David Tait. Branson decided that his new airline should not be all business class, but combine an economy section with a first class section at business class prices. His goal was clear: 'To provide all classes of travellers with the highest quality travel at the lowest cost.' Richard Branson also leased a second-hand 747. The contract he negotiated with Boeing had a sell-back option at the end of the first, second or third year; a clause protected Virgin against currency fluctuations. Another priority was to recruit air crew. Fortunately, British Airways had recently lowered the optional retirement age for its crew, creating a pool of experienced pilots from which Virgin could draw; this gave it the most experienced crew of any British airline.

Obtaining permission to fly to New York from American regulatory bodies was not easy; authorization to land at Newark was granted only three days before Virgin's first flight was scheduled. Forbidden to advertise in the US until the approval, Virgin decided to launch a teaser campaign. Skywriters festooned the Manhattan sky with the words 'WAIT FOR THE ENGLISH VIRGI . . .'.

Virgin Atlantic's inaugural flight took off from London on 22 June 1984, packed with friends, celebrities, reporters and Richard Branson wearing a World War I leather flight helmet. Once the plane had taken off, passengers were surprised to see on the video screen the cockpit, where the crew – Richard Branson and two famous cricket players – greeted them. Although this was obviously a recording, it was a memorable moment for passengers.

Early years (1984–89)

Virgin Atlantic's early years were slightly chaotic. 'I love the challenge,' Richard Branson said. 'I suspect that before I went into the airline business, a lot of people thought I would never be able to make a go of it. It made it even more challenging to prove them wrong.' Richard Branson's determination and enthusiasm, as well as the experienced management team that he assembled, made up for the initial amateurism.

Virgin Atlantic extended its operations progressively. Its early routes, all from London, were to New York (Newark since 1984 and John F. Kennedy Airport since 1988), Miami (1986), Boston (1987), and Orlando (1988). Flights to Tokyo and Los Angeles were added in 1989 and 1990. In 1987, Virgin celebrated its one millionth transatlantic passenger. Until 1991, all Virgin flights left from

London's Gatwick Airport, which was much smaller than Heathrow. Virgin countered this commercial disadvantage with a free limousine service for Upper Class passengers and a Gatwick Upper Class lounge, inaugurated in 1990.

While Richard Branson had always befriended rock stars, he had otherwise kept a low profile. This changed when he launched the airline: 'I knew that the only way of competing with British Airways and the others was to get out there and use myself to promote it,' he explained. Richard made a point of being accessible to reporters and never missed an opportunity to cause a sensation, wearing a stewardess's uniform or a bikini on board, or letting himself be photographed in his bath. What really caught the public's attention were his Atlantic crossings. In 1986, his 'Virgin Atlantic Challenger II' speedboat recorded the fastest time ever across the Atlantic with Richard Branson on board. Even more spectacular was the 1987 crossing of the 'Virgin Atlantic Flyer' – the largest hot-air balloon ever flown and the first to cross the Atlantic. Three years later Richard Branson crossed the Pacific in another balloon from Japan to Arctic Canada, a distance of 6700 miles, breaking all existing records with speeds of up to 245 miles per hour.

The years of professionalization (1989–94)

The professionalization of Virgin Atlantic's management began in 1989. Until then Virgin Atlantic had had a flat structure, with 27 people reporting to Richard Branson directly. As the airline expanded, it had outgrown its entrepreneurial ways, and needed to become customer-driven.

Richard Branson asked Syd Pennington, a veteran Marks & Spencer retailer, to look into the airline's duty free business in addition to his other responsibilities at Virgin Megastores. Some time later, Pennington, coming back from a trip, learned that he had been promoted to co-managing director of the airline. When Pennington expressed his surprise, Richard explained: 'It's easier to find good retail people than good airline people.' Syd Pennington saw that Virgin Atlantic lacked controls and procedures, and he devoted himself to professionalizing its management. His objective was to infuse the business with Richard Branson's charisma and energy while also making it effective enough to succeed. Tables 4.1 and 4.2 present a five-year summary of Virgin Atlantic's financial performance and labour force. Table 4.3 shows the three-year evolution of passengers carried and market shares.

After years of campaigning, Virgin Atlantic was granted the right to fly out of Heathrow in 1991. Heathrow, Britain's busiest airport, handled 100,000 passengers a day – a total of 40 million in 1990, compared with 1.7 million at Gatwick. Virgin Atlantic was assigned to Heathrow's Terminal 3, where it competed with 30 other airlines serving over 75 destinations on five continents. In Richard Branson's eyes, gaining access to Heathrow was a 'historic moment and the culmination of years of struggle'. His dream to compete with other

Table 4.1 Financial results and labour force of Virgin Atlantic Airways

Financial year	Turnover (£m)	Profit (loss) before tax (£m)
1988/89	106.7	8.4
1989/90	208.8	8.5
1990/91	382.9	6.1
1991/92	356.9	(14.5)
1992/93	404.7	0.4

Note: The reporting year ends on 31 July until 1990, and on 31 October as of 1991. The 1990/91 period covers 15 months.

Table 4.2

Year	Number of Employees*
1988	440
1989	678
1990	1104
1991	1591
1992	1638
1993	1627
1994	2602

* as of 31 December (31 May for 1994).
Source: Virgin Atlantic

Table 4.3 Market shares of Virgin Atlantic Airways (revenue passengers)

Route	1993	1992	1991
New York (JFK & Newark)	19.6%	17.2%	18.0%
Florida (Miami & Orlando)	33.2%	30.6%	25.2%
Los Angeles	23.6%	21.8%	25.8%
Tokyo	18.4%	15.5%	16.0%
Boston	22.2%	20.0%	15.3%
Total Passengers Carried	1,459,044	1,244,990	1,063,677

Note: Flights from Gatwick and LHR
Source: Virgin Atlantic

long-haul carriers on an equal footing had come true. A new era began for Virgin. Flying from Heathrow enabled it to have high load factors all year and to attract more business and full-fare economy passengers. It could also carry more interline flyers and more cargo, since Heathrow was the UK's main air freight centre. On the morning of the airline's first flight from Heathrow, a Virgin 'hit squad' encircled the model British Airways Concorde at the airport's entrance and pasted it over with Virgin's logo. Richard Branson, dressed up as a pirate, was photographed in front of the Concorde before security forces could reach the site. A huge party marked the end of the day.

In April 1993, Virgin ordered four A340s from Airbus Industries, the European consortium in which British Aerospace had a 20 per cent share. The order, worth over £300m, reflected the airline's commitment to new destinations. 'We are proud to buy an aircraft which is in large part British-built, and on which so many jobs in the UK depend,' said Richard Branson. The A340, the longest range aircraft in the world, accommodated 292 passengers in three cabins, and had key advantages such as low fuel consumption and maintenance costs. When the first A340 was delivered in December, Virgin became the first UK carrier to fly A340s. Virgin also ordered two Boeing 747–400 and took options on two others. It also placed a $19 million order for the most advanced in-flight entertainment system available, featuring 16 channels of video, which it planned to install in all three sections. In keeping with the airline's customization efforts, the new aircraft's cabin was re-designed. Upper Class passengers would find electronically-operated 54-inch seats with a 55 degree recline and an on-board bar. There was a rest area for flight and cabin crew.

In June 1993, Virgin scheduled a second daily flight from Heathrow to JFK. 'We've given travellers a wider choice on their time of travel,' said Richard Branson. 'The early evening departure is timed to minimize disruption to the working day, a welcome bonus to both busy executives and leisure travellers.' In March 1994, Virgin put an end to British Airways' and Cathay Pacific's long-standing duopoly on the London–Hong Kong route, launching its own A340 service.

Virgin's first Boeing 747–400 was delivered in May 1994. Only days later, Virgin opened its San Francisco line (until then a British Airways-United duopoly). In a press release shown in Figure 4.2, Virgin emphasized the continuation of its expansion plans, the renewal of its fleet, and the 'better alternative' that it offered customers on both sides of the Atlantic. During the inaugural flight 150 guests – and some fare-paying flyers who had been warned that it would not be a quiet flight – were entertained with a fashion show and a jazz band. In San Francisco the aircraft stopped near a giant taximeter. The door opened, Richard Branson appeared, and inserted a huge coin in the taximeter, out of which popped the Virgin flag. Airport authorities offered Richard Branson a giant cake decorated with a miniature Golden Gate Bridge. Guests were entertained for a whirlwind five days which included a tour of the Napa Valley and a visit to Alcatraz prison where Richard Branson

17th May 1994

NEW SAN FRANCISCO ROUTE MARKS CONTINUED EXPANSION FOR VIRGIN ATLANTIC

A new service to San Francisco, its sixth gateway to the US, was launched today (17th May 1994), by Virgin Atlantic Airways, marking another stage in the airline's development as it approaches its tenth anniversary.

The daily Boeing 747 service from London's Heathrow airport follows further route expansion in February 1994 when the airline introduced a daily service to Hong Kong, using two of four recently acquired Airbus A340 aircraft.

Virgin Atlantic Chairman Richard Branson said: 'San Francisco was always on our list of the 15 or so great cities of the world that we wanted to fly to, so it's a very proud moment for us finally to be launching this new service today.

'We regularly receive awards for our transatlantic flights so I hope that this new service will be able to provide consumers on both sides of the Atlantic with a better alternative to the current duopoly which exists on the San Francisco/London route.

'Today's launch is also the culmination of a number of significant developments at Virgin Atlantic, not least of which is our recent acquisition of two new Boeing 747–400s and four Airbus A340s. This comes on the back of our $19 million investment in new 14 channel in-flight entertainment, which, unlike other airlines, we have made available to all of our passengers.'

Mr Branson added that it was the airline's intention to have one of the most modern and passenger-friendly fleets in the world. Virgin's current fleet comprises: eight B747s, three A340s, and an A320 and two BAe 146 Whisper Jets which are jointly operated with franchise partners in Dublin and Athens.

A daily service will depart Heathrow at 11.15, arriving in San Francisco at 14.05 local time. Flights leave San Francisco at 16.45, arriving in the UK the following day at 10.45. For reservations call 0293 747747.

For further information:

James Murray
Virgin Atlantic Airways
Tel: 0293 747373

Figure 4.2 Press release for the opening of the San Francisco route. © 1995 INSEAD, Fontainebleau, France

was jailed in a stunt prepared by his team. Virgin also took advantage of the launch to unveil a recycling and environmental programme. A stewardess dressed in green – rather than the usual red Virgin uniform – gave passengers information on the programme, which had delivered savings of £500,000 since it was launched in late 1993.

At the time of Virgin's tenth anniversary, its fleet comprised eight B747–200s, a B747–400 and three A340s. The airline awaited delivery of its second B747–400 and fourth A340 and also planned to retire two older B747–200s by the end of 1994. By then, half of its fleet would be brand new. By comparison, the average age of British Airways' fleet was eight years.[3] Richard Branson planned to expand his fleet to 18 planes which would serve 12 or 15 destinations by 1995. Proposed new routes included Washington DC, Chicago, Auckland, Singapore, Sydney, and Johannesburg. The London–Johannesburg licence, granted in 1992, had been a major victory for Virgin: when exploited, it will end a 50-year duopoly enjoyed by British Airways and South African Airways.

All Virgin Atlantic planes were decorated with a Vargas painting of a red-headed, scantily dressed woman holding a scarf. The names of most Virgin aircraft evoked the 'Vargas Lady' theme, starting with its first aircraft, *Maiden Voyager*. (Table 4.4 lists the aircraft's names). The first A340, inaugurated by the Princess of Wales, was christened *The Lady in Red*.

Table 4.4 Virgin Atlantic fleet

Aircraft	Type	Name	Into service
G-VIRG	B747-287B	Maiden Voyager	1984
G-VGIN	B747-243B	Scarlet Lady	1986
G-TKYO	B747-212B	Maiden Japan	1989
G-VRGN	B747-212B	Maid of Honour	28/08/89
G-VMIA	B747-123	Spirit of Sir Freddy	09/05/90
G-VOYG	B747-283B	Shady Lady	10/03/90
G-VJFK	B747-238B	Boston Belle	06/03/91
G-VLAX	B747-238B	California Girl	28/05/91
G-VBUS	A340-311	Lady in Red	16/12/93
G-VAEL	A340-311	Maiden Toulouse	01/01/94
G-VSKY	A340-311	China Girl	21/03/94
G-VFAB	B747-4Q8	Lady Penelope	19/05/94
G-VHOT	B747-4Q8		delivery 10/94
G-VFLY	A340-311		delivery 10/94

[3] BA's fleet had 240 aircraft, including some 180 Boeings, 7 Concordes, 10 A320s, 15 BAe ATPs and 7 DC10s.

Virgin classes

Richard Branson originally proposed to call Virgin's business and economy classes Upper Class and Riff Raff respectively; in the latter case however he bowed to the judgement of his managers, who urged him to desist. Virgin Atlantic strove to offer the highest quality travel to all classes of passengers at the lowest cost, and to be flexible enough to respond rapidly to their changing needs. For instance, Virgin catered to the needs of children and infants with special meals, a children's channel, pioneering safety seats, changing facilities, and baby food.

'Offering a First Class service at less than First Class fares' had become a slogan for Virgin Atlantic. Marketed as a first class service at business class prices, Upper Class competed both with other carriers' first class and business class. Since its 1984 launch, this product had won every major travel industry award.

The Economy Class promised the best value for money, targeting price-sensitive leisure travellers who nevertheless sought comfort. It included three meal options, free drinks, seat-back video screens, and ice cream during movies on flights from London.

After years of operating only two classes, business and economy, Virgin had introduced its Mid Class in 1992 after realizing that 23 per cent of economy passengers travelled for business. Mid Class was aimed at cost-conscious business travellers who required enough space to work and relax. This full fare economy class offered flyers a level of service usually found only in business class, with separate check-in and cabin, priority meal service, armrest or seat-back TVs, and the latest in audio and video entertainment. Table 4.5 shows Virgin's three sections: Upper Class, Mid Class and Economy.

Virgin's B747 configuration on the Heathrow/JFK route consisted of 50 seats in Upper Class, 38 in Mid Class, and 271 in Economy. The typical British Airways B747 configuration on the same route was 18 First Class seats, 70 seats in Club World, and 282 in World Traveller Class.[4]

Service the Virgin way

Virgin Atlantic wanted to provide the best possible service while remaining original, spontaneous and informal. Its goal was to turn flying into a unique experience, not to move passengers from one point to another. It saw itself not only in the airline business but also in entertainment and leisure. According to a staff brochure:

[4] As of April 1994, the Club World and World Traveller – Euro Traveller for flights within Europe – were the names given to British Airways' former Business and Economy Classes respectively.

Table 4.5 Virgin Atlantic's three classes

UPPER CLASS

- Reclining sleeper seat with 15" more legroom than other airlines
- Latest seat arm video/audio entertainment
- Unique Clubhouse lounge at Heathrow featuring health spa (includes hair salon, library, music room, games room, study and brasserie)
- Virgin Arrival Clubhouse with shower, sauna, swimming pool and gym
- Inflight beauty therapist on most flights
- Onboard lounges and stand up bars
- 'Snoozzone' dedicated sleeping section with sleeper seat, duvet and sleep suit
- Complimentary airport transfers including chauffeur-driven limousine or motorcycle to and from airport
- Free confirmable Economy ticket for round trip to US/Tokyo

MID CLASS

- Separate check-in and cabin
- Most comfortable economy seat in the world with 38" seat pitch (equivalent to many airlines' business class seat)
- Complimentary pre-take off drinks and amenity kits
- Frequent Flyer programme
- Priority meal service
- Priority baggage reclaim
- Armrest/seatback TVs and latest audio/video entertainment

ECONOMY CLASS

- Contoured, space-saving seats, maximizing legroom, seat pitch up to 34"
- Three meal option service (including vegetarian) and wide selection of free alcoholic and soft drinks
- Seatback TVs and 16 channels of the latest inflight entertainment
- Pillow and blankets
- Advance seat selection
- Complimentary amenity kit and ice cream (during movies on flights from London)

> 'We must be memorable, we are not a bus service. The journeys made by our customers are romantic and exciting, and we should do everything we can to make them feel just that. That way they will talk about the most memorable moments long after they leave the airport.'

Virgin Atlantic saw that as it became increasingly successful, it risked also becoming complacent. The challenge was to keep up customers' interest by keeping service at the forefront of activities. Virgin was often distinguished for the quality and consistency of its service (as shown in Figure 4.3); it won the

1994

Executive Travel
Best Transatlantic Airline
Best Business Class
Best Inflight Magazine

Travel Weekly
Best Transatlantic Airline

1993

Executive Travel
Airline of the Year
Best Transatlantic Carrier
Best Business Class
Best Cabin Staff
Best Food and Wine
Best Inflight Entertainment
Best Airport Lounges
Best Inflight Magazine
Best Ground/Check-in Staff

Travel Weekly
Best Transatlantic Airline

Travel Trade Gazette
Best Transatlantic Airline

TTG Travel Advertising Awards
Best Direct Mail Piece

1992

Executive Travel (awards given for 91/92)
Airline of the Year
Best Transatlantic Carrier
Best Long Haul Carrier
Best Business Class
Best Inflight Food
Best Inflight Entertainment
Best Ground/Check-in Staff

Business Traveller
Best Airline for Business Class
– Long Haul

Travel Weekly
Best Transatlantic Airline

Travel Trade Gazette
Best Transatlantic Airline

Courvoisier Book of the Best
Best Business Airline

ITV Marketing Awards
Brand of the Year – Service

Frontier Magazine
Best Airline/Marine Duty Free

BPS Teleperformance
UK Winner
Overall European Winner

Meetings and Incentive Travel
Best UK Base Airline

Ab-Road Magazine
Airline 'Would most like to fly'
Best Inflight Catering

1991

Executive Travel
(Awards Given in 1992)

Business Traveller
Best Business Class – Long Haul

Travel Weekly
Best Transatlantic Airline

Travel Trade Gazette
Best Transatlantic Airline
Most Attentive Airline Staff

Avion World Airline Entertainment Awards
Best Inflight Videos – Magazine Style
Best Inflight Audio – Programming
Best Inflight Audio of an Original Nature

Which Airline?
Voted by the readers as one of the Top Four Airlines in the World (the only British airline amongst these four)

The Travel Organization
Best Long Haul Airline

Conde Nast Traveller
In the Top Ten World Airlines

Air Cargo News
Cargo Airline of the Year

1990

Executive Travel
Airline of the Year
Best Transatlantic Carrier
Best Inflight Entertainment

Business Traveller
Best Business Class – Long Haul

Travel News (now Travel Weekly)
Best Transatlantic Airline
Special Merit Award to Richard Branson

Travel Trade Gazette
Best Transatlantic Airline
Travel Personality – Richard Branson

Avion World Airline Entertainment Awards
Best Overall Inflight Entertainment
Best Video Programme
Best Inflight Entertainment Guide

Onboard Services magazine
Outstanding Inflight Entertainment Programme
Outstanding Entertainment
(For Sony Video Walkmans)

The Travel Organization
Best Long Haul Airline

1989

Executive Travel
Best Transatlantic Airline
Best Business Class in the World
Best Inflight Entertainment

Business Traveller
Best Business Class-Long Haul

World Airline Entertainment Awards
Best Overall Inflight Entertainment
Best Inflight Audio Entertainment
Best Inflight Entertainment Guide
(Outside Magazine)

Onboard Services Magazine
Overall Onboard Service Award
(Upper Class)

Which Holiday?
Best Transatlantic Airline

Nihon Keizai Shimbun (Japan)
Best Product in Japan – for Upper Class

1988

Executive Travel
Best Business Class – North Atlantic

Business Traveller
Best Business Class – Long Haul

Travel Trade Gazette
Best Transatlantic Airline

1986

The Marketing Society
Consumer Services Awards

What to Buy For Business
Business Airline of the Year

Figure 4.3 Awards won by Virgin Atlantic. Source: Virgin Atlantic

Executive Travel Airline of the Year award for an unprecedented three consecutive years. Service delivery, in other words 'getting it right the first time', was of key importance. The airline was also perceived to excel in the art of service recovery, where it aimed to be proactive, not defensive. It handled complaints from Upper Class passengers within 24 hours and those from Economy Class flyers within a week. If a flight was delayed, passengers received a personalized fax of apology from Richard Branson or a bottle of champagne. Passengers who had complained were occasionally upgraded to Upper Class.

Innovation

Virgin's management, who wanted passengers never to feel bored, introduced video entertainment in 1989. They chose the quickest solution: handing out Sony Watchmans on board. Virgin later pioneered individual video screens for every seat, an idea that competitors quickly imitated. In 1994, Virgin's on-board entertainment offered up to 20 audio channels and 16 video channels including a shopping channel and a game channel. A gambling channel would be introduced at year end. In the summer, a 'Stop Smoking Programme' video was shown on all flights – Virgin's contribution to a controversy over whether smoking should be permitted on aircraft.

The presence of a beauty therapist or a tailor was an occasional treat to passengers. The beautician offered massages and manicures. On some flights to Hong Kong, the tailor faxed passengers' measurements so that suits could be ready on arrival. In 1990, Virgin became the only airline to offer automatic defibrillators on board and to train staff to assist cardiac arrest victims. A three-person Special Facilities unit was set up in 1991 to deal with medical requests. Its brief was extended to handle arrangements for unaccompanied minors or unusual requests such as birthday cakes, champagne for newly-weds, public announcements, or mid-flight marriage proposals. The unit also informed passengers of flight delays or cancellations, and telephoned clients whose options on tickets had expired without their having confirmed their intention to travel. Another service innovation was motorcycle rides to Heathrow for Upper Class passengers. The chauffeur service used Honda PC800s with heated leather seats. Passengers wore waterproof coveralls and a helmet with a built-in headset for a cellular phone.

In February 1993, Britain's Secretary of State for Transport inaugurated a new Upper Class lounge at Heathrow: the Virgin Clubhouse. The £1 million Clubhouse had an unusual range of facilities: Victorian style wood-panelled washrooms with showers and a grooming salon offering massages, aromather-apy and hair cuts; a 5000-volume library with antique leather armchairs; a games room with the latest computer technology; music room with a CD library; a study with the most recent office equipment. Many of the furnishings came from Richard Branson's own home: a giant model railway, the Challenger

II Trophy, a 3-metre galleon model. A 2-ton, 5-metre table, made in Vienna from an old vessel, had to be installed with a crane. Upon the opening of the Hong Kong route, a black jack table was added at which visitors received 'Virgin bills' that the dealer exchanged for tokens. There was also a shoe shine service. Passengers seemed to enjoy the lounge. One remarked in the visitors' book: 'If you have to be delayed more than two hours, it could not happen in a more pleasant environment.'

Customer orientation, Virgin style

Virgin tried to understand passengers' needs and go beyond their expectations. While it described itself as a 'niche airline for those seeking value-for-money travel', its standards and reputation could appeal to a broad spectrum of customers. It managed to serve both sophisticated, demanding executives and easy-going, price-sensitive leisure travellers in the same aircraft. According to marketing director Steve Ridgeway, Virgin attracted a broader range of customers than its competitors because it managed this coexistence between passenger groups better. This had enabled the airline to reach high load factors soon after opening new lines, as shown in Table 4.6.

Virgin Atlantic initially had marketed itself as an economical airline for young people who bought Virgin records and shopped at Virgin stores, but gradually its target shifted. The danger, which Richard Branson saw clearly, was that people would perceive it as a 'cheap and cheerful' airline, a copy of the defunct Laker Airways. Richard Branson knew that his airline's survival depended on high yield business travellers. After establishing a strong base in leisure traffic, Virgin turned to the corporate segment and strove to establish itself as a sophisticated, business class airline that concentrated on long-haul routes. The idea of fun and entertainment, however, was not abandoned. Upper

Table 4.6 Load factors of Virgin Atlantic Airways

Year	Newark	Miami	Tokyo	JFK	Los Angeles	Boston
1990–1991	82.0%	89.5%	65.9%	76.9%	84.5%	83.3%
1989–1990	83.3%	92.1%	68.3%	74.2%	79.8%	
1988–1989	82.8%	86.7%	52.4%			
1987–1988	77.1%	85.0%				
1986–1987	74.4%	76.4%				
1985–1986	72.9%					
1984–1985	72.0%					

Source: Virgin Atlantic promotional materials. This information is no longer made public since 1991.

Class was upgraded and incentives were added to attract the business traveller. By 1991, 10 per cent of the airline's passengers and 35 to 40 per cent of its income came from the business segment. Virgin's competitive advantage was reinforced through the combination of corporate travel buyers' price consciousness and the rising service expectations of travellers. Richard Branson actively wooed business customers by regularly inviting corporate buyers to have lunch at his house and seeking their comments.

As part of Virgin's drive to meet customers' standards, on each flight 30 passengers were asked to fill out a questionnaire. Their answers formed the basis of widely distributed quarterly reports. Virgin's senior managers flew regularly, interviewing passengers informally, making critical comments on the delivery of service and circulating their reports among top management. Richard Branson himself, who welcomed every opportunity to obtain feedback from customers, took time to shake hands and chat with passengers. The preoccupation with service was so strong that staff were often more exacting in their evaluation of each other than the customers were.

Business executives, unlike younger leisure travellers, did not readily relate to other aspects of the Virgin world: the records, the Megastores, the daredevil chairman. Their good feelings about Virgin stemmed mainly from their positive experiences with the airline. These tough and demanding customers appreciated Virgin's style, service, innovations and prices. Some were enthusiastic enough to rearrange their schedules in order to fly Virgin despite punctuality problems. Aside from complaints about flight delays, their only serious criticism was that Virgin did not serve enough destinations.

Virgin's people

Virgin Atlantic attracted quality staff despite the relatively low salaries it paid. In management's eyes, the ideal employee was 'informal but caring': young, vibrant, interested, courteous and willing to go out of his or her way to help customers. Richard Branson explained:

> 'We aren't interested in having just happy employees. We want employees who feel involved and prepared to express dissatisfaction when necessary. In fact, we think that the constructively dissatisfied employee is an asset we should encourage and we need an organization that allows us to do this – and that encourages employees to take responsibility, since I don't believe it is enough for us simply to give it.'

Richard Branson believed that involving management and staff was the key to superior results: 'I want employees in the airline to feel that it is they who can make the difference, and influence what passengers get,' he said. He wrote to employees regularly to seek their ideas and to ensure that relevant news was communicated to them. His home phone number was given to all staff, who could call him at any time with suggestions or complaints.

Virgin Atlantic's philosophy was to stimulate the individual. Its dynamic business culture encouraged staff to take initiatives and gave them the means to implement them. Staff often provided insights into what customers wanted or needed – sometimes anticipating their expectations better than the customers themselves. Virgin Atlantic had a formal staff suggestion scheme and encouraged innovation from employees, both in project teams and in their daily work. Employees' suggestions were given serious consideration; many were implemented, such as the idea of serving ice cream as a snack, although formal marketing research had never shown the need for such a service.

Richard Branson himself was open to suggestions and innovations. He talked to everyone and was a good listener, inquisitive and curious about all aspects of the business. He spent time with passengers, and visited the lounge without any advance notice. While he personified a 'hands-on' approach to management, he never appeared controlling or threatening. His constant presence was a sign of involvement and a source of motivation for staff, who felt a lot of affection for him. It was not unusual to hear crew discuss his recent decisions or activities, mentioning 'Mr Branson' or 'Richard' with admiration and respect.

In the difficult environment of the late 1980s and early 1990s, most airline employees were anxious to keep their jobs. With most operating costs – fuel prices, aircraft prices, insurance, landing and air traffic control fees – beyond management's control, labour costs were the main target of cut backs. In 1993, the world's top 20 airlines cut 31,600 jobs, or 3.6 per cent of their workforce, while the next 80 airlines added nearly 14,000, or 2.4 per cent. That same year, Virgin Atlantic maintained its labour force, and was in the process of recruiting at the end of the year. In June 1994, Virgin Atlantic had 2602 employees and recruited 880 cabin crew members. Opening a single long-haul line required hiring about 400 people.

The airline industry

Deregulation of the US air transport industry in 1978 had reduced the government's role and removed protective rules, thereby increasing competition among American airlines. A decade later, deregulation hit Europe. The liberalization movement began in an effort to end monopolies and bring down prices. In fact, European carriers had been engaged in moderate competition in transatlantic travel while the domestic scheduled market remained heavily protected through bilateral agreements. European airlines were mostly state-owned, in a regulated market where access was denied to new entrants. In April 1986, the European Court of Justice ruled that the

Treaty of Rome's competition rules also applied to air transportation. Deregulation took place in three phases between 1987 – when price controls were relaxed and market access was opened – and 1992, when airlines were allowed to set their own prices, subject to some controls.

In this atmosphere of deregulation and falling prices, traffic revenue grew briskly until 1990, when a global recession and the Gulf War plunged airlines into their worst crisis since World War II. The 22-member association of European airlines saw the number of passengers plummet by 7 million in 1991. Traffic recovered in 1992, when the world's 100 largest airlines saw their total revenue, measured in terms of tonnage or passengers, increase by just over 10 per cent. However, the airlines recorded a net loss of $8 billion in 1992, after losses of $1.84 billion in 1991 and $2.66 billion in 1990. Some experts believed that the industry would ultimately be dominated by a handful of players, with a larger number of mid-size carriers struggling to close the gap. Tables 4.7 and 4.8 show financial and passenger load data for some international airlines, while Table 4.9 ranks Europe's top twenty airlines.

Virgin's competitors

Virgin's direct competitor was British Airways (BA). Both carriers were fighting each other intensely on the most attractive routes out of London. BA, the number one British airline, was fifteen times the size of second placed Virgin. Tables 4.10 and 4.11 compare Virgin's and British Airways' flights and fares.

British Airways became the state owned British airline in 1972 as the result of a merger between British European Airways and British Overseas Airways Corporation. In the early '80s, it was the clear leader in the highly lucrative and regulated transatlantic route, where operating margins were approximately 15 per cent of sales. However, its overall profitability was shaky when Lord King became Chairman in 1981. He transformed BA into a healthy organization and prepared it for its successful privatization in 1987. Since this time, BA has remarkably out-performed its European rivals.

British Airways traditionally benefited from a strong position at Heathrow, but competition toughened in 1991 when TWA and Pan Am sold their slots to American and United Airlines for $290 million and $445 million respectively. In the same year, Virgin also received slots at Heathrow. These slot attributions so infuriated Lord King that he scrapped its annual £40,000 donation to Britain's ruling Conservative Party. At the time of the Heathrow transfer, BA scheduled 278 flights a week across the Atlantic from London, with 83,000 seats, while American had 168 flights with 35,000 seats and United 122 with 30,000. Virgin had 84 flights with 30,000 seats.

Despite these competitive pressures and the recent airline recession, British Airways remained one of the world's most profitable airlines. The largest

Table 4.7 Financial results of selected international airlines

Airline company	Ranking 92	91	Sales US$ Million 1992	% change	Operating results US$million	Net results US$million 1992	Net results US$million 1991	Net margin % 1992	Jet and turbo fleet	Total employees	Productivity sales/employee $000
American	1	1	14,396	11.7	(25.0)	(935.0)	(239.9)	-6.5	672	102,400	140
United	2	2	12,889	10.5	(537.8)	(956.8)	(331.9)	-7.4	536	84,000	153
Delta	3	4	11,639	15.7	(825.5)	(564.8)	(239.6)	-4.9	554	79,157	147
Lufthansa	4	5	11,036	7.1	(198.5)	(250.4)	(257.7)	-2.3	302	63,645	173
Air France	5	3	10,769	-1.1	(285.0)	(617.0)	(12.1)	-5.7	220	63,933	168
British Airways	6	6	9,307	6.5	518.4	297.7	687.3	3.2	241	48,960	190
Swissair	16	16	4,438	7.0	152.8	80.7	57.9	1.8	60	19,025	233
TWA Inc	18	18	3,634	-0.7	(404.6)	(317.7)	34.6	-8.7	178	29,958	121
Singapore	19	19	3,443	5.4	548.0	518.5	558.4	15.1	57	22,857	150
Qantas	20	20	3,099	2.9	79.1	105.7	34.6	3.4	46	14,936	207
Cathay Pacific	21	21	2,988	11.3	464.0	385.0	378.0	12.9	49	13,240	225
Southwest	34	41	1,685	28.3	182.6	103.5	26.9	6.1	141	11,397	148
Virgin Atlantic	62	62	626	7.3	(22.0)	Not reported	3.8	Not reported	8	2,394	261

Source: *Airline Business*, September 1993, 'Much Pain, No Gain'. Productivity computed for this exhibit.

Table 4.8 Passenger load factors of selected international airlines

Airline company	1992 revenue Tonne Km million				1992 revenue passenger Km		1992 passengers		Passenger load factor		Year end	1992 rank
	Passenger	Freight	Total	% change	Million	% change	Million	% change	1992 %	1991 %		
American	14,223	2,176	16,399	19.7	156,786	18.3	86.01	13.3	63.7	61.7	Dec. 92	1
United	13,489	2,522	16,010	12.0	149,166	12.6	67.00	8.1	67.4	66.3	Dec. 92	2
Delta	11,761	1,765	13,525	20.2	129,632	19.6	82.97	11.8	61.3	60.3	Dec. 92	3
Lufthansa	5,882	4,676	10,725	14.4	61,274	17.1	33.70	14.2	65.0	64.0	Dec. 92	4
Air France	5,238	3,970	9,208	5.3	55,504	4.0	32.71	3.4	67.4	66.8	Dec. 92	5
British Airways	7,622	2,691	10,313	13.2	80,473	15.6	28.10	10.5	70.8	70.2	Mar. 93	6
Swissair	1,573	1,063	2,684	9.1	16,221	7.0	8.01	0.4	60.3	61.6	Dec. 92	16
TWA Inc	4,258	734	4,992	1.4	46,935	1.8	22.54	8.5	64.7	64.7	Dec. 92	18
Singapore Air	3,675	2,412	6,086	14.2	37,861	8.5	8.64	6.3	71.3	73.5	Mar. 93	19
Qantas	2,684	1,220	3,904	4.9	28,836	7.2	4.53	9.4	66.2	66.0	Jun. 92	20
Cathay Pacific	2,695	1,671	4,366	13.3	27,527	12.7	8.36	13.1	73.5	73.6	Dec. 92	21
Southwest Air	2,032	49	2,082	23.4	22,187	22.0	27.84	22.6	64.5	61.1	Dec. 92	34
Virgin Atlantic	984	285	1,269	27.4	9,001	8.7	1.23	5.6	76.1	81.6	Oct. 92	62

Source: Airline Business, September 1993, 'Much Pain, No Gain.'

Table 4.9 Europe's top 20 airlines (1993)

Rank	Airline company	Sales US$ million	Global rank
1.	Lufthansa	11,036.5	4.
2.	Air France Group	10,769.4	5.
3.	British Airways	9,307.7	6.
4.	SAS Group	5,908.2	12.
5.	Alitalia	5,510.7	14.
6.	KLM Royal Dutch	4,666.3	15.
7.	Swissair	4,438.5	16.
8.	Iberia	4,136.7	17.
9.	LTU/LTU Sud	1,836.1	31.
10.	Sabena	1,708.3	33.
11.	Aer Lingus	1,381.0	38.
12.	Aeroflot	1,172.1	43.
13.	Finnair	1,132.2	45.
14.	TAP Air Portugal	1,110.1	47.
15.	Austrian Airlines	1,003.8	49.
16.	Britannia Airways	924.0	53.
17.	Olympic Airways	922.5	54.
18.	Turkish Airlines	736.5	59.
19.	Airlines of Britain Hldgs	687.7	61.
20.	Virgin Atlantic	626.5	62.

Source: Airline Business, September 1993, 'Much Pain, No Gain.'

carrier of international passengers, serving 150 destinations in 69 countries, it was making continuous progress in terms of cost efficiency, service quality and marketing. BA recruited marketing experts from consumer goods companies who implemented a brand approach to the airline's classes. Some of the actions undertaken by BA in the early 1990s included the relaunching of its European business class Club Europe with £17.5 million and spending £10 million on new lounges (with a traditional British feel), check-in facilities and ground staff at Heathrow. It was also rumoured that BA was preparing to spend nearly £70 million on an advanced in-flight entertainment and information system for its long-haul fleet before the end of 1994.

British Airways and Virgin had fiercely competed against one another from the onset. One major incident that marked their rivalry was what became known as the 'dirty tricks campaign'. In 1992, Virgin Atlantic filed a lawsuit against BA, accusing it of entering Virgin's computer system and spreading false rumours. In January 1993, Virgin won its libel suit against BA in London. The wide press coverage caused much embarrassment to British Airways. Later that year, Virgin filed a $325 million lawsuit in the Federal Court of New York, accusing BA of using its monopoly power to distort competition on North American routes.

Table 4.10 Virgin Atlantic and British Airways: comparison of routes

Destination from London to:	Airline	Frequency	Departure–arrival (local times)	Aircraft
New York (JFK)	Virgin Atlantic	Daily (LHR)	14:00–16:40	747
			18:35–20:55	
	British Airways	Daily (LHR)	10:30–09:20	Concorde
			11:00–13:40	747
			14:00–16:40	747
			18:30–21:10	747
			19:00–17:50	Concorde
		Daily (Gat)	10:40–13:20	D10
New York (Newark)	Virgin Atlantic	Daily (LHR)	16:00–18:40	747
	British Airways	Daily (LHR)	14:45–17:40	747
Boston	Virgin Atlantic	Daily (Gat.)	15:00–17:10	A340
	British Airways	Daily (LHR)	15:45–18:00	747
		Daily (LHR)	09:55–12:30	767
Los Angeles	Virgin Atlantic	Daily (LHR)	12:00–15:10	747
	British Airways	Daily (LHR)	12:15–15:15	747–400
		Daily (LHR)	15:30–18:30	747–400
Miami	Virgin Atlantic	W,F,S,Su (Gat.)	11:15–15:45	747
		Th (Gat.)	11:15–15:45	747
	British Airways	Daily (LHR)	11:15–15:40	747
		Daily (LHR)	14:30–18:55	
Orlando	Virgin Atlantic	Daily (Gat.)	12:30–16:40	747
	British Airways	Tu,W,Su (LHR)	11:15–19:15	747
		M,Th,F,S (Gat.)	11:00–15:10	747
San Francisco	Virgin Atlantic	Daily (LHR)	11:15–14:05	747
	British Airways	Daily (LHR)	13:15–16:05	747–400
		Daily (LHR)	10:50–13:40	747
Tokyo	Virgin Atlantic	M,T,Th,F,S,Su (LHR)	13:00–08:55 (next day)	747/A340
	British Airways	Daily (LHR)	12:55–08:45 (next day)	747–400
		M,T,Th,F,S,Su (LHR)	16:30–12:15 (next day)	747–400
Hong Kong	Virgin Atlantic	Daily	20:30–16:35 (next day)	A340
	British Airways	F	13:55–09:55 (next day)	747–400
		M,T,W,Th,S,Su.	14:30–10:30 (next day)	747–400
		Daily	21:30–17:30 (next day)	747–400

Sources: The Guide to Virgin Atlantic Airways, Issue May/June 1994
British Airways Worldwide Timetable, 27 March–29 October 1994

Table 4.11 Virgin Atlantic and British Airways fares (£)

Route	Virgin Atlantic				British Airways			
	Upper Class ①	Mid Class ①	Economy 21 Day Apex ②	First Class ①	Club ①	Economy	21 Day Apex ③
New York	1195	473	489	1935	1061	620	538
San Francisco	1627	595	538④	2179	1627	920	638
Los Angeles	1627	604	538	2179	1627	920	638
Tokyo	1806	783	993	2751	1806	1580	993
Hong Kong	979	600	741	3280	2075	1808	741
Boston	1082	473	439	1935	1061	620	538
Miami	1144	529	498	2085	1144	780	598
Orlando	1144	529	498	2085	1144	780	598

Note:
① One-way weekend peak-time fares in Pounds Sterling (£).
② Economy fare for Virgin is 'Economy 21 day Apex' (reservation no later than 21 days prior to departure).
③ 21 day Apex round trip ticket.
④ Between May 17 and June 30, 1994 a special launch fare round trip ticket was sold at £299.

In addition to British Airways, Virgin competed with at least one major carrier on each of its destinations. For instance, it was up against United Airlines to Los Angeles, American Airlines to New York and Cathay Pacific to Hong Kong. Most of its competitors surpassed Virgin many times in terms of turnover, staff and number of aircraft. Yet Virgin was not intimidated by the size of its competitors; it saw its modest size as an advantage that enabled it to react quickly and remain innovative.

Virgin Atlantic's management structure

Virgin Atlantic's headquarters were in Crawley, a suburb near Gatwick. The airline had a loose organization combined with a high level of dialogue and involvement, as well as strong controls. A senior manager explained: 'Our business is about independence, entrepreneurial flair, and people having autonomy to make decisions; yet we pay a great deal of attention to overhead and cost levels.' Members of the management team, whose structure is shown in Figure 4.4, came from other airlines, other industries, or other divisions of the Virgin Group. The three top executives – co-managing directors Roy Gardner and Syd Pennington and finance director Nigel Primrose – reported directly to Richard Branson.

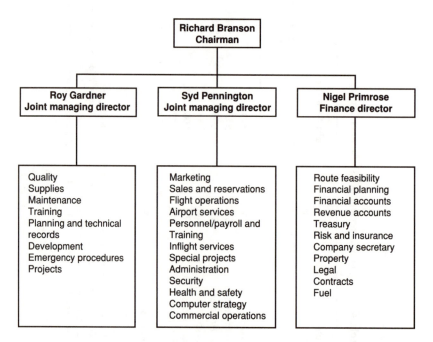

Figure 4.4 Virgin Atlantic Airways Ltd: organizational structure. Source: Virgin Atlantic

Gardner had joined Virgin Airways as technical director in 1984 after working at Laker Airways and British Caledonian Airways. He was responsible for the technical aspects of operations: quality, supplies, maintenance, emergency procedures. Pennington oversaw commercial operations, marketing, sales and flight operations. Primrose, a chartered accountant with 20 years of international experience, had been part of the senior team that set-up Air Europe in 1978 and Air UK in 1983 before joining Virgin Atlantic in 1986. He was Virgin Atlantic's company secretary with responsibility for route feasibility, financial planning, financial accounts, treasury, and legal affairs.

Steve Ridgeway headed the marketing department. After assisting Richard Branson in several projects, including the Transatlantic Boat Challenge, he had joined the airline in 1989 to develop its frequent traveller programme, becoming head of marketing in 1992. Paul Griffiths, who had 14 years of commercial aviation experience, became Virgin Atlantic's director of commercial operations after spending two years designing and implementing its information management system. Personnel director Nick Potts, a business studies graduate, had been recruited in 1991 from Warner Music UK where he was the head of the personnel department.

Marketing activities

Steve Ridgeway's marketing department covered a variety of activities, as shown in Figure 4.5. Some traditional marketing disciplines, such as advertising, promotions, planning and the Freeway frequent flyer programme, reported to Ruth Blakemore, head of marketing. Catering, retail operations (for example, duty free sales), product development and public relations reported directly to Steve Ridgeway.

Virgin Atlantic spent 2 per cent of turnover on advertising, well below the 5 to 7 per cent industry norm. Virgin's advertising had featured a series of short campaigns handled by various agencies. The winning of a quality award was

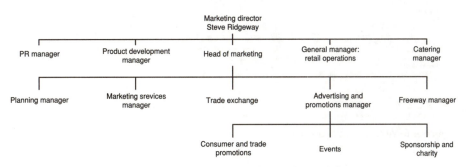

Figure 4.5 Virgin Atlantic: marketing department. Source: Virgin Atlantic

The world's favourite airline?

They must be on a different planet.

It's a brave airline that claims to be the world's favourite.

Now it seems the world has a different idea.

For at the 1989 Executive Travel Airline of the Year Awards, Virgin Atlantic have emerged victorious.

Those most demanding and, dare one say, discerning of people, the readers of Executive Travel Magazine voted Virgin Atlantic, Best Transatlantic Carrier.

It's not just over the Atlantic that they hold sway.

For Virgin were also named Best Business Class in the World, above airlines they admire such as Singapore and Thai.

A choice that was quickly seconded by Business Traveller Magazine.

It's not hard to see why Virgin's Upper Class commands such respect.

AIRLINE OF THE YEAR
AWARDS 1989

VIRGIN ATLANTIC AIRWAYS
EXECUTIVE TRAVEL MAGAZINE

Best Transatlantic Carrier
Best Business Class in the World
World's Best Inflight Entertainment

BUSINESS TRAVELLER MAGAZINE

World's Best Business Class

Passengers enjoy a free chauffeur driven car* to and from the airport plus a free economy stand-by ticket.†

On the plane there are first class sleeper seats that, miraculously, you can actually sleep in and on-board bars and lounges.

And your own personal Sony Video Walkman with a choice of 100 films.

As you might expect from Virgin, this entertainment is truly award winning. It helped scoop a third major award. Best In-Flight Entertainment.

So the next time you want to travel across the world in style, you know who to favour.

For details call *0800 800 400* or for reservations *0293 551616*, or see your travel agent.

*First 40 miles with our compliments. †Not available on Tokyo route.

LONDON   ·   NEW YORK JFK AND NEWARK   ··   MIAMI   ·   MOSCOW   ·   TOKYO

Figure 4.6 Virgin Atlantic: advertising (1990)

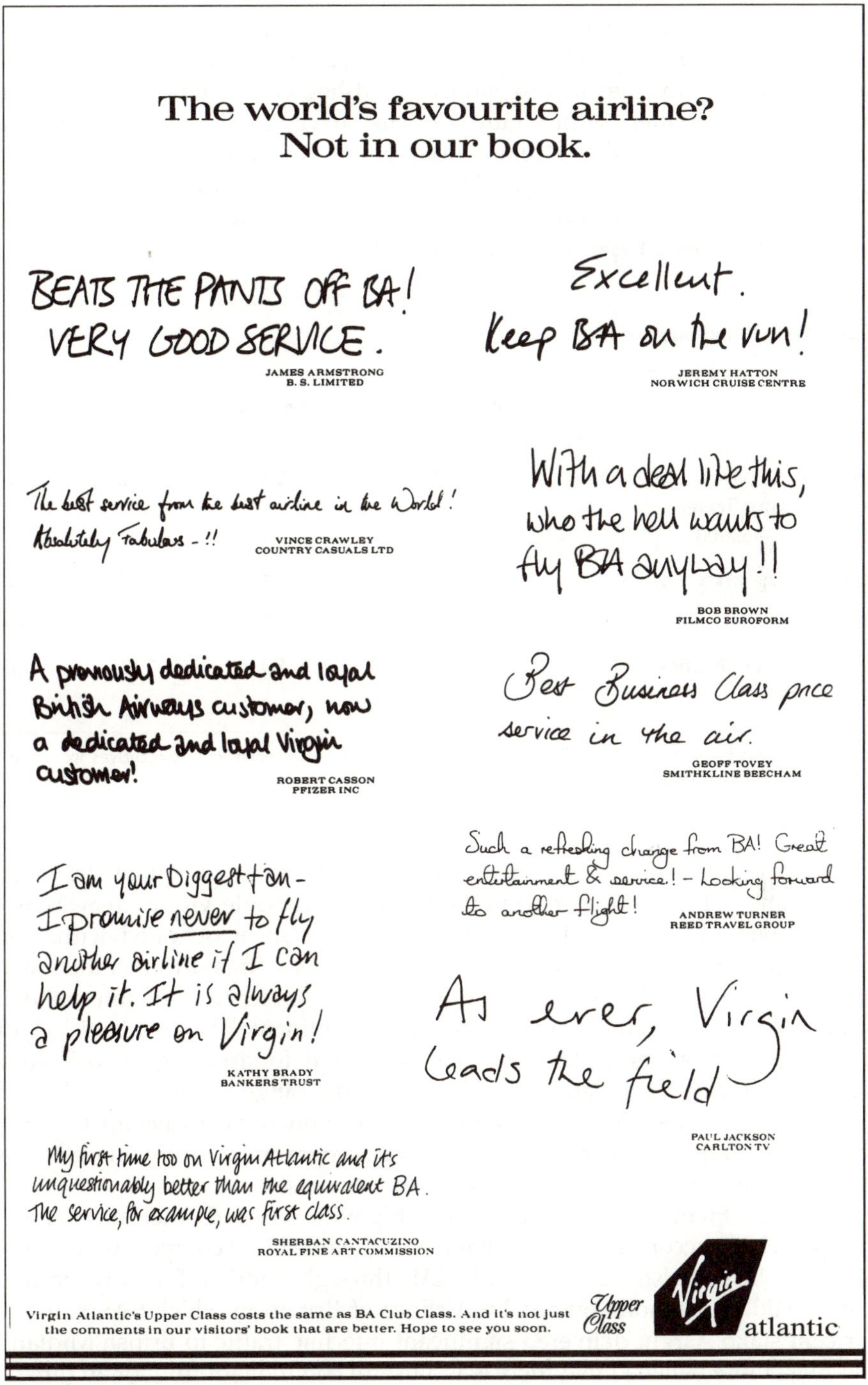

The world's favourite airline?
Not in our book.

BEATS THE PANTS OFF BA! VERY GOOD SERVICE.

JAMES ARMSTRONG
B. S. LIMITED

Excellent. Keep BA on the run!

JEREMY HATTON
NORWICH CRUISE CENTRE

The best service from the best airline in the World! Absolutely Fabulous - !!

VINCE CRAWLEY
COUNTRY CASUALS LTD

With a deal like this, who the hell wants to fly BA anyway !!

BOB BROWN
FILMCO EUROFORM

A previously dedicated and loyal British Airways customer, now a dedicated and loyal Virgin customer!

ROBERT CASSON
PFIZER INC

Best Business Class price service in the air.

GEOFF TOVEY
SMITHKLINE BEECHAM

Such a refreshing change from BA! Great entertainment & service! - Looking forward to another flight!

ANDREW TURNER
REED TRAVEL GROUP

I am your biggest fan - I promise never to fly another airline if I can help it. It is always a pleasure on Virgin!

KATHY BRADY
BANKERS TRUST

As ever, Virgin leads the field

PAUL JACKSON
CARLTON TV

My first time too on Virgin Atlantic and it's unquestionably better than the equivalent BA. The service, for example, was first class.

SHERBAN CANTACUZINO
ROYAL FINE ART COMMISSION

Virgin Atlantic's Upper Class costs the same as BA Club Class. And it's not just the comments in our visitors' book that are better. Hope to see you soon.

Upper Class *Virgin* atlantic

Figure 4.7 Virgin Atlantic: advertising (spring 1994)

often a campaign opportunity, as in Figure 4.6, as was the opening of a new line. On one April Fool's Day, Virgin announced that it had developed a new bubble-free champagne. It also launched ad-hoc campaigns in response to competitors' activities, as in Figure 4.7. The survey in Table 4.12 shows that Virgin Atlantic enjoyed a strong brand equity, as well as a high level of spontaneous awareness and a good image in the United Kingdom. In order to increase the trial rate, its advertising had evolved from a conceptual approach to more emphasis on specific product features.

Table 4.12 Brand equity survey

	British Airways	Virgin Atlantic	American	United
Perceived Strongest Brand Name in Transatlantic Travel (% of Respondents)	70	24	2	1
Spontaneous Awareness (%)	96	74	49	22
Usage (%)	93	48	44	23
Rating of Brand Names (0–100 scale)	85	80	61	58

Source: Business Marketing Services Limited (BMSL). Based on 141 interviews of executives from the UK's top 500 organizations.

In 1990, the airline launched its Virgin Freeway frequent travellers programme in Britain (it started in the US in 1992). While Virgin Freeway was an independent division of the Virgin Travel Group, it operated within the airline's marketing department. Freeway miles were offered to members who flew Mid Class or Upper Class or who used the services of international companies such as American Express, Inter-Continental Hotels, British Midland, SAS and others. Miles could be exchanged for free flights to Europe, North America and Japan, as well as a wide range of activities: hot air ballooning, polo lessons, rally driving, luxury country getaways for two, five days skiing in the US. As part of the Freeway programme, Virgin offered a free standby ticket for every Upper Class ticket purchased .

The Virgin Freeway was run in partnership with SAS and other international groups, which, according to Ruth Blakemore, enabled it to compete with British Airways. Virgin also had ties with SAS through another Freeway partner, British Midland, wholly-owned by Airlines of Britain in which SAS had a 35 per cent stake. Virgin delivered significant interline traffic to British Midland, and Blakemore believed that there was a useful common ground for all three to join forces against British Airways.

In May 1993, Virgin Atlantic unveiled a promotional campaign targeted at BA passengers who had never tried Virgin. Members of BA's Executive Club USA programme who had accumulated 50,000 miles or more qualified for a free Upper Class Companion ticket on Virgin; those with 10,000 to 49,999 miles qualified for a free Mid Class ticket. The campaign was launched with a radio commercial in which Richard Branson said: 'In recent years, Virgin has done about everything we can think of to get those remaining British Airways' passengers to try Virgin Atlantic.'

The marketing department handled the franchising of the Virgin Atlantic brand, which included two routes. London–Athens, launched from Gatwick in March 1992 in partnership with South East European Airlines of Greece, was transferred to Heathrow seven months later. London City Airport–Dublin, with City Jet, was launched in January 1994. In both cases, the aircraft and crew bore Virgin's name and colours, but Virgin's partner was the operator and paid royalties to Virgin for the use of its brand, marketing and sales support, and for assistance in the recruitment and training of flight staff.

In April 1994, Virgin announced a partnership with Delta Air Lines – its first alliance with a major international airline. Delta would purchase a set percentage of seats on Virgin flights between London and Los Angeles, New York (Newark and JFK), Miami, San Francisco, Orlando, and Boston which it would price and sell independently. The alliance, which increased Virgin's annual revenue by $150 million and gave Delta access to Heathrow, had received the blessing of the British government and was awaiting US approval.

Virgin Atlantic's public relations department, known as 'the press office' and led by James Murray, played an important role. 'We are not here just to react to press inquiries,' explained Murray. 'We also try to gain publicity for the airline's products and services and to show how much better we are than the competition.' Virgin Atlantic enjoyed excellent relations with the media – not the rule in the airline industry – because of a combination of factors: Richard Branson's persona, the airline's openness in dealing with the press, its 'David vs. Goliath' quality, the news value of its innovations, and a good management of media relationships.

For instance, Virgin had readily accepted an invitation to participate in BBC television's prime time Secret Service series, in which investigators posing as customers test service at well known firms. Failures in service delivery were exposed and discussed. British Airways, which the BBC had approached first, had declined. While the programme did identify some shortcomings in Virgin's operations, including delays in meal service (due to oven problems) and in answering passenger calls, it gave a lively demonstration of the quality of service in Upper Class and of Virgin's willingness to take corrective action.

The public relations department comprised three people in Crawley and two in the group press office, where James Murray spent two days a week. Originally set up in Richard Branson's own house, the group press office had to move next door as the amount of work increased. Staff were on call round-the-clock, sometimes taking calls from journalists in the middle of the night.

During a one-hour car ride with James Murray, the casewriters watched him handle a constant flow of requests ranging from invitations to the inaugural San Francisco flight to questions on Virgin's position on privatizing the Civil Aviation Agency or the possible banning of peanuts on flights after reports of allergy risks – all on the car phone.

A five-member product development department evaluated and developed innovations. It handled a broad range of new product activities – a new identity programme for the aircraft, selection of seat design and internal decoration, the catering system, or new lounges – and coordinated the input from other departments. Typically, the marketing, engineering, commercial and sales departments also participated in developing new products. For example, Airport Services played a crucial role in setting up the Clubhouse lounge.

By June 1994, Virgin had taken steps to correct its main weaknesses: the age of its fleet and its punctuality problems. More than half the fleet would be renewed by the end of the year, and Virgin was undertaking an 'On-Time Initiative' in which cabin crew were to shut doors exactly 10 minutes before departure time, even if late passengers had not boarded – even Richard Branson, who was notorious for being late. Virgin was also implementing a new corporate identity programme. In addition to the Virgin logo and the 'Vargas Lady', all aircraft would bear the words 'virgin atlantic' in large grey letters, as shown in Figure 4.8.

Figure 4.8 Virgin Atlantic aircraft after the new corporate identity programme (1994)

Challenges for the future

During its first decade Virgin Atlantic had confronted great challenges and survived the worst recession in the history of air transportation. Amidst rumours over the airline's financial health, Richard Branson had always stressed his personal commitment. 'I would put everything I had into making sure that Virgin Atlantic was here in twenty years time,' he said.

Virgin Atlantic had demonstrated its capacity to innovate, to satisfy customers, and to be financially viable in difficult times. As the world economy began to recover, the airline was poised for a quantum leap in the scale of its operations. When Richard Branson had founded it in 1984, his ambition had been to build an airline unlike any other. Ten years later, what set Virgin apart was its reputation for giving customers what they wanted at prices they could afford, pioneering new concepts in service and entertainment, and restoring a sense of pleasure and excitement to long distance travel.

The main challenge the airline faced as it celebrated its tenth anniversary was to foster this difference throughout the 1990s. What sort of airline should it be? How could it achieve that goal? How could it remain profitable? How could it retain its competitive edge in innovations? Was it possible to grow while retaining the organizational advantages of a small entrepreneurial company? How could it keep employees motivated and enthusiastic? How would it keep the momentum of its success? These were some of the questions that went through Richard Branson's mind as his 400 guests and himself watched a Virgin 747 Jumbo fly over the Thames and Westminster to mark Virgin's first decade.

Chapter 5

Land Rover: the Discovery success story

Vivienne Shaw

Since the launch of the Discovery on 15 November 1989 Land Rover's newest vehicle has been an unprecedented success. The first new vehicle to be launched by the company in 19 years has transformed not only the company's performance but also the 4 × 4 leisure market. This case study looks at the background to the Discovery's success and how Land Rover has managed to beat the Japanese at their own game.

Background

Formed in the late 1940s, Land Rover has become the acknowledged world leader in 4 × 4 technology. The workhorse of the company, recently re-branded the Defender range, gained the company a reputation for solid performance in all terrain conditions. Popular with farmers, utilities and the military the vehicle has been the foundation of Land Rover's success in this niche market. With the launch of the Range Rover in 1970 the company created a further niche in the 4 × 4 market targeting those individuals who required a rugged all terrain vehicle, but who demanded levels of comfort not available in the workhorse Defender range. The Range Rover is firmly targeted at the top end of the luxury 4 × 4 sector and continues to dominate this segment with high levels of customer loyalty.

Land Rover was a two-product company operating in clear niches within the 4 × 4 market. It was the Japanese, however, who spotted a gap in the market

– a broader leisure 4 × 4 sector somewhere between the upper class image of the Range Rover and the utilitarian Defender range. It was Mitsubishi with the Shogun, Isuzu with the Trooper and Daihatsu with the Fourtrak who really started the market segment now known as the leisure 4 × 4 market. It was the Discovery, however, which developed that segment and in the UK cornered the market for Land Rover. The launch of the Discovery was to change the face of the 4 × 4 leisure sector and to create the fastest growing segment in an otherwise slowing car market.

Discovery's performance

Whilst Discovery cannot claim to have created the leisure 4 × 4 market, it can be said that the Discovery grew a substantial niche within the car market as a whole. Whilst Europe was experiencing a severe recession and the mainstream car manufacturers were severely hit, the leisure 4 × 4 market continued to grow and the Discovery was instrumental in that growth.

The leisure 4 × 4 market has changed considerably since the launch of the Discovery. New entrants such as the Vauxhall Frontera have grown the market further. Within the 4 × 4 leisure segment there are now sizeable sub-segments each targeting different customer needs with different product offerings. In spite of increased competition, the market has continued to grow and Discovery's sales growth has been impressive, in most years exceeding the growth rate in the leisure 4 × 4 market as a whole. As Table 5.1 shows, Discovery has achieved a high market share in the segment of the car market in which it competes, and, in spite of intense competition since 1993, has maintained that share of the market. The success of the Discovery in market share terms is even more impressive when it is considered that much of that

Table 5.1 Market Shares in the 4 × 4 Leisure Market in the UK

Competitor	1990 %	1991 %	1992 %	1993 %	1994 %	1995 %
Land Rover Discovery	25.33	28.73	26.28	27.89	29.22	28.77
Mitsubishi Shogun	14.28	14.24	9.35	6.69	5.94	8.45
Isuzu Trooper	13.04	11.49	11.07	7.58	3.25	2.58
Daihatsu Fourtrak	5.85	6.56	6.05	2.38	2.92	1.82
Vauxhall Frontera		1.20	14.27	15.54	16.50	11.65
Ford Maverick				3.11	7.32	5.13
Jeep Cherokee				6.18	5.45	7.40
Share of Japanese mfrs	39.25	36.02	30.10	22.54	18.50	18.06

Figures supplied by Land Rover, 1996

share came not just from growth in the market but from the Japanese competitors in the market. As Table 5.1 shows, the market share of Japanese manufacturers in the leisure 4 × 4 segment has been in decline ever since the vehicle's launch.

Although the market is still growing, growth rates are slowing down especially in the sub-segments traditionally served by Discovery. New competitors like the Rav4 from Toyota are taking over from Discovery in new sub-segments of the market and in their first full year of manufacture have already taken nearly 10 per cent of the total 4 × 4 leisure market. In order to continue with their high levels of success Land Rover needs to maintain a good market focus and to develop new products which, whilst building on the organization's marque values, serve the new sub-segments of the market which are showing the fastest growth rates.

The annual growth in sales enjoyed by Discovery is quite remarkable and is shown in Table 5.2. This also shows that the high levels of market share have not just been achieved as a result of growth in the market but that the Discovery has genuinely taken share away from its Japanese competitors. It also shows how much Discovery has helped grow the 4 × 4 leisure market. The exceptionally high growth achieved in 1993 can be directly attributable to the re-launch of the Discovery in that year. The sustained growth of Discovery sales enjoyed between 1989 and 1995 is virtually unheard of in the car market.

Developing the Discovery

Market research played an important role in the development of the Discovery. In order to launch a new vehicle against existing Japanese competitors, the Discovery project team had to get the vehicle right first time. Thus, for the first time, Land Rover adopted a market-focused approach to the development of a new product and it has paid off. Extensive research was conducted throughout the design and development phase of the project. Research was commissioned

Table 5.2 Discovery and Market Growth Rates

Growth	1991 %	1992 %	1993 %	1994 %	1995 %
Land Rover Discovery	26.9	23.6	47.7	23.4	13.8
4 × 4 Leisure Market Growth	11.9	35.1	39.2	17.8	15.6

Based on figures supplied by Land Rover, 1996

at the product and market level with specific research into the existing competitors, customer needs and attitudes. At the time the major rivals to Discovery were the Mitsubishi Shogun, Isuzu Trooper and the Daihatsu Fourtrak.

One of the main aims of the Discovery project team was to create a 4 × 4 vehicle with all the necessary performance capabilities but which was more like a car than a truck. This was achieved through a heavy focus on the interior design. The development of the Discovery represented a departure from normal product development approaches at Rover in that a small project team was set up comprising both marketers and engineers in order to combine the necessary engineering performance with the needs of potential customers. Land Rover's research showed that the Japanese models on the market at the time only scored average marks for ride, interior design and facia with spaciousness scoring below average. Potential customers clearly disliked the dull, black interiors of existing 4 × 4 vehicles.

Armed with this data, the Discovery team, with the aid of Conran, created a radically different interior for Discovery. Lots of windows and a high roof, together with light coloured seats and light coloured fascia created an airy, roomy feel to the vehicle. Further small innovations were added to the interior to make the vehicle stand out from its competitors. Magazine racks were introduced above the rear seats and storage space was added above the front visors. The rear seat, also a minor innovation, was designed to be 'theatre style' so as to be slightly higher than the front seats, giving the rear passengers a better view.

Further innovations were introduced inside the vehicle with neat foldaway seats in the back. The seat design itself was innovative as was the mechanism for folding it away without compromising the luggage space in the back. These foldaway seats in the seven-seater version have become the prized 'possession' of the children in the Discovery family. All of this could be achieved without losing any of the rugged off-road capabilities of a 'Land Rover vehicle'. The exterior styling was also a departure from the normal boxed image of the competitors. The higher, more curved exterior created a very distinctive looking vehicle. The shape was so different in a market where exterior styling was converging that it made people's heads turn.

The mechanical design of the Discovery was not particularly innovative, but built on tried and tested 4 × 4 technology. There was, however, a deliberate policy on behalf of Land Rover to create a different image for Discovery from that of the Range Rover. The Discovery should not be seen as a baby Range Rover. Much of the styling on Discovery is innovative though and does make the vehicle stand out from the crowd. The Discovery, according to Terry Donovan, a member of the development and launch team, 'knocked the Japanese competition sideways' as, in terms of customer needs, it was the ideal vehicle at the time.

Prior to launch, the company made extensive use of clinics to test potential customers' reactions to both the vehicle itself and the positioning to be adopted. Using the Shogun as the benchmark, 18 months before launch, clinics were held to gauge the reaction of individuals to a new 4 × 4 vehicle. Initially participants of the clinics were not informed which company was developing the vehicle, although a blank oval badge on the steering wheel led many people to believe that the prototype Discovery was a Ford. They were then concerned as to whether the vehicle really could deliver the capabilities being promised. Yet others thought that it had to be a Japanese vehicle. Most participants actually dismissed the possibility that the vehicle was a Land Rover because the styling was perceived as being too radical and the design was seen as being too feminine. On learning that it was actually a Land Rover those concerns disappeared immediately, showing the strength and image Land Rover had already built up in terms of off-road capability. The reaction surprised even Land Rover marketers as customers exclaimed 'This is it!' meaning that Discovery is the vehicle they had been waiting for.

In Discovery customers finally had a vehicle which could be driven comfortably both across fields and on motorways without any compromise in comfort. From the drawing board to market took one third of the usual development time. Although this may have resulted in some quality related problems post launch, the speed of development and commercialization were vital to the success of Discovery.

The launch

Land Rover knew that the launch of the Discovery in the UK would be vital for the vehicle's success. Get it wrong here and they would not be able to make up for it in Europe or the rest of the world. Given Land Rover's British heritage it was clear from the early stages that the UK would be the vehicle's biggest market.

The launch in the UK was a success because extensive market research had shown that targeting existing 4 × 4 drivers would not secure the long term success of the Discovery and that targeting 'normal car' drivers would yield the best results. The launch itself took place in a Plymouth warehouse converted into a theatre with an off road track, to put the Discovery through its paces, on the nearby moors.

Given that it was Land Rover's first new product launch for 19 years there was considerable media interest which helped to create a high level of public interest. The launch advert (Antarctica), which was shown on television in seven European countries, was full of intrigue and helped the Discovery marketing team build a strong position against the existing Japanese competitors. Interest levels were so high that some customers had to wait up to nine months for a vehicle. Sales of the Discovery outpaced the expectation of the development team. Launched in recessionary times, Discovery made Land Rover one of very few car companies increasing production and employing new workers whilst other manufacturers were laying off their workforce. Following launch, sales of Discovery in the UK soared and have been increasing year on year and are still increasing seven years after the initial launch. A strategic decision was taken to make the Discovery a competitive purchase. A launch price of £15750 was set for a base three-door model, which either matched or was slightly below the price of Discovery's benchmark vehicle the Shogun. This competitive pricing strategy has no doubt been influential in the success of the Discovery.

Publicity played a major role in the initial launch of Discovery. Land Rover created heightened awareness of the vehicle prior to launch with the 'leak' of a photograph of the vehicle to the press six months ahead of launch. In the run up to the launch further pieces of information were 'leaked' creating a sense of anticipation. So much publicity was given to the imminent launch of Discovery in the UK that the interest levels in the vehicle were high. The story is told that so many people put down a deposit of £1000 for a vehicle before launch that the company had generated sufficient orders to cover nine months production of Discovery.

Everyone, not least members of the Discovery project team, was stunned by the vehicle's immediate and continued success. Initial sales estimates had been based on a maximum production run of 750 cars a week. Production has now exceeded 2000 vehicles a week. Land Rover forecasting clearly left a lot to be desired! The company admits, however, that it lacked the confidence to produce a better forecast attributing some of this to the organizational culture, which existed at the time within Rover, which was not accustomed to such success.

Customer profile

Discovery has always been targeted at families, but the vehicle is more than just a family car. Seventy per cent of Discovery owners came from the traditional car market, with only a very low level of substitution from other Land Rover products. Within the segment there is also a high degree of loyalty with a repeat purchase rate of 49 per cent. This goes to show that Discovery is not just a fad.

Seventy per cent of Discoveries are bought by individuals. The customer profile, which was developed before launch using extensive market research, is as follows. Average age is mid 40s, affluent but not as rich as Range Rover owners. Customers typically come from family households. They work hard and are still achieving. Most come from managerial or professional backgrounds and are concerned with the running costs of their car. Males purchase 85–90 per cent of Discoveries, but 30–40 per cent are driven by females. It is often the customer's second or third car.

This customer profiling has proved to be very accurate and still describes the typical Discovery owner today.

Developing the Discovery brand

Market research at Land Rover has not been limited to the development of the Discovery and is perceived as an important on-going activity. Given the success of Discovery it would be easy for the company to become complacent, but, as far as market research is concerned, this has certainly not been the case. Research continues to be conducted at four main levels:

1 Product level – research is regularly conducted into the current product compared with the competition, customer characteristics, market trends and new vehicle concepts.
2 Quality – quality is researched in detail both at supplier and customer level.
3 Communications – regular research is undertaken to assess the image of the Discovery vis-à-vis its competitors. There is a strong quality focus to the research, which is mainly of a syndicated nature on a pan-European scale.
4 Dealer level – customer satisfaction surveys are conducted regularly. The dealer research is used to incentivize the dealers with financial benefit accruing to the best dealers.

The actual quantity of research conducted by Land Rover in the development phase and post launch was unusual for the company, although continuous research on the Discovery, and now on other Land Rover products, has helped the company to achieve a greater market focus throughout the organization.

Marketing mix

Clearly the Discovery was the right product at the right time. The pricing of the vehicle also added to the success as a clear strategic decision was adopted by Land Rover to make Discovery a competitive purchase. The remaining two elements of the marketing mix – distribution and promotion – also had to be right to ensure the success of Discovery. Dealers within the UK were scrutinized very carefully. Market research showed that many of Land Rover's existing dealers had a pretty poor reputation and were not perceived as being very customer oriented. As a result the number of dealerships was pared from 350 to 120 with a requirement on the part of each of the remaining dealers to invest £100,000 in the franchise prior to the launch of Discovery. This would ensure the commitment of the dealers to Discovery. The initial advertising of Discovery concentrated on the mystique of the vehicle with tracks through the snow across all kinds of terrain ending with a vehicle covered in snow. Dramatically a helicopter lifts and clears the snow to reveal the Discovery. Post launch advertisements have built on the vehicle's positioning as a family vehicle which is more than just a car and which can be used to provide the whole family with fun and adventure. Only television advertisements were used in the early days and were designed purely to create awareness and not to sell the product.

The promotion and positioning were innovative as Land Rover moved away from the traditional focus on the capabilities of the vehicle to a more aspirational approach. It is this aspirational approach which created a strong image for Discovery which has not really been matched by its competitors. This approach led the way for the company to create a set of marque values for the organization and the complete Land Rover product range.

Innovations within the dealership network are also taking place in the USA. Although a small player in the US 4 × 4 leisure market, Discovery, since its launch in 1993, has created a niche position for itself, not least in the way it is now approaching its dealerships. In the last couple of years Land Rover have introduced Land Rover Adventure Centres throughout the USA. Within the dealership there is a heavy emphasis on lifestyle and aspirational issues. All dealer staff are required to attend a training course called 'Creating the Magic' designed to create a unique Land Rover culture. Following a deal with Timberland, the footwear and clothing specialist, all Land Rover personnel in the USA wear Timberland clothing. The dealerships are themed, for example as the wild west, and all aspects of the dealers' premises follow this theme, with log cabin effect in the show room. Perhaps the most innovative part of this approach is the inclusion in each of these centres of a mini 'demo track' where prospective customers can put the Discovery through its paces. This approach has been highly successful in the US and there are plans to transfer the idea to other markets. The major constraint in the UK is space. Whilst the inclusion of a jungle track is desirable, most dealers do not have the necessary land on which to build one.

Marque values

One important facet of the Discovery's success has been the creation of a set of marque values, not just for the Discovery but for the Land Rover organization as a whole. Driven by the Discovery, these values have now been applied across the range of Land Rover vehicles and throughout the Land Rover organization. Developed on the back of extensive research, six marque values have been identified (Table 5.3).

Of the six marque values, the ones most closely aligned with the Discovery are freedom and adventure. In the early days, owning a Discovery made an individual stand out from the crowd as the vehicle itself looked so different to anything else on the market and made heads turn when one drove past. Adventure is also a key Discovery value as it opens up a whole range of possibilities for individuals who previously owned a car, which in turn feeds into freedom as the Discovery driver has greater freedom to go where she/he wishes.

Table 5.3

Individualism	Knowing your own mind; independence
Authenticity	Specialist 4 × 4 manufacturer: fit for purpose
Freedom	Go where you want to: choice
Adventure	Exploring the unknown: confidence
Guts	Giving everything you've got: endurance
Supremacy	Superior 4 × 4 performance: leadership

As the literature produced and circulated to all Land Rover employees notes 'Successful marques trigger a strong mental image – a set of values and associations – that helps the decision-making process . . . We have to shape this image through everything we do. Make the values of the Land Rover marque work powerfully for us in the purchase decision.' It is recognized that car purchases are not necessarily entirely rational 'which is why the emotional values of the Land Rover marque are so important . . .'

Each Land Rover brand makes a contribution to the marque values which, in turn, feed into the other brands. The marque values are seen as being the 'DNA of the organization'. There is an interrelationship between the values and all products, which come under the Land Rover banner. All future development within the company should be informed by the marque values, enhance some of them, but must not go against any of them. Whilst the notion of marque values is a useful way to develop and inform the marketing strategy for the Discovery and other Land Rover brands, they have served a wider purpose which underpins the continued success of the Discovery.

Developed by the Land Rover marketing team, in consultation with their advertising agency Bates Dorland and communications agency Cricket, the marque values have been seen as a way of instilling a sense of shared values within the Land Rover organization as a whole. Initially targeted at the dealers, a cascade effect was created throughout the organization as John Russell, former managing director, Sales and Marketing, Rover Group, insisted that everyone within the organization be invited to attend the same presentation. Talk to people on the assembly line or development engineers and they can tell you what the marque values are and identify with them. The creation and communication of the marque values has reinforced a sense of pride within the Land Rover organization. Instilling a sense of shared values within Land Rover is not about training, but as John Stubbings of Bates Dorland notes 'is seen almost as a form of evangelism'.

The development of the marque values followed on, however, from the successful launch of the Discovery. Had the Discovery not been so successful, it might have been more difficult to establish the marque values and create the vision which now informs other market and product development activities within Land Rover. The marque values are under constant review, but concentrate on the strength and character of each brand and not on quality and reliability.

Management at Land Rover

Management, and in particular marketing management, at Land Rover, has been instrumental in effecting a change to a more marketing oriented organization. John Russell was seen as being an instinctive marketer – a person with vision who is committed to using new and exciting approaches to marketing not just Discovery but all Land Rover vehicles. Although innovations at Land Rover are small, the team approach has encouraged free thinking and idea generation. It was Russell who was instrumental in the development of marque values within Land Rover and he has personally ensured that all individuals are fully informed of those values and how they can and do contribute to the success of the Discovery and of Land Rover.

Discovery, and consequently Land Rover, have been successful because individuals are committed to the brand. This has enabled the company to develop a clear long-term strategy with clear brand commitment and integrity.

Although there is still a strong manufacturing orientation within the organization, Land Rover is clearly becoming more market focused. There is a pride in those who work for the company and the public image is of a company which has been transformed. The Discovery can also take some credit in the organizational transformation which is taking place, because had the Discovery not been so successful then instilling a sense of value within the company would have been much more difficult.

The take-over of Rover by BMW is seen as a good opportunity for Land Rover and, in particular, Discovery. BMW does not have the 4 × 4 expertise which Land Rover has, so this part of the company can make a very positive contribution to the BMW Group. BMW also adopt a long-term perspective to their markets and have already invested significantly in plant and equipment at Land Rover's Solihull facilities. BMW value investment in both product and markets, which can only be a positive sign for the continued success of Discovery and Land Rover.

Future developments

Since the launch of the Discovery and its subsequent success Land Rover have not rested on their laurels. Following the development of the sub-segment of the leisure 4 × 4 market currently dominated by Toyota's RAV4 and Suzuki's

Vitara Land Rover has been determined to maintain its strong market position. To this end the new Freelander was developed to compete in the lighter end of the 4 × 4 market. As with the Discovery, the Freelander is a relatively late entrant into a market dominated by Japanese manufacturers. Formally unveiled at the Frankfurt Motor Show in September 1997, the question on everybody's lips is 'can the Freelander repeat the success of its stable mate the Discovery?'

Chapter 6

Rank Xerox: DocuTech

Veronica Wong

Background

The Xerox Corporation of the USA developed the commercial uses of the electrostatic copying process from a 1938 invention of Mr Chester Carlson, an American patent lawyer. It launched its first viable xerographic office copier in 1959. Protected by patents, the company grew phenomenally and completely dominated the world copier market through the 1960s and into the early 1970s. Xerox became a multi-product international company marketing a wide range of document processing equipment including copiers/duplicators, facsimile machines, laser printers, scanners, electronic publishing systems, workstations, networks and software. Currently it has sales of US$16.6bn (1 ECU = US$1.12 or UK£0.66) and profits of US$1.1bn.

Rank Xerox Ltd is owned jointly by the Xerox Corporation of the US and The Rank Organisation plc of the UK. The US company has a majority (80 per cent) stake in the group. The business of the group and its associates is research, development, manufacture, marketing and maintenance of document processing systems and equipment. This is supported by a portfolio of document services. The group's activities also include the marketing of paper and the manufacture and marketing of toner and related supplies. In 1995, the group's turnover was £3693 million, a 12 per cent increase over 1994, while profit before tax grew to a record level of £616 million in the same year. Profit after tax was £363 million, a 69 per cent increase over 1994.

Xerox Corporation enjoyed a monopoly of the plain paper photocopier (ppc) market right up to the early 1970s. Over the years, however, its monopoly culture, large bureaucracy and forays into new businesses, led to an organization that became increasingly out of touch with the new competitive pressures in its flagship copier business. Xerox had become too product-oriented, at the expense of a customer focus. Customers had become disappointed with Xerox quality and service. Costs and product prices were higher than the competition's. The company lost significant market share to domestic and Japanese competitors.

Beginning in 1980, Xerox undertook an ambitious programme to regain its eroded leadership in the copier industry. The first phase of recovery involved restructuring the entire corporation in the US and the UK and developing a philosophy emphasizing quality. Competitor benchmarking was used to establish goals, plans and procedures to improve quality and to achieve cost reductions. The quest for quality was communicated forcefully throughout the organization. A corporate-wide 'Leadership through Quality' total quality management programme was in place by 1983. All employees were trained in quality tools and processes to ensure that they could meet quality targets set for each year.

The second phase involved the development of a 'Customer Satisfaction' initiative in 1987. The customer satisfaction goal for 1990 was that:

'100 per cent of Xerox customers are very satisfied or satisfied with
our products and services through the elimination of defects and
errors in our work processes and the achievement of world-class
benchmark quality and value in our products and other deliveries to
the customer.'

Based on identifying the best methods in use, the corporation developed 'core' procedures that could be used by all operating units world-wide for measuring, managing and improving customer satisfaction.

The business underwent another major restructuring in 1988, refocusing its document-processing line on its core copying business. In the course of refocusing the organization on the document-processing business, Xerox/RX began to style itself 'The Document Company', a name used hereafter in the case, and equipped itself with a new logo and mission – to 'provide total document solutions to customers thereby enhancing their productivity and business performance'.

Xerox/RX's obsession for quality, restructuring, cost reductions, customer satisfaction and innovations over the last decade has led to positive results. The corporation has been able to stem the decline in market share. Currently it is the market leader, with 38 per cent stake in the UK copier market, in terms of copy volume, compared to Canon's 18 per cent and Kodak's 12 per cent. Ten other firms have shares between 3 per cent and 8 per cent. Not only has it received prestigious awards for total quality strategies and customer satisfaction delivery (namely, the Malcolm Baldridge National Quality Award in 1989 the European Quality Award in 1992), Xerox Corporation's 99.9 per cent customer satisfaction performance is unrivalled in the industry. The corporation has continued to invest in new products, ranging from colour copiers and digital production publishers to 'smart' multifunction machines, to remain competitive in a difficult and entrenched market. It has achieved this through an organization and culture that is inherently marketing oriented.

The Document Company: leadership, management process and culture

Leadership and management process

The company regards innovation leadership – being first in a technology or market – as critical for competitive success. Product, service and distribution channel innovations are viewed as means to achieve business growth objectives and long-term business performance. Technological innovations must be continually supported by product improvements (continual innovation). A balance is sought between radical (major) and incremental innovations, between short- and longer-term business goals. The corporation has evolved a Business Excellence Management Model – a framework to guide the determination of the firm's business directions and how best to achieve these. The model embraces six categories: 'management leadership' (vision setting and organizational culture); 'human resource management'; 'process management'; 'customer and market focus'; 'quality support and tools' and 'business priorities and results'. For each management category, an annual formal planning process produces a set of desired states (mission), priorities and objectives and the strategies and 'enablers,' which help the firm to achieve these. A 'Policy Deployment' document (also known as The Blue Book) is used to build and communicate the key programmes and support actions required to close the gap between the firm's current position and its targets. The Blue Book is aligned to the Business Excellence Management Model used by the company and all its business units world-wide. It is an essential vehicle for incorporating goals and priorities set by management into missions, plans and strategies.

The Blue Book clearly spells out a vision of what the company must become if it is to prosper and serve customers better. It is the starting point for all the firm's planning and investment, including innovation decisions. It guides the formal planning embraced by each management category. For example, the Rank Xerox 2000 vision states that:

'The Document Company will be the leader in the Global
Document market, providing Document Services that enhance
Business Productivity.'

The Blue Book also outlines the company's key goals for customer satisfaction, employee satisfaction, market share and return on assets.

The role for senior management is explicitly stated in The Blue Book:

'(to) display a customer focus, exhibit role model behaviour,
establish clear long term goals and annual objectives, establish
strategic boundaries and provide an empowered environment to
achieve world class productivity and business results.'

Culture: market-orientation, employee empowerment and a learning organization

Top management recognized that, to achieve the vision and goals it had set for The Document Company, it needed market-driven business strategies, product strategies and innovations that were determined by customer requirements and expectations. The restructuring programme and quality and customer satisfaction initiatives pursued in the 1980s would not have borne fruit without a fundamental shift from a product- to customer-oriented culture. This meant that everyone in the organization must 'look towards the marketplace, where we can be continually interested in our customers, aware of our competitors and in touch with the relevant technologies. Our success is measured by our results, which means an absolute improvement in each of our priorities – externally benchmarked.' At The Document Company, employees are rewarded when they meet customer satisfaction and market performance targets.

Top management also strongly encouraged teamwork, supported by a strong belief in people 'empowerment' whereby 'diverse opinions are valued in active and constructive debate and people closest to the action are empowered to make decisions. Responsibility is then shared by all with managers accountable for achieving results through the expertise of the teams.'

A learning culture has also been created. Top management asserts that ' We learn from our own mistakes', so strongly encourage risk-taking and show tolerance of failure. A number of schemes have been introduced to encourage employees to innovate, such as the 'inspiration programme' that rewards staff with a bonus or a percentage of profits generated by their idea. Additionally, to communicate the importance of innovation, 'leadership in innovation' is one of the key performance measures used to appraise and reward staff performance. Mistakes and conflicts, on the other hand, are accepted and solutions found quickly through open and honest communications.

The Document Company has also cultivated a strong culture for benchmarking and implementing best practice. The firm has a charter for both external benchmarking (learning from world-class players within and outside its own industry) and internal benchmarking (standardized procedure for sharing best practice within the organization).

Networking and training are heavily stressed to ensure staff continually acquire the knowledge, skills and attitudes they need to do the job better. Internal 'formalized' networks exist, such as the 'network of business process champions and sponsors', 'customer service network' and specific communications networks which operate as channels for sharing ideas and information on 'best practices'. External networks are particularly relevant for successful innovation. Xerox/RX recognizes the role that partnerships and alliances play in facilitating innovation and securing global leadership in new and emerging markets. External networks often provide the basis for productive and fruitful alliances and partnerships

The Document Company is currently a competitive business. It has fostered a culture that is market led, customer oriented and highly competitor focused. Innovation is seen as central to its revival strategy. The DocuTech systems were the first fruits of the corporation's new innovation strategy.

DocuTech

In October 1990, the company launched the DocuTech Production Publisher. Business observers cite this as an innovation that 'will ignite a revolution as profound as the introduction of the first plain paper copier in 1959'.

Features

The DocuTech is an electronic document processing and printing system that consists of a high speed, high-resolution digital scanner, a microprocessor, a high resolution, high speed laser printer and on-line finishing equipment. The laser printer produces superior quality documents and at a faster rate than a conventional desktop laser printer. The standalone system scans hard-copy documents, turns these into digital masters which are then 'made ready' for printing, and then finally prints and finishes off (e.g. staple, stitch, bind) the document, all in one process. Additional finishing equipment can be incorporated into the system, such as a booklet maker and perfect binders, thus providing a range of finishing options. The DocuTech machine allows the user to manipulate text and images easily and quickly before the documents are printed. The system also allows jobs to take place concurrently (e.g. one job can be printing whilst another is being scanned and edited). Jobs can be put in a job queue and the machine working all the time, leaving the operator free to do other jobs. The documents can be stored, retrieved, altered and reprinted at a later date. The DocuTech can also be upgraded, thus reducing buyers' fear of technological obsolescence.

DocuTech's significance to the firm

The innovation has successfully penetrated the market for professional document production (that is, the 'professional production publishing environment'). It is a major innovation based on digital, as opposed to traditional offset and light lens technology, and has been instrumental in creating new growth opportunities for the corporation. The innovation was very significant to the firm, as it surfaced at a time when the corporation's core black and white plain paper copier business faced a mature and intensely competitive international market. Since launching the DocuTech, digital publishing has become a billion-dollar-a-year business for the corporation, with sales of digital products, along with colour printing and other copying equipment, growing more quickly than black-and-white plain paper copiers. Revenues from digital products have been growing at an annual rate of 22 per cent. By 2000, management predicts that the company's revenues will be 80 per cent digital. The DocuTech is hence a 'flagship' product.

In black and white professional production publishing, offset printing has been the dominant technology, with 62 per cent share of the UK market in 1995. Light lens xerography technology holds a 26 per cent share, while new digital systems such as the DocuTech account for 12 per cent of the market. By 1999, digital production printing is expected to account for 29 per cent of the production publishing market, with light lens technology share dropping to 15 per cent. Offset's share of black and white production will drop to 56 per cent in the same period. In 1995, 10 per cent of jobs in black and white production publishing were short runs. With the availability of the DocuTech and digital technology, this figure will rise to 20 per cent by 1999. In terms of realizable volume of black and white production pages, the company anticipates its volume will rise from 78 billion, in 1995, to 216 billion pages in 1999 (a compound annual growth of 29 per cent). This evolution will be achieved through technologies such as the DocuTech to transform the dynamics and economics of production publishing. The introduction of further innovations, which integrate colour with black and white production, will also accelerate the adoption and diffusion of the technology.

The document production market

The company segments the document market according to five main product usage environments:

- **Data centre sites:** These are data processing agencies and organisations in which the majority of document production is done within the data centre. Traditional equipment includes line/dot matrix printers, inkjet and other printers and reprographic machines.

- **In-plant locations:** These are central reprographic departments within firms, which have their own reprographic machines. Users rely on offset printing technology to produce documents. In recent years, work handled by such departments is being shifted to the general office/service room environments and outsourced to commercial printers.

- **Quick printers:** These are the high street operators who offer relatively fast reprographic services to clients. However, the industry is declining as volume stays in the office or is transferred to commercial printers to reduce/avoid associated high cost of using quick printers.

- **Commercial printers and service bureaux:** These provide a range of document production services, which primarily use traditional offset printing technology. In general, the volume of long runs is rising, but there has been an increase in demand for specialist, shorter run jobs, which are more suited to quick printer contracts. There is also a move towards the use of reprographic and electronic technologies in this environment.

- **General office:** This is the office environment where a multitude of data processing equipment caters for a range of document processing needs of office users. The technologies involved range from line/dot matrix printers, inkjet and other printers, to fax machines, copiers, personal computers and, increasingly, laser printers and digital copiers. There is also a trend towards the 'networked' office environment, a phenomenon that is forecast to increase from 35 per cent LAN (local area network) penetration in 1994, to 55 per cent penetration by 2000.

Individual country statistics vary. In the UK, there is a shift in the volume of data and document processing from data centres and central reprographic departments to the general office environment. There is also an increase in the flow of work from 'home office' environments to commercial printers and service bureaux. Forty per cent of all documents produced are outsourced to commercial printers and service bureaux.

The key factor for DocuTech's success lies in the ability of the firm to target specific segments in the industry and to innovate and deliver total document processing and production solutions to customers in these segments. DocuTechs are particularly suitable for usage environments, such as commercial print houses, service bureaux, printers (including quick, specialist forms and book printers) and central corporate reprographic departments. These targets have been singled out as environments where the DocuTech systems will deliver superior value and meet customers' needs and requirements more effectively than traditional technologies.

Relative advantages and creation of customer satisfaction: DocuTech versus traditional offset printing and high volume copiers

DocuTech's benefits are best illustrated by comparing the new technology to alternative and traditional techniques used in production publishing. Here, document producers want to create high quality production prints and distribute high quality finished documents in a fast and cost effective manner. Documents can range from administrational forms, leaflets and manuals to publicity material, directories and books.

Traditionally, offset printing is used to achieve high quality reproduction. Offset printing gives excellent quality and can handle vast volumes, but has considerable set-up time, which makes short runs (from less than 1000 prints) prohibitively expensive. Hard copies must be 'made-up' and reset to give a typeset master for printing. Manipulations and changes are time-consuming as they are done by hand, resulting also in more opportunity for error. The DocuTech rivals black and white offset print quality. However, many of the disparate elements of traditional printing – electronic 'pre-press' activities, image and text manipulation facility, electronic storage and easy retrieval – can be integrated into one machine. This makes it possible for a job normally done on offset to be accomplished in dramatically less time and at much lower cost, for short runs (see Exhibit 1).

Furthermore, DocuTechs simplified many of the jobs that were normally tedious and time-consuming in offset printing. For example, scanned originals become digital master copies, eliminating the need to cycle a hard-copy master through the system for every print. Document producers can therefore improve overall efficiency, and even increase revenue by taking on extra business. Moreover, in many instances, to reach the right economies, producers end up printing more documents than needed. This increases costs not just in storage, but also wastage of overruns and outdated materials. DocuTechs, by contrast, can handle different size print runs, anything from a single proof (that is 'print-for-one') to thousands of multiple documents. The stored digitized documents can be amended and printed/reprinted as and when required (that is, 'printed-on-demand'). Clearly, DocuTechs have an edge over offset in terms of their ability to handle varying volumes and where volumes are difficult to predict on a day-to-day basis. Like 'just-in-time' delivery, DocuTechs enable document producers to be more flexible and responsive, offering a more customized service to clients. 'On-demand' printing therefore meets both document producers and their clients' needs for inventory containment, shortened schedules and reduced expenses. Users have claimed that, where there is a minimum feasible volume, as much as 60 per cent to 1000 per cent reduction in costs can be achieved through switching to in-house digital DocuTech systems from traditional printing technologies.

Another important strength of the DocuTech is that it can be upgraded, hence reducing the fear of technological obsolescence for many potential buyers. More recent facilities added to the basic DocuTech such as multiple distribution formats (that is, finished documents can be electronically transmitted anywhere by fax and to personal computers via a network, for viewing at the point of need and/or printed out on paper) further increases DocuTech's scope and flexibility.

Additionally, DocuTechs bridge the gap between high volume copiers and offset printing machinery. Copiers are less expensive than offset for short run work, are easy to use and can handle small volumes well, but quality is often limited. DocuTechs produce superior quality documents compared to high volume paper copiers, and they offer a 'one-stop' job.

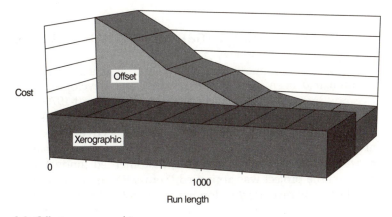

Figure 6.1 Offset vs xerographic

Senior management sees the success of the DocuTech system as being based on value creation: the machine offers greater operational efficiency and flexibility, thereby enhancing productivity and improving business perform-ance. As the DocuTech is regarded a radical innovation, the senior management team realized that it was necessary to educate customers on DocuTech's vast potential (the unique benefits) and to raise their perceived value of the new product. The benefits the DocuTech system offered to customers – enhanced productivity, increased customer value and improved business performance – became the dominant message in customer communications. The 'print-on-demand' and 'print-for-one' benefits have become very powerful marketing and positioning themes for promoting the DocuTech to target markets.

Birth of the 'digital production publisher' concept

Until 1979, Xerox's business was primarily based on light lens technology. The question was how to change from the existing complicated analogue lens system to digital technology and to make a very high speed digital photocopier that would be used in a production environment. Senior management's vision – 'that the future will inevitably be digital' – was a major driving force behind the corporation's investment in, and commitment to, the digital production publisher programme. The belief in digital technology's dominance is backed by industrial research, which suggests that by 2000, only 42 per cent of firms will be using analogue equipment, compared to 58 per cent using digital. Eventually, the concept of a machine that could capture black and white text and images, electronically store these for later retrieval and manipulation, then print and finish-off the document in one operation, emerged. This eventually became the DocuTech Production Publisher 135 introduced 1990.

Shaping the technology: market focus and customer orientation

The corporation had been investing in research and development of digital scanners, computing and printing technologies since the mid-1970s. Although, in that sense the DocuTech was technology led, the project was ultimately driven by top management's vision of a cost-effective, integral, digital document production system. R&D was very much led by a market focus, consistent with the corporation's emerging customer-led innovation ethos in the 1980s. When the project was approved, Xerox/RX set up a 'council' in the early years of the new product development project to test the product concept with industry members/potential customers. Early feedback indicated to management the potential for DocuTech in big, central corporate reprographic departments that were Xerox/Rank Xerox's 'bread and butter' copier markets. The key users in this environment were already speculating on the growing importance of computer technology and the trend towards working in a broad computing and a 'network' environment. A high speed, high quality, flexible digital document production system that does the job in one process would potentially raise the organization's productivity and improve performance.

The team had also used focus groups involving key or lead users from commercial printing environments to discuss the corporation's future business direction. These discussions highlighted the tremendous opportunity for DocuTech to meet all the key requirements of the printing industry, particularly commercial printers and service bureaux, quick printers and reprographic houses, which relied on offset technology. Lead users in the UK printing industry were facing increasing pressure to shorten schedules, lower costs, provide higher quality and to secure greater process integration and flexibility. The DocuTech team realized that the printing industry represented an even more significant target for DocuTechs. However, the standalone machines, priced at around US$250,000, were more expensive than conventional copiers and printing machines. To justify an investment, buyers must be convinced that their organization's specific requirements can be fully realized with the new technology. The team recognized that subsequent development of the DocuTech system must be geared to potential customers' key concerns and requirements. The focus groups and 'councils' provided just the sort of 'customer insights' that were critical to help shape the technology for users. From there on, the potential target markets (namely, commercial printers, service bureaux, quick printers, reprographic houses and in-house reprographic departments) were clearly defined and these customers began to 'drive' the application.

The innovation process

Balancing technical and marketing goals

RX/Xerox's new product development ethos strongly reflects corporate recognition of the need to strike a balance between technological and market focus. This is achieved through managing both technical and marketing staff's awareness of environmental trends. All four research centres in the US and Europe are expected to scan the technological environment and to use market research to discover ways to harness technologies to provide document solutions to target customers. Technical centres are also encouraged to work closely with corporate functions to achieve a stronger market focus for innovation. As senior managers imply, 'It (technological innovation) very much is about managing market demand and supply.' According to John Seely Brown, Xerox's chief scientist and its Palo Alto Research Centre (PARC) director, research should guide corporate strategy, which leads, in turn, to R&D.

Managing the risks of technological innovation: the critical role of marketing

Marketing's awareness of technical and broader environmental conditions is essential in helping the project team manage the risks and reduce the uncertainty of technological innovation. Feedback is systematically obtained from sales and service staff using a 'field engagement process', trade shows and seminars run with customers. The company also identifies competitors' strengths and weaknesses, yielding a competitor database, based on information provided by customers/users. Systematic and regular (quarterly and annual) competitive reviews are conducted to identify key trends and market drivers (e.g. legislation, change in needs, new technology, etc.) in the company's operating environment. Groups of individuals, including marketing staff, become dedicated 'experts' on specific markets or competitors, and are seen as the 'line of sight' for product developers, guiding the development of product and marketing strategies and policies. The information collected is invariably disseminated via feedback reports/documents and internal seminars throughout the organization. In the case of DocuTech, for instance, competitor information was gathered specifically about its major rival, Kodak. This led to the team designing a superior product, which successfully differentiated the Xerox offering. Furthermore, as the DocuTech approached commercialization, on-going customer feedback confirmed that 'on-line finishing', notably stapling, facilities, were particularly important. Xerox/RX took this on board and built up a strong alliance programme for third party finishing companies. This resulted in the development of an on-line finisher for the DocuTechs, which became one of the main selling features of the innovation. In this way the marketing function plays a significant strategic role in the innovation process.

Marketing's involvement in new product development was clearly manifested in another way in the DocuTech project. The project was noted for its monthly 'sunrise meetings' in which marketing managers from all key country markets, together with engineers and technical staff, evaluated and monitored the launch programme to keep track of progress. As noted earlier, the multinational launch team played a critical role in new product development. Today 'sunrise meetings' have evolved into a 'cultural thing' for Xerox/RX.

Systematic but flexible new product development process

A systematic new product development process is pursued, but flexibility and responsiveness to customer/market requirements or changes are maintained. (The outstanding potential for the DocuTech to serve the printing industry's document production needs was recognized later in the new product process. When this was realized target customers' requirements drove further product development.)

In terms of the organization of innovation, the corporation has moved from a multi-domestic structure (national affiliates doing everything from product design to distribution on its own) to a complex, but more integrated global organization. The company has standardized its operations across borders, introduced global product-development teams and centralized procurement, resulting in a more efficient new product process. The DocuTech project embraced the new approach to innovation organization, as seen in the involvement of a cross-functional, multinational team throughout the project.

With regard to the new product process, outline plans are developed in the initial stage of the new product project, reviewed and approved. Pre-launch activities, including concept and product testing, product strategy development and planning, competitor analyses and the development and implementation of support systems and actions, are all executed. Where necessary, staff training to deliver product and customer service support strategies is initiated and conducted on an ongoing basis whenever required. Launch strategies for local and global markets are developed, reviewed and approved.

Prior to full scale market launch, trial tests are undertaken and feedback used to refine strategy and tactics. In the DocuTech project, one year before launch, the machines were market-tested to obtain customer feedback. The trial tests were conducted in 50 sites around the world.

As with other business processes in The Document Company, innovation processes are benchmarked against 'best practice'. The key element focused on is 'time-to-market'. Cycle time is reduced through overlapping new product development stages, open communications and the involvement of focused cross-functional teams, that are 'empowered' to take and implement decisions quickly. The early involvement of multinational managers also helps to secure commitment and commercialization targets. Comparable with world class standards, the company's new product development cycle time is 3–5 years, depending on the type of product being developed. A breakthrough product like DocuTech was developed within 5 years. The development cycle for an enhancement of an existing product takes about 12 months. There is, however, a trade-off between speed and quality. The company's goal – to achieve 99.9 per cent quality and 95 per cent customer satisfaction ratings – is not sacrificed for speed.

Alliances/partnerships

Alliances and partnerships with suppliers and customers were important in encouraging new ideas, sharing risks and leveraging resources and creating marketing opportunities for the DocuTech. The DocuTech project relied on collaborations and partnerships with suppliers of hardware/software and customers to deliver cost-effective document production solutions. For example, Intergraph, a leading supplier of computer-aided design, manufacturing and engineering (CAD/CAM/CAE) and geographic information system (GIS) solutions, reengineered its document process by putting greater emphasis on digital electronic processes. The two firms formed a strategic alliance to bring together Intergraphs' hardware-software product and an upgraded DocuTech, the Network Publisher, creating an opportunity to co-market CAD/CAM/CAE, mapping and publishing solutions to the companies' mutual customers. To make networking possible, Xerox struck an agreement with Sun, a workstation maker, Novell, a networking company and Abode, a software house, to work on common standards. The company also teamed up with AT&T to work on solutions to overcome cost and performance barriers to sending digitized documents over computer networks. Today, the company regards current partnerships and alliances with such companies as Deutsche Telekom, Scitex, EFI, Colorbus and others, as essential to secure the technologies required for success in tomorrow's markets.

Product champion and high performance work teams

Initially, Xerox's digital strategy was regarded with suspicion by those inside the analogue photocopier camp as they saw the innovation as a real threat to the 'annuity' – the recurring sales of service, parts, paper and rentals – obtained from copiers, and which account for two-thirds of Xerox's document business revenues. Peter van Cuylenburg, who directed Xerox's digital strategy, however, argued that new software and upgrades could make the annuity from digital products even greater than that from existing copiers.

DocuTech had a 'champion,' or 'guardian angel,' who worked with the team of managers to resolve problems and to achieve project goals. Putting a champion in charge gave the technology the right focus and marketing input to ensure the successful completion of the DocuTech project.

The organization today recognizes the value of such 'product champions' in developing radical and difficult innovations. These 'specialists' are empowered to work through high performance work teams to bring innovations to market.

Continual innovation

The DocuTech production publisher was not a one-off innovation. Its long-term success relies on the firm's commitment to continual product development and improvements and to upgrade the system over time. The first DocuTech introduced in 1990 was a standalone system, which accepted work only in hard-copy formats. The system was upgraded, within a year of launch, to accept digital input from a variety of sources via devices called 'DocuTech Media Servers'. The DocuTech processor could be connected to a DocuTech Media Server (essentially a personal computer) which made it possible for the system to accept documents on magnetic media, that is, floppy disks or tapes. This increased significantly the flexibility of the machine in terms of document feeding.

Within a year of DocuTech's launch, plans were underway to introduce networking so that the computer system could be linked to workstations and personal computers throughout an organization. The DocuTech Network Server, introduced in 1992, allows multiple remote users in sites spread over the building, country or the globe, to concurrently submit print jobs to the Network Server, generating even greater reductions in document production, printing and distribution costs and turnaround time. The Network Server also allows the DocuTech to be networked to customers' PCs or Apple Mac systems, accelerating further turnaround times.

Further enhancements such as the XDOD (Xerox Documents on Demand) were added to the DocuTech product family in 1994. This involves attaching a high-speed XDOD scanner and archiving facility (basically a PC coupled to an optical disk) to a DocuTech. The XDOD enables, in particular, rapid reprinting of very old documents and archived materials.

In early 1995, the company introduced the DocuTech 6135, a new system controlled by a DocuSP software, based on an 'open' system (the Sun Workstation), as opposed to the original DocuTech's proprietary software. This enables the scanners, processors and printers in different locations to communicate over PC networks regardless of differences in the computers' software. This allows even more open access for users and wider distribution of documents, improving further customer value and performance.

More recently, the company introduced the DocuColor for use in colour production, which would spearhead corporate growth in the colour, digital document production sector. For the future, the company's focus will be on integrating colour and black and white printing, extending colour capabilities, increasing speed and improving document production scheduling and dispatching.

Conclusions

Senior managers at The Document Company are aware that many factors have contributed to the successful commercialization of the DocuTech. Management vision was instrumental in channelling the investment in digital technology. Market focus and attention to customer needs ensured that new offerings were designed ultimately to deliver unique and superior customer value more effectively than competition. Top management commitment and focus on corporate priorities sustained a dominant position in the global document market by delivering solutions that enhance customers' productivity. Clear targets were provided for innovation achievement. There was a quality oriented and innovation driven culture and a strong project team accomplished the task of product development and commercialization effectively. Management recognizes how crucial it is to sustain the process of innovation, acknowledging that the success of the DocuTech will invariably trigger retaliations from the competition. The issue for the firm is how they should protect their position as technological pioneers in the global document market and reap the benefits of their long-term investment in product innovation.

Chapter 7

British Steel's success in the construction industry

Vivienne Shaw

Background

British Steel is Europe's largest steel producer and the third largest in the world with total sales exceeding £8 billion. Since privatization the company has improved efficiency such that independent analysts now rate it as the most cost-efficient, integrated steel producer in the world. With pre-tax profits of over £1.1 billion in 1996, British Steel is also the world's most profitable steel producer. This enviable position has been achieved through a programme of continuous investment in production efficiency and market development.

Steel is often perceived as a commodity used in a wide range of applications from cars to power stations, packaging to construction. Organized into product-related divisions, British Steel employs 55,000 people world-wide producing over 14 million tonnes of steel per annum, over half of which is exported throughout the world. In 1996 three of the company's businesses won the Queen's Award for Export including special sections, of which 82 per cent of sales are accounted for by exports.

British Steel has traditionally been seen to be a production-oriented company. This view extends back to the post war years when steel was effectively manufactured under government licence and all producers could sell everything they made. There was, therefore, little need for the adoption of a high level of market orientation.

This case study focuses on the Sections, Plates and Commercial Steels division of British Steel which, whilst achieving high levels of production efficiency gains, also displays a high degree of market orientation. The Plates and Sections Division of British Steel represents a very important part of the organization as a whole. It makes up 45 per cent of all British Steel's sales in the UK and 24 per cent of all tonnage of steel produced.

The construction market

In the early 1970s, masonry and reinforced concrete dominated building frames and structures. Whilst steel had been used in construction (the first recorded steel framed building was in 1796) it was not considered to be a cost-effective solution for buildings of more than one storey. A throwback to the post-war days in which demand for steel outstripped supply allowed concrete producers to gain a strong foothold in the construction market. Reinforced concrete (using steel as the means of reinforcement) offered builders a low tech, engineering solution with the added advantage of high levels of fire resistance. Concrete was also relatively easy to work with and was fashionable with the architects and developers at that time. By comparison steel was a mature, higher cost product requiring additional, expensive coatings (often of concrete) to make it fire resistant. On average steel was 20 per cent more expensive than reinforced concrete.

It would appear, therefore, that this would be a market in which steel would always be at a severe cost disadvantage and offer little opportunity for a company like British Steel. Research carried out by the company in the mid-1970s identified, however, that if they could address the cost issues, customers would be more willing to consider steel structures as an alternative to reinforced concrete.

A number of events were set to ensure that steel became a more competitive choice in the construction market. In the mid-1970s British Steel experienced what might be termed, with the benefit of hindsight, a piece of luck. Industrial unrest and organizational issues meant that British Steel nearly went bust. The price of steel plummeted by a third thereby, making steel a more cost effective alternative to concrete. Although still slightly more expensive, concrete no longer enjoyed a significant cost advantage. This changed situation led to a concerted effort on the part of a small team at British Steel to set out to demonstrate to the construction industry that steel was now a feasible alternative to other materials. The approach this team adopted was quite unique and forward thinking in the mid-1970s. Rather than just relying on the opinions of building specifiers to determine the factors which affected the choice of structure, the idea was to conduct extensive market research into exactly how decisions for particular projects were made, i.e. who actually decided which materials to use in the frames of buildings. This research, repeated on a regular basis since, came up with some interesting findings, which enabled British Steel to develop a marketing plan.

Buyer behaviour in the construction industry

Traditionally contractors or developers were considered to be the main buyers of concrete or steel for the frames of buildings. The research, however, revealed a number of key players in the decision making process (see Figure 7.1). Whilst the contractors, developers and even the client might influence the decision, the key players were the architects and civil engineers. Whilst the controlling authorities and government bodies played an important role in determining the necessary legislation on building regulations, their direct involvement on which material to use for individual projects was minimal. This discovery allowed British Steel to adopt a very clear targeting policy in the construction market and has without doubt contributed to their success. Whilst the architects and structural engineers are the key decision-makers they have quite different needs. The architects want to design buildings which meet their clients' needs, but which have an original identity and are going to win them recognition. The structural engineers, meanwhile, need to design buildings for structural stability with materials, which meet building regulations and can cope with the stress under which the building will be put. The research also established that the specification process lasted on average 12–18 months and British Steel aimed to influence this at every stage possible.

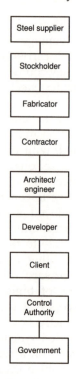

Figure 7.1 Specifier chain for structural steel

British Steel's approach was not particularly new by consumer marketing standards, but was very innovative in the steel industry and heavy engineering in general. The old approach was 'we'll tell you what you need' which has been replaced by 'we'll work together to find the right construction solution for you'.

But it was not just a case of identifying the key decision makers in the construction industry; British Steel also need to sell the idea of using steel as an alternative to concrete.

British Steel's response

British Steel, therefore, set about, in an almost evangelical way, to change the tide of opinion in favour of concrete into a wave of sales for steel. The main objective was 'to secure or enhance the share of steel in construction compared with alternative materials and products'. The company set out to develop the market through the appointment of regionally based advisory engineers to take the message to the architects and structural engineers. The advisory engineers were supported by the company with technical literature and further market research and through their participation in promotional seminars and technical conferences outlining the advantages of steel. The aim with the key decision-makers was 'to make them comfortable in specifying steel'.

Although the cost of steel had fallen by about 40 per cent, it was still necessary to use expensive coatings on the steel in order to meet the necessary fire protection standards. Further market research in 1980 with the key decision-makers highlighted that this was still perceived as a serious disadvantages for steel over concrete. Running parallel to the market development activities, therefore, was a series of incremental product improvements to make steel frame constructions more attractive in the construction industry. As Figure 7.2 shows, the three main cost items in a multi-storey frame were the fire protection, the steel itself and the fabrication. In the early 1980s these three accounted for over 80 per cent of the total cost. The challenge for British Steel was to reduce these costs to more manageable levels. By 1995 the cost of each of these inputs had been reduced significantly with the cost of fire protection being reduced by a massive 60 per cent. Greater production efficiencies enabled the cost of steel production to fall by nearly 40 per cent and improved efficiency by the fabricators brought the cost down further to 56 per cent of the 1981 cost. By comparison the cost of using reinforced concrete has remained relatively static.

The huge decrease in the cost of fire resistance can be attributed to the high levels of investment by British Steel into research to improve performance in this area. The company has invested over £1 million in new fire resistance techniques and coatings to achieve this level of performance. Furthermore, it has also been heavily engaged in activities to educate and influence the control authorities and government bodies in revising building regulations so as to improve the prospects for steel as a solution to construction problems.

The attempt to persuade architects and engineers to use steel was a great success. Architecture is to some extent based on fashion so again there was some luck, in the fact that architects took to steel so well. Architects seek elegance and originality and steel, particularly structural hollow sections, has allowed them to create both elegant interiors and exteriors through the use of exposed steel tubes to make a statement about their building. One danger for the future is that architects may move away from steel in favour of other materials to try again to be different.

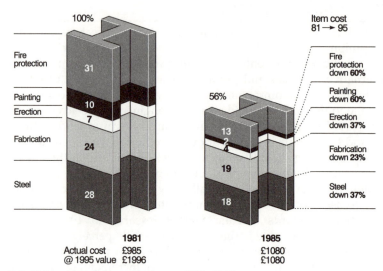

Figure 7.2 Multi-storey frame cost change 1981–1995

British Steel's performance

Construction is British Steel's largest market accounting for 24 per cent of UK sales. Steel sections are found in a wide range of buildings throughout the world, from Kansai Airport in Japan to Canary Wharf in London. As Table 7.1 shows, in the early 1970s steel had around 60 per cent share of the building frames market for single storey buildings compared with only 15 per cent for multi-storey buildings. The main reason for this was that the fire resistance requirements for single storey buildings were less stringent than for multi-storey buildings, allowing British Steel to compete without the need for further expensive coating of the steel sections. The low levels of share in the multi-storey market were directly attributable to the high cost of a steel solution.

By 1983 steel's share of the construction market has increased significantly even in the single-storey market. A market share, in 1983, of 86 per cent even exceeded British Steel's expectations. However, further penetration of the

Table 7.1 Steel's share of the construction market

Year	Single-storey buildings (%)	Multi-storey buildings (%)
1970	59	15
1980	n/a	33
1985	86	43
1990	n/a	51
1996	95	62

Figures supplied by British Steel

market was achieved with the company taking 95 per cent of the single storey market by 1996. Meanwhile, significant progress was also being made in the multi-storey market, a market previously considered unsuitable for steel. British Steel's share of this market has also steadily increased, levelling out to around two-thirds of the market. The challenge facing the company is to maintain these high levels of market share in an increasingly competitive environment. British Steel's innovative approach to the market has enabled them to dominate the steel in construction market for over 20 years. It is only in more recent years that their competitors, both in the concrete market and other steel producers, have woken up and have started to challenge British Steel. Much of the growth in the share of steel in the construction industry can be directly attributable to British Steel's market focused approach to the industry. They have led the market and others, after much delay, have started to follow.

One of the amazing observations behind British Steel's success in the construction industry has been the lack of competitive response from concrete and other steel producers. It has taken concrete manufacturers nearly 20 years to wake up to the changes in the market and to respond. Meanwhile other steel producers, mainly from overseas, have also been slow to react, although that is now changing.

British Steel's success in the construction market has not been confined to the UK. The construction markets, however, differ in other countries, with steel only being used in 24 per cent of buildings in Germany compared with 78 per cent in France. The French and German industries are now taking a similar approach to that adopted in the UK. British Steel is identifying the key decision makers in overseas markets and are hoping to emulate the success they have achieved in the UK market.

The success in the construction market has served as a good guide to other parts of the organization. In each of British Steel's divisions a forum for product and market development activities, along the lines of that adopted in the Sections and Plates Division, has been established comprising both technical and commercial people. The hope is that British Steel will be able to emulate their success in the construction market in other key sectors.

The future

Although steel's share of the construction market is higher than ever in the 1990s, British Steel is not complacent. The company is aware that they need to invest in order to maintain their enviable position. Their main priorities for the future remain a high focus on cost as a contributory factor to the steel solution in the construction market. They continue to look at ways to make incremental improvements to their sections to maintain a good cost position. Research into fire protection and structural systems development is ongoing. British Steel is designing and developing new shapes for sections, which will allow architects to make more imaginative use of steel structures. They are also concentrating heavily on environmental considerations making steel the environmentally friendly solution to construction as well as continuing with their research into customer needs and wants.

The importance of environmental issues cannot be underestimated. In half of all new buildings, environmental concerns are voiced, which was not the case when British Steel first grew the market. Developers are even prepared to pay a little extra to have a 'green' building. Concrete is perceived to be 'greener' than steel. One challenge facing British Steel now, therefore, is to persuade decision-makers that steel is more environmentally friendly than concrete. There is a slight turn in opinion towards concrete because it is a natural product, unlike steel, and architects increasingly want to use natural products, although there is still a high environmental cost to quarry for concrete. Steel by comparison is one of the most recyclable products in the world.

The latest research conducted in 1996 shows how far British Steel has come in the construction market. The main concerns of architects and engineers are less the cost of steel or concrete and less the issue of fire resistance but now features such as design and speed of erection – two areas where British Steel are again leading the competition.

British Steel acknowledge that they now find themselves in a defensive position in the construction market and that the key issue is one of protecting and maintaining their strong position. The aim for the future, in the words of Bob Latter, is 'to create a dynamic of continuous improvement'. New ideas and steel sections should be developed each year, giving the team of regional advisory engineers new material with which to go and preach to the decision makers and influencers.

Chapter 8

BAA: specialist shops

Veronica Wong

Background

BAA is the world's largest commercial operator of airports. It owns and operates seven UK airports – Heathrow, Gatwick, Stansted, Glasgow, Edinburgh, Aberdeen and Southampton – which handle 71 per cent of air passenger traffic and 81 per cent of air cargo. BAA has successfully expanded into overseas markets and currently manages the Indianapolis Airport system and the shops and catering facilities at Pittsburgh Airport, both in the USA. BAA operates in four businesses: airport terminal management, retailing, project management and construction and property development.

BAA's airport management is responsible for all aspects of airport (both terminal and airfield) operations. Terminal staff look after security, engineering and customer services. Airfield staff's main responsibility is to ensure that the airfield environment is safe and secure for airline customers. The retailing business is responsible for managing all commercial facilities at BAA airports, including shops, restaurants, bars, bureaux de change and car parks. In project management and construction, BAA is reputed to be one of the UK's main developers of infrastructure and a major player in the management of construction projects. It currently manages over one hundred projects to improve airport facilities. As for property development and management, BAA currently has an extensive property portfolio, both on-airport and off-airport. Its property development company, Lynton, for example, concentrates on working with business partners to develop new buildings, ranging from office complexes to hotel developments. Currently BAA has revenue of £1,253m and pre-tax profits of £418m.

Prior to privatization in 1987, BAA operated as a nationalized company that depended solely on government funding and sponsorship. BAA's culture was primarily internally focused, with a strong engineering-orientation and little awareness of customer needs and demands. Following privatization, BAA had to develop a more market-oriented business, while seeking to maintain profitability and satisfy shareholders' demands. Almost half of the corporation's income (e.g. airport/traffic charges) is regulated by the Civil Aviation Authority (CAA), however, and this income is steadily decreasing over the years as a result of constraints imposed by regulation on prices. Since 1989, BAA has sought to improve revenue earnings through cost control, building its retailing business and developing new businesses outside its core activities. As a nationalized company, BAA had invested relatively little in retail activities. It was working with concessionaires and took a percentage of airport retail turnover, exploiting duty and tax free sales. With the additional threat of the proposed abolition of duty free sales, by 1999, BAA recognizes the need to seek alternative opportunities for business growth in the 1990s and to steadily reduce its dependency on duty free business over the years. BAA targeted its retail business as a source of revenue growth and developed a strategy for retailing which has brought results. The retail business revenue of £556m accounts for 44.4 per cent of total BAA revenue (£1253m, year to 31 March 1996), compared to £434m earned by airport/traffic charges (that is, 34.6 per cent of total revenue).

Creating a market-led, customer-focused, innovation-oriented culture

Mission

The business of operating and developing airports, as a profit-making enterprise that provides a return to shareholders as well as serving customers and satisfying other stakeholders' interests, is driven by the company's mission. The mission is to make BAA the most successful airport company in the world. This means:

Always focusing on customers' needs and safety

When BAA customers were asked what they want, they have always stated both higher quality and lower cost. BAA finds out what its customers want through its Quality of Service Monitor (QSM) research programme, which involves interviewing 150,000 passengers each year about every aspect of their experience at its airports. After several years of doing this, the company has built up an extensive bank of information about the business and how its airports are performing compared with competitors. To meet customers' concerns for airport safety and security, BAA has involved a high proportion of staff who work constantly to improve security both by ensuring that the company meets the highest standards and that the measures taken cause the minimum inconvenience to passengers.

Achieving continuous improvements in costs and the quality of processes and services

To deliver higher quality at competitive costs, requires total commitment to continuous improvement of processes and services. Regulation has caused BAA to hold down the charges to airlines using its airports. This has forced BAA to look at how to improve its productivity, which it has succeeded in doing through continuous improvement programmes resulting in productivity gains of more than 45 per cent in the last four years. Independent reviews of airport charges for 1996 show that Heathrow and Gatwick are among the lowest of any major European airport.

Enabling employees to give of their best

Continuous improvements in processes and services can only be achieved through the full commitment of the company's employees. Through two-way communication and training, BAA encourages employees to fulfil their potential and contribute directly to the success of the company.

Realizing the mission

To realize its mission, BAA has to firstly create a culture that embraces change and thrives on innovation. It has achieved this through empowerment of its staff (that is, giving them the 'freedom to manage'), a focus on teamwork, simpler structures and functional leadership.

Freedom to manage is a philosophy of work that allows every individual the chance to maximize their contribution to the business. Employees participate in the development and success of the company through their contact with airline customers and passengers, so employee involvement and empowerment are key. They enable front-line staff, who are best equipped to understand individual customers' needs, to improve customer service at the point of delivery. This way of working essentially means getting managers and workers to behave as though they are their own boss. They are empowered to use their full range of skills and their own initiative, without tight or unnecessary controls and administrative hurdles. This means revolutionizing two-way communications in the firm, removing barriers between senior management and front-line staff.

To build a motivated and committed workforce, BAA has introduced new training programmes and schemes to involve all managers in the company's mission. BAA's philosophy has been to urge all employees, whatever their level in the organization, to be proactive and participate in training. There are internal and external courses for cultivating functional skills and imbuing corporate values to help employees maximize their contribution to corporate goals. Special training schemes such as 'Sharing the Vision' are aimed, for example, at senior managers to socialize them into BAA's vision and mission. Courses, namely 'Growing the Business', are used to develop managerial skills in strategic planning and implementation. These initiatives aim to create organization-wide awareness of the company's vision and how business goals can be achieved through effective teamwork. Coaching and self-study schemes have also been established to ensure that employees' competencies can be improved and continuously developed. More recently, new career development programmes for middle managers and customized programmes for managers in key business areas such as projects, retailing and property, have been introduced.

BAA aims to become a learning organization, seeking where appropriate to implement best practice management systems and processes. The company also recognizes that, to ensure passengers and customers receive excellence and good value for money in all the services BAA provides, the company must work together with its customers and business partners to create added value for all concerned. The ultimate goal in all this is to become a world-class player and the best airport company in its industry. To date, BAA has successfully achieved annual increases in productivity. In 1996, this has gone up by 6.3 per cent in terms of passengers per employee. Unique standards of customer service have helped BAA airport malls, in particular, become the world benchmark by which air passengers judge airport retailing.

BAA's chief executive, Sir John Egan, has been a major driving force behind the successful transformation of the company. In forcefully advocating the doctrine: 'The route to a world class company is customer satisfaction, continuous improvement and committed people able to give of their best,' the corporation has been principally driven to concentrate on its core airport business, to continually innovate and pursue excellence in customer safety and security, and service quality delivery. Through attracting and retaining highly committed employees, the company has sought to achieve world-class standards across all of its business activities, which will enhance both the quality and growth of the corporation.

Growing retail revenue through innovation

Retail performance

BAA has grown retail to be its largest single source of revenue. In 1995/96, retail revenue grew by 10.5 per cent to £556m, accounting for 44 per cent of BAA's total income. By contrast, the revenue from airport and traffic charges accounted for 35 per cent of BAA's income, with price regulation at Heathrow, Gatwick and Stansted airports holding charges down. BAA's income from retailing operates on a concessionaire- or turnover-related basis, that is, BAA takes a percentage of the retailers' sales, except for car parking, advertising and duty free, where the operator is paid a management fee. BAA has recently formed a new company, World Duty Free, which will take over the running of airport terminal tax and duty free shops as contracts with existing operators expire over the next three years. This allows better control of the entire retail process, from buying to selling of tax and duty free goods. The new company can also be used as a platform to expand into the world duty free market. Concessionaires operating on a turnover-related basis are normally given three- to five-year contracts so as to allow flexibility on both sides. In recent years, retailers operating at BAA airports have enjoyed sales growth that outperforms high street sales growth, and new companies are joining the ever expanding range of airport retailers.

BAA's retail revenues by product area are shown in Table 8.1. According to senior management, BAA's strong retailing growth and performance is a result of:

- the quality of the offer to the customer – making available an unparalleled choice of leading brands with value for money;
- consistent investment over the past years in increasing retail space. Currently, BAA airports have up to 825,000 square feet of retail space; and
- the development of product markets in partnership with retailers.

Table 8.1 Retail revenue by product area 1995/6 (£ millions)

	(£ millions)
Duty and tax free shops	335
Book shops	20
Tax free specialist shops	33
Bureaux de change	26
Car parks	64
Catering	20
Car rental	16
Advertising	14
Tax paid specialists shops	9
Other	19

Retail strategy

BAA's retail strategy is strongly market-led. Ninety per cent of passengers surveyed indicated that they expected to see high quality shopping facilities at airports. The strategy for quality improvement was initiated in 1990 and this has been enhanced regularly since. Its main components are:

- use of market research to uncover customer needs;
- introducing more competition in products and services;
- commitment to deliver high levels of customer service;
- offering value for money in the duty and tax free shops through regular price checks and independent high street pricing surveys to guarantee fair prices;
- introducing international brand names to the airports;
- providing a wide range of high quality products;
- creating quality retail environments; and
- working in partnership with retailers to satisfy customers' needs profitably

An important element that complements BAA's quality improvement drive is innovation. To improve quality and create more added value for customers, BAA had to pay particular attention to the introduction of new retail concepts and services in selected airport terminals. Over the last five years, a record number of innovations have been launched, including:

- The introduction of specialist shops, ranging from Dixons, Boots The Chemist and The Body Shop to Bally, Burberry and Harrods, to create a 'truly international high street' within airport terminals.
- The launch of the world's first airport loyalty – BonusPoints – scheme at Gatwick Airport, which enables passengers to earn points for car parking, eating or drinking, shopping and currency exchange at the airport, as well as exchange points for money-off vouchers, goods or miles in the frequent flyer programmes of several airlines.
- The launch of a unique Worldwide Value Guarantee that gives a full refund from anywhere in the world to a passenger who is not satisfied with any product bought at any one of BAA's airports. This is backed up by international Freephone and Freepost facilities for customer queries or returned purchases, preordering services, computerized information desks and frequent shopper incentives. The retail service innovation minimizes the costs and risks for passengers and enables them to buy at BAA airports with confidence.
- The setting up of a 24 hour Freephone helpline to enable passengers to check in advance if an item is in stock and reserve or pre-order. New shopping information desks in terminals also help solve passengers' queries.

- The introduction of long-term management contracts with airport duty and tax free shops in order to secure better control of product selection, pricing and promotion, which has allowed BAA to broaden choice and encourage competition, to the benefit of customers.

These efforts have paid off, as evidenced by the international recognition achieved by BAA's airports. Specifically, in 1996, Heathrow was voted the best airport in the world for shopping, the UK magazine *Retail Week* awarding it the 'Retail location of the year award'. BAA's differentiation in terms of offering unique standards of customer service and satisfying customer needs has turned its airport malls into the world benchmark by which air passengers judge airport retailing.

Specialist shops

Tax free specialist retail outlets are currently the third largest revenue earner for BAA and a growing source of funds for the company.

Amongst the first specialists to open in Heathrow's Terminal 4 were: Caviar House (1987), Bally (1990), Tie Rack and Hamleys (both in 1991). Harrods opened in Heathrow's Terminal 3 in 1990 and then in Terminal 4 in 1992. Specialist units were not granted tax-free status until 1992. This led to their proliferation across the BAA estate. Also, since the successful introduction of these units, BAA has attracted more and more leading brands to its departure lounges as demand for a wider range of products in each terminal continues to grow. In addition to the specialist retailers mentioned above, the following are amongst the key retailers and upmarket international brand names that currently operate in one or more of BAA's airport terminals: Austin Reed, The Body Shop, Boots The Chemist, Burberry, Crabtree & Evelyn, The Disney Store, Dixons, Ferragamo, The Gap, Gucci, Hermes, HMV, Liberty, Marlboro Classics, Selfridges, Swatch, Tie Rack and Virgin.

At BAA's Heathrow International Airport, therefore, quality international brand names such as Hermes, Gucci and Ferragamo are available to the travelling customer within a few seconds walk of the best British high street, with stores such as Dixons, Boots, Liberty and Selfridges.

The innovation process

The following reflects the typical process involved in the introduction of new specialist retail shops in BAA's airport terminals. Generally, such a process is also used in the development of new retail outlets for catering, bureaux de change and books.

Strategy determination
The whole approach to developing specialist retailing within BAA's airport terminals has been, as with the company's wider retail strategy, strongly

customer-driven. Guided by market research which highlighted the range of top quality branded merchandise that airport customers wanted, a specialist shops team was set up to work closely with hundreds of retailers to bring quality and choice to travelling passengers. The results of extensive market research helped BAA's retail team to build up a detailed picture of the range of products and quality brands that airport customers wanted in terminals. They were able to identify the specific gaps that existed in the current retail portfolio and develop a long-term strategy for new specialist shop development.

Organization structure for innovation

A major thrust in BAA's specialist retail development initiative was the adoption of a completely new structure to enable BAA and retail partners to work together to meet customers' needs. In the first instance, BAA management listened to retailers' concerns about its organization and responded by reorganizing the retail business according to product sectors rather than geographic location. Retail teams were subsequently organized by product-markets such as clothes, books, shoes and so forth. This enabled BAA to be more efficient in its retail relationships and to develop centres of excellence within the airport retail group. A more product-market structure allowed BAA to plan the retail mix in each terminal and work with individual retailers, providing them with relevant information about passengers using the terminal – age, sex, nationality, socio-economic profile, spending and destination. Each team subsequently focused on developing a merchandise strategy for each product that would satisfactorily match customer wants to available terminal retail space. Teams looked after each product sector, and their target was to gain maximum penetration of their market. A holistic approach was also taken in the sense that new specialist shops introduced must be carefully balanced against the needs and requirements of existing retailers in the terminal in question.

Project management

A project manager was appointed to prepare a timing and capital plan for approval by a project board. Within the project, the teams engaged in a formal process of planning and management so as to maximize efficiency. Marketing, including communications planning, was more informal and autonomous, although a process existed which entailed a clear definition of marketing objectives, with cost-benefit and break-even analyses conducted to evaluate returns on promotional spending.

Throughout the process, successful contractors and the retail development project team were involved in every element of new retail outlet development, ranging from store design, to construction.

Retailer selection

Following strategy development and project approval, potential retailers were invited to tender for shop space in the terminal. An information pack on the terminal, including details of BAA's terms and conditions for concessionaires, was sent to these retailers. Interested parties responded with their own proposed 'deal'. BAA management then evaluated and screened proposals based on several key criteria:

- the financial benefits sought by BAA;
- the financial benefits sought by the retailer;
- the attractiveness of the retailer in terms of the expertise, products and brands it brought to the partnership; and
- customers' priorities and their product and brand preferences.

Project design

In the early stages of the project, shop designers were involved and consulted to determine space allocation with a view to maximize total space utilization in the terminal concerned. These decisions occurred early in the project, in parallel with project planning and scheduling, and well before construction work was completed or got too far, to ensure that project objectives would be realistically fulfilled.

Winning through partnership and team effort

Teamwork and partnership underpinned BAA's successful introduction of new specialist retail shops in airport terminals. Within the project each focused product team worked hard to build a close relationship with the new retail partner to maximize the benefits to both parties as well as to airport customers. The overriding issue was to create a win-win situation for all concerned – the customers, the retailers or 'suppliers' and BAA. It was therefore important for the BAA team to build a strong level of trust between itself and the retailer for the partnership to work.

New retailers operating in an airport terminal environment typically ride a steep learning curve. There are considerable differences in trading conditions between the high street and airport terminal retailing. Specifically, store opening hours are much longer, staying open for airport customers throughout the day and night. The customer profile tends to be biased towards the higher socio-economic categories but segments such as business, non-business or holiday travellers, just as the nationality bias of travellers across all flights handled by the terminal, must be taken on board in each firm's merchandising policy. For example, market research suggested that there are marked differences in the product and brand preferences of Far Eastern and western European air travellers. Differences are also apparent between business and holiday travellers. New retail operators, therefore, had to familiarize themselves with these differences and adapt merchandising strategy to the varying needs of different customer groups within the terminal. Additionally, security requirements are particularly stringent compared to high street environments and new retail partners had to learn to accommodate these requirements in their daily operating environment.

The success of the partnership approach had very largely relied on regular communications between the parties concerned. There were regular review meetings where extensive customer data and market intelligence were shared between members of the BAA teams and retail partners. Review sessions continually monitored project progress and the achievement of targets. The meetings were also instrumental in generating and evaluating new ideas that would help improve customer satisfaction and maximize opportunities for both BAA and retailers. 'Away-days' are the norm at BAA – the concept was introduced to encourage BAA's retail teams and shop partners to proactively seek ways to improve the existing portfolio and identify innovation opportunities.

Role of marketing

Invariably, marketing research played a key role in generating customer insight, which directed BAA's strategy for new specialist retail store development. Marketing, however, contributed in other significant ways. Segmentation and targeting skills were important in ensuring that merchandise and brand offerings were effectively matched with the customer profile of the terminals concerned. For example, the more exclusive outlets like Ferragamo or Harrods were first introduced at Heathrow Terminals 3 and 4, which heavily target the more discerning international, inter-continental travellers.

BAA had invested, and continues to make a substantial investment, in advertising and promotions to support airport retailers and other service providers. Such activities have a clear role in communicating to target customers the improvements and innovations BAA has introduced to its terminals. In 1995, BAA launched its first ever TV advertising campaign aimed at increasing understanding, awareness and use of the range of new services available at its airports as passengers travel through them. Research before and after the campaign showed a high level of awareness and a substantial improvement in customer attitudes to airport shopping. In recognition of BAA's successful marketing, the magazine *Retail Week* awarded the company the title 'Retail Location of the Year 1996'. More recently, BAA also won the prestigious *Frontier Magazine* award for successful marketing.

Rapid, ongoing innovation

BAA's philosophy was, and still, is to strive for continual, on-going improvements and innovation. Each year, and since the introduction of the first specialist shops in its terminals at Heathrow and Gatwick in 1992, new retail shops continue to be added to the portfolio. Feedback from customers and competitor research is regularly disseminated, with the pressure put on teams to respond fast and to try out new ideas quickly. Importantly, innovations are market-led and strategies consistently guided and modified by customer reaction.

Managing the transition and beyond

BAA has undergone a great learning experience and has successfully managed the change from delivering a dull shopping experience to airport travellers to becoming 'the best airport in the world for shopping' within six years of privatization. Managers involved in this transformation stress that top management's commitment to the innovation ideals of the corporation is key. According to Anna Haynes, BAA's group duty free retail marketing manager, top management's enthusiasm, when transmitted to key staff and workers, helps to bring about 'a feeling of excitement ... there is a buzz about the business. Retail staff act as a team, are a part of the team and we all feel we are making a real contribution!'

She adds that the remarkable thing about BAA's transformation is that the recent changes and retail innovations have evolved despite the absence of a formal reward system for innovation. A shared value and strong belief in innovation and profits from customer satisfaction have been the primary motivating force behind people's participation and the successful execution of BAA's new specialist shops concept.

The professionalism and proficiency with which the BAA team handled new specialist retail store development in airport terminals could not have been accomplished without the support of an organization and management that were dedicated to learning and training. BAA had benchmarked competitor airport operators worldwide, as well as quality-oriented and independent retailers, to identify best practice. Training for retail staff has been forcefully emphasized throughout. Concurrent with the implementation of its new retail strategy, shared learning and training initiatives have enabled BAA to realize its dream goal of becoming the best airport in the world for shopping. Unique standards of customer service have helped BAA airport malls become the world benchmark by which customers judge airport retailing.

BAA's management recognizes that the corporation cannot stand still, but must maintain the momentum for innovation if it is to continue to satisfy its customers and shareholders profitably. But what are the innovation challenges facing the company? What new market opportunities lie ahead for the organization? How might BAA ensure that it remains among the best airport companies in the world?

Chapter 9

Virgin Direct: personal financial services

Susan Bridgewater

> 'People ask us: 'why are you getting into life insurance? It's a dreary, discredited business.' And we say: 'Yup, that's why.'
>
> Richard Branson, Virgin Direct Life Insurance

In March 1995, the Virgin Group made yet another bold step when it set up a joint venture with Norwich Union to enter telephone financial services marketing. In entering the market, Virgin said its strategy was:

> 'to advertise itself as the friendly face in a world of financial cowboys. The combination of easy-to-understand products and low initial charges will soon be applied to pensions and life insurance, where public faith has been shaken by accusations of mis-selling and over-charging.'
>
> Wolffe, 1995

The Virgin PEP was Richard Branson's attempt to attract new customers into a market, which he felt to be over-complicated. After experiences in trying to invest his own money, Mr Branson said of the financial services market:

> 'My impression was that it was packed with hidden charges, pushy salesmen, poor performance and meaningless jargon. I couldn't believe it could all be so complicated, so I put together a team to do it better.'
>
> Wolffe, 1995

With its initial product, the Personal Equity Plan (PEP), Virgin made innovative use of index-tracking, a technique of investment which shadows the performance of the All Share stock market index, rather than using fund managers who pick and choose the companies in which they invest. At the time of its launch this was the lowest price PEP, with no entry and exit charges (*Financial Times*, 1995). Within six months of its launch, the Virgin PEP had attracted an estimated £100m of customers' money (Wolffe, 1995). By July 1997, Virgin Direct managed over £1 billion on behalf of its 200,000 customers and the Virgin Growth PEP had established itself as the UK's most popular PEP. Virgin's entry into this market forced established firms to review their charges and brought a number of other non-financial services firms into the 'no-frills' sector:

> 'The success of the upstart Virgin Direct, a financial services offshoot of Richard Branson's leisure empire, in selling personal equity plans based on tracker funds has triggered important responses. Thus, Fidelity, one of the major leading traditional groups, has recently moved into this market with a Footsie tracker fund. This is significant because until now Fidelity has been a leading exponent of the stockpicking 'active' management style based on extensive research.'
>
> Riley, 1996

> 'Traditional PEP providers have had to cut margins following the entry into the market of companies such as airline and leisure group Virgin, through its Virgin Direct joint venture launched last year with Norwich Union (. . .) The pressure on margins is likely to intensify as a result of Direct Line's move. Like Virgin Direct, it aims to attract a new range of investors.'
>
> Smith, 1996

In June 1996, Virgin launched life insurance, health and critical illness plans and on 1 November 1996, entered the pensions market. The introduction of these new, complex financial products was a significant step. Virgin's PEP products were sold on an 'execution-only', basis, that is customers chose to make their own decisions about the suitability of the product to meet their specific needs. However, once Virgin Direct had a core product range in place, Virgin Direct introduced a service to advise customers about the best financial choices for their own particular circumstances. Although it is early days to judge the success of the move into life insurance and pensions, Virgin received 6000 phone calls a day during the launch of its pensions and has over twice the industry conversion rate from interest into purchase.

The Virgin brand

'You bought the record, you drank the cola, you took the aeroplane
to New York, Richard Branson's Virgin empire is more than a casual
assortment of consumer goods; in marketing terms, it is a whole
way of life. But Branson's baby boomers are about to grow up. With
all the pre-publicity of a Hollywood film premiere, Virgin is set to
enter its least glamorous market: the personal equity plan.'

Wolffe, 1995

Ask any member of the Virgin Direct team why Richard Branson was
interested in the financial services market and you are likely to get the answer
that if an industry needs 'sorting out' Richard Branson is interested in doing so.
The brand image of 'good service', 'good value for money' and 'challenging the
status quo' has led Richard Branson's Virgin Group to diversify into a variety
of seemingly unrelated sectors. The answer to why lies in this strong
identification with the needs of the customer. In deciding which market to
enter, the company policy is to 'find the big, bad wolf, then slay it'. If the
customers' needs could be better met by taking on the industry, there is a
challenge for the Virgin brand. As Jayne-Anne Gadhia, Operations Director of
Virgin Direct, expresses it:

'The Virgin brand is about taking on the rest of the industry. It is a
brand with personality. Richard Branson is seen by the public as a
customers' champion, who is allowed to question how to do things
better and differently.'

David Ramsbottom, marketing manager, agrees that the Virgin brand has a
personality which people can relate to. This can be very useful in markets such
as pensions, where Virgin Direct is experiencing high levels of success in the
self-employed market among customers who have a strong affinity with
Richard Branson. The brand image has also been internalized by the Virgin
Direct team to create a clear vision for financial services:

'Let's take the customer's perspective, understand the complexity,
simplify it and offer a life raft of financial services which meet their
needs.'

The feeling is that the traditional financial services providers see the brokers
and sales force as their customers. They are product-driven and so involved in
creating clever products. Managing director of Virgin Direct, Rowan Gormley
sees this as expensive and ineffective:

'They create new options, new bells and whistles. Once these have
been sold, they need to pay administration costs to run a massive

number of variants. The customer is paying for this and for the sales force. Resources are going into keeping the business ticking over. Yet the fundamentals are so simple. Obviously we need to communicate with the customer. We do this via the telephone rather than by employing agents or a salesforce. And we take a jigsaw approach to products: no gaps, no overlaps. That way there is real value creation.'

In contrast, Virgin Direct's approach to financial services is a virtuous circle. Identify a genuine customer need, design products which meet that need, offered by a company that can be trusted. In this way the maxim that financial services must be sold, because they are not voluntarily bought, can be broken.

The launch of Virgin Direct

The idea

The managing director of Virgin Direct, Rowan Gormley, joined the Virgin Group from venture capital firm Electra. His role with the group was to identify new business opportunities. One of his first challenges was to look at the Virgin Pension Scheme. In doing so, he spoke to bank managers and salesmen from the big life insurance firms who proposed complicated deals. Despite his three degrees in finance he still ended up bamboozled, although the fundamentals are simple. The idea of entry into the financial services market was born, in late September 1994, out of the belief that the majority of customers must also find the existing products impenetrable. They are paying for a lot of overheads, which are unnecessary. Therefore this was a market in which Virgin could achieve their aims of providing a better value service for customers.

The idea of entry into personal financial services was presented to and agreed by Richard Branson on 16 December 1994. It was decided that a joint venture with one of the existing life insurance firms would provide access to capital and to an initial pool of staff with experience of the market. Several possible partners were considered. After speaking to each of them, Richard Branson and Rowan Gormley set up a 50 per cent joint venture with Norwich Union mainly because Virgin identified a group of people, principally Jayne-Anne Gadhia, with whom they struck a chord.

The launch process

On 6 January 1995, a team of eight was set up. Besides Rowan Gormley, the remaining seven team members were drawn from Norwich Union. Jayne-Anne Gadhia worked alongside Rowan Gormley to get the operation up and running. The infrastructure was set up over an intensive three-month period. In parallel, market research and public relations for the new venture were carried out from London. Virgin Direct began operating in Norwich on 6 March 1995. Jayne-Anne had the task of selecting which Norwich Union staff should be involved in the new venture. One of the main reasons why she feels that Virgin Direct has been successful is because of these people. When she originally made her selection, senior Norwich Union staff showed surprise at her choice. They were not the group of people who they would have expected her to choose. In Norwich Union they had been classed as 'trouble-makers' who rocked the boat by questioning the status quo.

One year on, when the 60 original staff of Virgin Direct had formed a committed and cohesive group, the same people from Norwich Union expressed surprise that it had worked. Jayne-Anne feels that it did because these people were exactly right for the Virgin Direct way of working. They are risk takers, who saw how they wanted things to be. Now that they worked for a smaller organization which was prepared to take risks, they had the chance to do the things they would always have loved to do:

> 'In a big company there is always a 'they'. It is easy to criticize
> because 'they' are too remote – here we are all 'they' we do not
> have a hierarchy. It is a meritocracy and 'we' have to make it happen'

Virgin Direct's initial launch, in March 1995, was based on an index tracking PEP and followed by an income PEP. The launch of life and health insurance products followed in June 1996 and pensions on 1 November 1996. Virgin Direct's chosen strategy is not that of cost leadership. It is no longer the cheapest PEP on the market, although it aims to give the lowest price that makes good business sense. Differentiation is achieved on the basis of the service which the customers receive, rather than solely on the products themselves.

Communication

Virgin Direct's target market naturally varies by product and reflects an individual's changing needs throughout their life. It can, however, be broadly described as 35+, ABC1, adults. The company has a wide appeal and, while viewed as a young brand, has been particularly successful in attracting the older age groups. The opportunity created by an often ill-served customer cuts right across the demographic groups.

Virgin have been successful in penetrating the existing market through more product focused ads in the personal finance pages of the national press, essentially competing head to head with the competition (see Figure 9.1). Elsewhere, to attract the broader market, they have used a more brand-led, needs-based approach but always presenting a key customer benefit. Television and high profile poster campaigns have played a key role in this.

Virgin have also been successful in moving outside the personal financial pages of the national press.

Virgin Direct has two main communication rules. The first is about what is said. Everything must be about the customer or for the customer and statements of fact should be used, not claims. The second is about the way

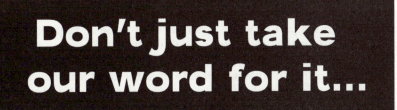

Don't just take our word for it...

Breath of fresh air in pensions

"Virgin...has put together a pension plan that in terms of charges is both outstanding value for money and as transparent as you will get. It is also simple, a refreshing change in a market renowned for making matters as complex as possible."

Mail on Sunday – 20.10.96

Life offices beaten by a brand and a beard

"Mr Branson has started from the premise that the customer has far more interesting things to do with his life than become an expert in financial services. He wants a simple, clear proposition that he can quickly understand. He hates being sold anything, especially by life assurance salesmen...
...So Virgin produced a tracker personal equity plan which was a straightforward way of getting into equities at minimum cost. Its recent performance has caused some embarrassment for those who are paid serious money to pick stocks. The tracker PEP unit is now the basis for the pensions plan, and once again, it is a product for those who get headaches when they even think about the subject."

Daily Telegraph – 19.10.96

If you'd like to know more about the Virgin Personal Pension, please give us a call. Tell us how much you want to tuck away each month. We'll send you a personalised information pack telling you everything you need to know.

Help fight financial jargon

"Virgin looks like mopping up in the retirement savings market. Its sales literature is clear, crisp and easy to understand. More important, the company's charges are among the clearest and cheapest around."

The Independent on Sunday (Business) – 20.10.96

Branson's pensions skyrocket

"The (Virgin Personal) pension...is unlike anything else currently on sale to the public. Its simplicity, flexibility and low charges were praised by leading pensions experts."

Sunday Express – 20.10.96

A new path through the maze

"Most important, in a labour market where no one can be sure of continuous employment to retirement age, the Virgin plan imposes no penalties for suspending or reducing premium payments."

Daily Telegraph – 19.10.96

direct
personal financial service

0345 95 95 95

Open seven days a week from 8am to 10pm

Virgin Direct Personal Financial Service Ltd is regulated by the Personal Investment Authority. The price of units and any income from them can go down as well as up and you may not get back all the money you invest. Past performance is not necessarily a guide to the future. The basis of tax may change and the value of the tax benefit depends on how much tax you pay. For your security all calls to Virgin Direct are recorded and randomly monitored.

Figure 9.1

things are said. For example, clear, straightforward, not patronising, witty, surprising and different.

Part of Virgin Direct's strategy is to put the customer firmly in control by giving the information they need. If a customer rings to ask about PEPs, an information pack will be sent. The application form has been simplified and will already be filled in with as many details as possible to reduce the time taken to fill it in. A follow-up call will be made to check that the pack has arrived, but the customer will never be asked when they are going to return an application. This is part of Virgin's 'no pester promise', a response to the hard sell tactics traditionally associated with the industry.

The Virgin Direct literature plays a key role in communication. In its simplicity and clarity, it differs markedly from the complex financial formulae usually found. Considerable effort is expended in making this accessible, as it is one of the major tools in conveying the differences in Virgin's approach to the business. Virgin Direct has an integrated communications strategy. The same agency, Consolidated Communications, is responsible for both advertising and public relations. Weekly meetings are held with all involved from Virgin Direct and with the advertising and PR people, the account managers and the creative staff. This ensures that everyone is working towards the same goals and allows decisions to be made on the spot.

The Call Centre

The Virgin Direct Call Centre is really the nerve centre of the operation. If Virgin differentiates itself on its service, then this is where the customers come into contact with the 'Virgin Experience'. Mark Barnes, customer service manager in the Call Centre, considers answering the telephones and dealing with the customer directly as a key part of understanding Virgin Direct:

> 'Everyone has been on the telephones at some stage. Richard
> Branson took some calls when he came down for the opening.
> Understanding what happens in the call centre plays a big role in
> understanding the business as everyone needs to speak the same
> language.'

The way in which the tele-operators deal with the customer is an important part of the Virgin Direct service. Mark says:

> 'There is always a way forward – even if it is a product which Virgin
> Direct does not offer we try to point them in the right direction.
> We have products, which we design to sell over the telephone.
> When people respond to the adverts, we try to give them the
> information which will help them to buy.'

In fact, Virgin Direct is designed from the customer interface outwards. The business concept is relatively simple. Direct contact with the customer keeps down the overheads. At the present time, this contact is best achieved by telephone. Managing director Rowan Gormley feels that this is the most accessible method of communication. Higher technology modes of contact such as modems might limit the number of customers in a position to do business with Virgin. As soon as the caller gives their postcode, their details can be called forward. A single database of customer transactions is used to give rapid access to details of any previous transactions with the firm. Virgin also guarantees not to supply this database to anyone else.

Anthony Mullan, business analyst, and Vincent Ballister, development manager, explain how this works. Virgin Direct's systems are designed to be user friendly and to offer quick routes to giving quotes to customers. Anthony Mullan's role in most organizations would be known as business process re-engineering, or reducing the business to the simplest and most effective processes. In Virgin Direct, he and Vincent Ballister have worked together to 'engineer' it that way from the beginning. Flow diagrams chart the series of steps that take place after the customer's phone call to ensure that there is a quick and efficient response. Every contact with the customer is important and is carefully thought through.

It is quite usual in life insurance to have to go through several stages of form filling before a quote can be given. At this stage the customer has already invested significant time and effort. Yet, at the end of this process, they might find out that they are not eligible for insurance from the firm in question. The definitions of what is covered are so woolly that a customer may have to wait a considerable length of time before discovering whether he or she is eligible.

Vincent Ballister has designed the computer systems to do away with the interim stages. For life and health insurance, there is an expert system, which allows the tele-operator to fill in the answers to a series of basic questions. In the majority of cases, this will result in an immediate guaranteed price, although if there are some pre-existing medical conditions, this may be provisional pending a medical examination. Here again, Virgin has taken an innovative approach. Rather than telling the customer to go away, have a medical and then begin the process again, Virgin has its 'nurse on a motorbike'. If a medical is necessary, a date can be agreed there and then with the customer and someone will come out to them to carry it out.

A challenge for any systems provider is the speed at which new and more complex products have been added to the Virgin portfolio. The systems were originally designed to handle 'execution-only' products. Now customers may need to be taken through a more complex set of processes. Vincent explains that the systems were designed to be flexible as it was clear that the range of products would expand. However, such has been the rate of change that he has had to scrap two systems and begin again to ensure that the service is customer driven and not constrained by the status quo. He is impressed that such an expensive course of action will be supported if it is in the customer interest.

Criteria for success

Rowan Gormley sees the success of Virgin Direct as being based on service and value creation. The aim is to retain customers. Success will be achieved when most of the customers are dealing with Virgin as a priority provider and have the full portfolio of Virgin products. He sums the recipe up as follows:

> 'There is a great brand. If we keep the price down and the service is good, then the value creation of Virgin Direct is better than competitors. The customers will keep on coming back to us.'

Jayne-Anne Gadhia reflects:

> 'Competitors and people who visit often want to know what the recipe for success is. They think there is a magic ingredient. But Virgin Direct's success is not based on a magic ingredient, it is down to hard work.'

She includes among factors which have played a role in Virgin Direct's success the systems which back up the call centre. Although the leading suppliers offered good systems, these would constrain Virgin's service. Instead, the firm opted to build its own systems to meet its exact requirements. The level of risk involved is typical of the firm. Jayne-Anne sums it up: 'If someone has an idea and there are twenty reasons why not, we do it anyway.'

Martin Campbell, Virgin Direct's product development manager, feels that the real innovation in Virgin Direct is to backtrack and to go back to what personal financial services should be about. Whilst the financial services firms are adding ever more sophisticated products, the customers are actually saying 'go in the opposite direction, make it simper'. To do so is a radical innovation. Virgin Direct now has a number of products, but the two types of PEP investment funds are the 'engine room'. The other products allow different ways in. So Virgin's recipe is 'make it simple to make it effective.' The savings are passed on to the customer.

Creating sustainable advantage

Perhaps the most innovative part of the Virgin Direct operation is the organizational culture. There is a strong, shared vision. Everyone shows a strong commitment to what Virgin is trying to do. Within a large conglomerate, Virgin Direct operates as a small, flexible unit. There is a team spirit of pulling together. Jayne-Anne Gadhia sums it up as 'a passion and obsession. We want Virgin to be the best.'

The real challenge for Virgin Direct lies in their success. On television advertising evenings, the Call Centre is organized to have the maximum number of tele-operators available to handle calls. Communication activity aims to achieve the right volume of calls. The business has already grown to take over the entire building in which they are based. Maintaining the informality of communication, cross-functional teams and service excellence of operators may be a challenge as numbers increase further.

Stop press: 17 October 1997 – the launch of Virgin One

In October 1997, a year after the launch of pensions, Virgin Direct entered the retail banking market with the words:

> 'We are delighted to announce that we're taking on the banks and building societies. The newspapers have been talking about it for months, our competitors have feared it for ages and our customers have been asking for it for years. We've teamed up with The Royal Bank of Scotland plc to launch the Virgin One account which could change the way you manage your money forever.'
> Launch announcement, October 1997

The Virgin One account offers the combined features of a mortgage, loan and current account (see Figure 9.2). Richard Branson says that it is:

> 'set to turn personal banking on its head by breaking down the artificial barrier between savings and borrowings (. . .) banking is inherently a very straightforward business: it astonishes me that it has been allowed to become so complicated.

This new form of banking is aimed at busy people: 'who have got better things to do than to chase around trying to get a return on their money. It sets a new challenge to traditional banks and building societies through the five principles which were used to create the account:

- One account, One statement and One phone number
- All borrowings at mortgage rate
- Your money works hard, you don't
- Its your money not ours
- You'll be treated as an adult

The Virgin Direct process of innovation continues, where will it end?

Key features of the One account:

Customers decide how much money they will need to meet their financial needs, including their mortgage, credit cards, other loans etc.

We'll agree a suitable credit limit with the customer. This is called their 'facility'

They pay their monthly income into the account.

There is no tax to pay whilst the One account is in net debit. This is because the customer is paying back borrowings rather than saving

The account can be used for all the usual financial transactions, including cash withdrawals, direct debits, cheque payments, Switch and Visa cards.

There's one rate of interest for the entire facility.

Interest will be calculated each day and charged to the account monthly.

Customers can run their One account over the telephone 24 hours a day, any day of the year.

Other important information:

Minimum facility is £50,000.

Customers must agree to use their home as security.

The facility must be repaid on, or before, retirement.

All accounts will be held by the Royal Bank of Scotland

Figure 9.2

References

Riley, B. (1996) FT Quarterly Review of Personal Finance, *Financial Times*, 26 January, p. 31.

Smith, A. (1996) Direct Line to compete with PEP providers, *Financial Times*, 17 February, p. 1.

Wolffe, R. (1995) Weekend Money: Putting pop into Peps – Virgin is about to expand into financial products but will sell them only by telephone, *Financial Times*, 11 February, p. 1.

Anonymous (1995) Midweek Money: Branson competes on price – Bond Peps / Smart Money, *Financial Times*, 4 October.

Chapter 10

First Direct telephone banking

Susan Bridgewater

Background

> 'By far the biggest change, and the one most likely to broaden customer choice in the personal current account banking market, has been the growth of telephone banking. The market leader is First Direct telephone bank, which is open 24 hours a day, 365 days a year.'
>
> Miller, 1994

On 1 October 1989, Midland Bank plc, operating in the mature UK banking sector, made a dramatic innovation. The First Direct telephone banking subsidiary in Leeds was the country's first telephone retail banking service. The success of First Direct far exceeded the original aim of building a niche position in the market. Since its launch, First Direct has attracted more than 650,000 cheque account customers (Key Note Report, 1997). This represents around 12 per cent of the 5 million people who chief executive officer, Kevin Newman, believes currently constitute the 'banking without branches market' (Kelly, 1990). The number of customers transferring to the new banking service stands at over 12,000 each month compared with an industry average of 5000. First Direct has recently announced plans to build a new call centre in Scotland, which will create up to 5000 jobs.

First Direct telephone banking: a benchmark case

A member of the original First Direct project team and chief executive officer from late 1991 to 1997, 38 year old Kevin Newman describes the retail banking sector of the late 1980s as mature and differentiated only by price:

> 'The domestic retail bank of the time was like a desert. It needed
> some rain to bring it back to life. Banking was believed to be a
> mature sector, wherein differentiation was only possible on the basis
> of price. This was not a sustainable means of achieving competitive
> advantage. Price changes were mirrored by competitors and led to
> price wars. Eventually all of the banks ended up back at equilibrium,
> but financially worse-off. The main threat was posed by firms 'new to
> banking.' Inertia was huge. There was a perception that all banks
> were the same.'

Against this climate, the introduction of First Direct's telephone banking service was a bold and innovative step. The budget allocated by Midland Bank for the launch of First Direct was £6 million. Of this, £2.5 million was spent on media advertising (O'Kelly, 1990). Kevin Newman sees this risk as wholly justified:

> 'If it worked we could change the business in a big way. The size of
> the financial stake required from Midland for First Direct was
> insignificant given the other issues which Midland was facing.'

Thus, the risk of the initial investment must be judged against the size of the parent organization. The stake put up by the parent company represented a relatively low risk, in the light of the possible gains. The risks for individual members of the launch team were much higher. The success or failure of the First Direct venture was likely to have a positive or negative impact on head office's perception of their abilities.

The key characteristics of the First Direct banking service are that it offers free banking, direct telephone banking and 24 hour access, 365 days a year. The service is targeted primarily at customers in the ABC1 socio-demographic segments, between the ages of 25 and 45.

At its launch, First Direct was the only bank to offer 24 hour access to banking services. However, Peter Simpson, commercial director of First Direct and also a member of the launch team, believes that service quality and features are less critical to success than the firm's aims and philosophy. He describes the core concept of the firm as:

> 'to develop intelligent relationships with customers on a one-to-one
> basis. Use of direct delivery by telephone is simply the means by
> which this is achieved.'

Having decided to remain within the banking sector, the way in which First Direct met these last three criteria has changed the dynamics of the retail banking market.

The number of direct and indirect imitators who have entered the market attests to First Direct's impact on the market:

> 'Innovations such as interactive electronic networks allowing 'home shopping' may allow retailers to mimic First Direct by cutting staff and buildings.'
>
> Gapper, 1990

> 'First Direct, the independent Midland offshoot launched in 1989, has shown the way for personal banking with a similar formula.'
>
> Hutton, 1994

> 'Significantly, the Prudential is not following Midland's First Direct in offering current accounts. At least, not yet.'
>
> *Financial Times*, 1995

> 'Banque Directe is modelled unashamedly on First Direct, the Midland Bank subsidiary in the UK that began in 1989 and now claims more than 500,000 customers.'
>
> Jack, 1995

Channel strategy

One reason for the success of First Direct is that it identified a latent dissatisfaction with the traditional branch system:

> 'The remarkable success of the telephone banking system, pioneered by Midland's First Direct, is testimony as much to the unpopularity of conventional branch banks as to the convenience of a 24-hour telephone service.'
>
> O'Connor, 1994

Market research no longer supports the traditional belief that the customer has a personal relationship with bank manager (See Figure 10.1). A MORI survey of British Banking in 1988 showed that 48 per cent of customers had never met their bank manager, 51 per cent would prefer to visit the branch as little as possible, whilst 38 per cent felt that banking hours were inconvenient. Based on these findings, First Direct set about radically rethinking the channels used to deliver banking services to the end customer.

Research also showed that customers prefer the telephone as a mode of direct communication to high-tech alternatives. Mike Harris, chief executive officer at the launch of First Direct, cites market research findings that 85 per cent of

> 20% of account holders had not visited their branch in the last month.
>
> 51% said they would rather visit the branch as little as possible.
>
> 48% had never met their bank manager.
>
> 38% said banking hours were inconvenient.
>
> 27% wished they were able to conduct more business over the phone.

Figure 10.1 MORI survey of British banking customers. Cited in Parmenter and Larréché (1997)

people prefer to talk to a person rather than a computer (Bradshaw, 1990). Computer technology may be the future of retail banking, but it would currently reach only a proportion of the target market, whilst telephones are familiar and readily accessible:

> 'The telephone is now the key interactive device. Not only are there telephones in almost every household, but many millions of people are using mobile phones.'
>
> Key Note Report, 1997

The success of First Direct and the difficulties encountered by other delivery modes suggest that this was the correct choice:

> 'Many of the banks which rushed to offer computer-based services in the late 1980s are giving up on the high-tech approach and going for real people instead.'
>
> Hutton, 1994

First Direct is acknowledged as the first creator of a new type of banking service which Ernst and Young describe as 'virtual banking' (see Figure 10.2). At the time of its introduction, no other bank offered a comparable service. Whilst there have been many imitators, First Direct's success can be judged by the frequency with which it is used as a benchmark by competitors.

Service portfolio

One of the key features of First Direct is a high standard of service quality, which reduces prices and also adds value to customers. Service accuracy is high:

> 'Midland Bank and National Westminster Bank are rated worst for overall satisfaction, while Abbey National, First Direct, Girobank and Yorkshire Bank are rated best.'
>
> *Financial Times*, 1993

Migration of Technology Usage by the Banking Industry

Traditional bank

Issues: Size of mainframe
         Communications between branches and central data centre

---

Emergence of the virtual bank
Issues: Cost reduction
         Improved service
         Identifying vendor alternatives

Choosing the right path to virtual banking
Issues: Delivery channels
         Operational redundancy
         Improved customer interface

Managing the virtual bank
Issues: Customer focus
         Changing the organization
         Changing the role of technology
         Redefining partner relationships
         Identifying cross-selling opportunities
         Managing multiple vendors/service providers – least cost, best service
         providers

Figure 10.2 Virtual banking: the technology challenge

The initial range of services was focused in order to keep costs low and spread the learning curve over time.

Kevin Newman divides the services offered by First Direct into three categories (Table 10.1) based on their level of complexity and frequency. Simple, routine operations can easily be automated. However, more complex issues, which would previously have required going to the branch, or even speaking with the bank manager, must be handled with greater sensitivity. These need to be dealt with in person and, preferably, by the same person at First Direct. They must also be tailored more to the individual so as to replicate a trusting relationship with the bank manager. Simple transactions can be dealt with using a standardized approach. Increasingly, automatic telling machines (ATMs) will handle these. Technological advances mean that ATMs will be able to have increasingly intelligent interaction with customers. They will be able to tell a customer, for example, that a cheque paid out last night will take them overdrawn. The customer will automatically be offered the opportunity to avoid this by transferring money between accounts.

Market research shows (Table 10.2) that as telephone banking has developed its portfolio of services, customers are increasingly happy to conduct

Table 10.1

Type of transaction	Routine transaction	Complex transactions	Complex products
Task	Balances Cash management Simple products Paying-in	Queries Bank loans Extend overdrafts	Insurance Mortgages Investment Complaints
Equivalent in traditional banking system	Automated	Largely automated but may wish to deal with same person	Bank managers

complex transactions such as mortgages and loan applications by telephone. Conversely, they are switching away from direct contact for routine operations such as balance enquiries and order of statements, which are most frequently handled via ATMs.

Communication

Creation of First Direct's 'virtual' organization poses distinctive challenges. First, customers must be made aware of the innovative nature of First Direct's banking service. First Direct's revolutionary launch adverts, designed by advertising agency Howell, Henry, Chaldecott, Lury, were first

Table 10.2 Facilities used in telephone banking

Facility used	1994	1997	Percentage change
Balance enquiry	84.2	65.5	−22.2
Arrange loan	na	9.9	
Arrange mortgage	na	2.4	
Financial advice	13.5	9.9	−35.2
Order cheque book or statement	51.7	33.5	−35.2
Pay bills	51.5	39.8	−22.7
Arrange standing order or direct debit	na	42.9	
Other	62.0	42.0	−32.1

Source: British Market Research Bureau's Target Group Index 1994–97

shown on television on 1 October 1989. The first advert took the form of a message from 2010 to the current day (see Figure 10.3). Second, First Direct had to overcome resistance to dealing with a bank via telephone rather than via a branch. The second phase of advertising offered optimistic and pessimistic views of First Direct, which were shown simultaneously on different channels. The optimistic highlights the positive features which the service offers, whilst the pessimistic addresses concerns which potential customers might have (see Figure 10.4).

The extraordinary nature of First Direct continued as an advertising theme throughout the launch phase. This promotional effort was of great importance to the successful launch of First Direct, which was less visible to customers than traditional banks:

> '"This means that marketing is our only form of visual
> communication with our customers", said Ms Jan Smith, First
> Direct's Marketing Director. "Getting it right from the start was
> vital."' (O'Kelly, 1990).

However, the target market comprised infrequent television viewers. Therefore, First Direct used a mix of promotional tools in a campaign carefully co-ordinated between HHCL, Option One Direct, the direct mail subsidiary of Gold, Greenless, Trott Communications, and Quentin Bell, First Direct's public relations consultancy.

Direct press advertisements featured 'tip-ons,' an origami-style envelope stuck to the page, which included First Direct's phone number and a business reply card. Every respondent received an explanatory brochure, a 'help card' giving details of how to open an account and an interest rate card for various types of account. A distinctive black and white corporate identity was used to attract attention and hopefully increase readership of the mailshot. The response rate for the direct mail campaign was 2.3 per cent compared with an average of less than 2 per cent. Whilst this sounds like a low response, Jan Smith insisted:

> 'Direct marketing works well for us. It is a good way of targeting
> accurately. Media advertising is more of a 'scatter-gun' approach.
> However, First Direct will continue media advertising throughout
> the next year.'
>
> O'Kelly, 1990

For the year ending June 1997, First Direct had the largest individual advertising spend of any retail bank, which amounted to £6.4 million or 14.6 per cent of the industry's total spend (Key Note Report, 1997).

An Announcement from the future: shown 1st October 1989

Breaks into Audi advert as an announcement from the year 2010:

'Please don't be alarmed. This is a first attempt to communicate across time. This experiment is being sponsored by First Direct to celebrate our 21st anniversary. For us it is the year 2010. To celebrate the 21st anniversary of First Direct we have returned to the year of our launch. We return you now to your own programmes with every best wish for your personal happiness in your own future.'

Figure 10.3 First Direct launch advertising

Optimistic and pessimistic scenarios

Charlotte Rampling presents factual information about First Direct's new telephone banking services using an interactive format.

'First Direct is a new banking organization that does things differently. For example, no branches. What is your reaction?'

'For an optimistic view, stay on this channel, for a pessimistic view, turn to Channel 4 now.'

Optimistic scenario
[Shot as a song and dance act with singer in London street dressed in white.]

'I'm going to have a place for my money, I can call both night and day.
I am going to speak to intelligent people there, who will do anything I say.
They will give me instant decisions. I get an overdraft automatically.
First Direct will be wonderful for you and me.
They don't have any branches. They can spend more on service for me.
First Direct will be wonderful for you and me. '

Charlotte Rampling:
'Because First Direct don't have any branches they can spend more on service, and it's free. '

Call 0800 22 2000 for a current account information pack.
First Direct is a division of Midland Bank plc.

Pessimistic scenario
[Shot as a blues song in London Street, with singer dressed in black.]

'You heard about First Direct, mm? Won't work for sure.
They say they're a new kind of banking, huh? No branches no more.
But we have had branches for years, what are they changing it for?
They say you can call their people, 24 hours a day.
They're far too new and different. They'll close down right away (like tomorrow, honey).
They're not an old institution, that's where my money stays.'

[shot of red herrings]

Charlotte Rampling:
'Phone your bank now . . . if nobody answers, ring First Direct instead'

Call 0800 22 2000 for a current account information pack.
First Direct is a division of Midland Bank plc.

Figure 10.4 The second phase of advertising

Criteria for success

The success of First Direct is apparent from the frequency with which its is used as a benchmark by competitors. Telephone banking as a sector of the banking market was initiated by First Direct and has grown to sizeable proportions (see Table 10.3).

Table 10.3 Adults using telephone banking

	1994	1997	Percentage increase
Adults using telephone banking (%)	4.5	12.7	354.3
Adults with a current account at a bank or building society using out of hours telephone banking (%)	20.7	38.0	83.6

Source: British Market Research Bureau's Target Group Index 1994–97

It is less easy to quantify in financial terms. Whilst it is a separate subsidiary of Midland Bank, now owned by HSBC Holdings plc, the financial results of First Direct are not disclosed separately. However, some indications of First Direct's performance can be established. Kevin Newman comments that the scale of the First Direct operation is much larger than originally envisaged and that building a critical mass was initially more important than returning a profit. Accordingly, First Direct's measure of success in the growth phase was the number of customers. This currently stands at around 650,000 (see Table 10.4).

Table 10.4 Data based on internal sources, Keynote Reports 1997 and Midland bank accounts

Date	Total number of customers
December 1989	11,000
December 1990	66,000
December 1991	136,000
December 1992	241,000
December 1993	361,000
December 1994	476,000
December 1995	550,000
December 1996	600,000
December 1997	650,000

Although precise levels of profit are not disclosed, Midland Bank's financial figures show that First Direct went into the black in the second half of 1994. The full year performance for 1995 was 'not to be sniffed at' (*Financial Times*, 1996) and made a significant contribution to the 10 per cent increase in the profits of Midland Bank. Longer-term success will be measured, according to commercial director Peter Simpson, by three measures:

1 **Shareholder returns to HSBC.**
2 **Customer satisfaction value:** recognition of changing customer needs. As trust in traditional institutions has broken down, First Direct aims to build a new type of organization in which the customer trusts the value of the service received.
3 **Individual values:** 100 per cent of employees saying that First Direct is a great place to work.

The challenge now facing First Direct is that of sustaining the competitive advantage which it gained from the 'big idea'. Peter Simpson describes the history of First Direct as comprising three phases:

1 **Launch:** 18 months spent introducing a 'revolutionary idea'.
2 **Development:** three and a half years to reach profit.
3 **Rediscovery:** the current 'evolution' of the business as it grows and develops. The aim now is 'evolution' or continuous innovation.

The continuous development phase is building upon computer technology. Although the interface with the customer is via telephone, a database is at the fingertips of every member of the call centre within First Direct. The demographic details and history of each customer's transactions is used to assess the likelihood that current customers will be interested in the broader portfolio of financial services offered by First Direct. Scores are assigned to each customer on their 'propensity to buy' each of the services. The database is used as the basis for sophisticated direct mail activity, determining which offers the customers should receive, with what frequency. Kevin Newman believes that future success will come from reaching that part of the target market which is not yet aware of First Direct and from achieving service excellence in a fuller range of financial services.

References

Anonymous (1993) Customers Report Banking Errors, *Financial Times*, 2 December.
Anonymous (1995) Leading Article: Prudential Step, *Financial Times*, 25 October.
Anonymous (1996) UK Company News: Midland Expands 10% to £998 million, *Financial Times*, 27 February.

Bradshaw, D. (1990) Technology: dial M for Money. Why Improvements in telephone Banking Should Increase Convenience, *Financial Times*, 8 March.

Dempsey, M. (1995) Survey of International Telecommunications: Virtual Banking on Trial, *Financial Times*, 3 October.

Gapper, J. (1990) The high price of customer contact: Innovations in the financial sector have not been matched by other service providers, *Financial Times*, 4 April.

Hutton, B. (1994) Finance and the Family: Ringing in the Revolution – A look at the way technology is affecting financial services, *Financial Times*, 15 January.

Jack, Andrew (1995) International Company News: Ringing the Changes in French Banking – Banque Directe has taken the telephone services initiative, *Financial Times*, 7 August.

Key Note Report (1997) Retail Branch Banking, October.

O'Connor, G. (1994) Quarterly Review of Personal Finance, *Financial Times*, 29 April.

O'Kelly, L. (1990) Survey of International Direct Marketing: Banking on phones – Case Study: First Direct, *Financial Times*, 18 April.

Miller, R. (1994) Quarterly Review of Personal Finance, *Financial Times*, 29 April.

Parmenter, D. and J.-C. Larréché (1997) *Firt Direct: Branchless Banking*, INSEAD, Fontainebleau, France.

Chapter 11

Orange mobile phones: the future is bright

Susan Bridgewater

Background

Prior to 1994, mobile telephones were largely the preserve of business executives. The *Financial Times* describes two categories of business user:

> 'In most populous mobile nations, the best analogy for the present state of the mobile phone market is that of a thin sandwich in search of a thick filling. Two thin slices of the business market are currently being serviced – namely senior executives on the one hand, and travelling sales people plus the self-employed 'roamers' (plumbers, electricians, and so on) on the other. In between lies a mass of the employees who get no closer to a mobile phone than overhearing banal conversations on the train home. Typically, a company will have a handful of mobile phones for staff on the move – but no policy of progressively extending their use.'
>
> Adonis, 1994

These business customers were largely price insensitive. They also represented a very small proportion of the populace. In the UK, Racal's Vodafone or British Telecom's Cellnet analogue mobile telephones had met the needs of these people since 1985. Both firms 'levied largely unchanged and almost identical tariffs' (*Financial Times*, 1994). The predicted growth of mobile telephones from the preserve of price insensitive innovators to a broader market had been slow to take place:

> 'Nonetheless, even in the west, the mobile phone has a long way to go before it becomes a standard business item, let alone a mass consumer product. For all the talk of mobile networks competing with, or replacing, fixed networks, virtually no organisation of any size make universal provision for their employees to have cellular phones.'
>
> Adonis, 1994

However, in 1994, three major trends offered opportunities for change in the mobile or cellular telephone market:

> 'First the tentative entry of the mobile phone into the consumer market. Second, the rise of competition between rival operators within countries. And third, the migration from analogue to digital networks offering greater capacity, enhanced features, improved reliability, and the capacity to 'roam' across national borders.'
>
> Adonis, 1994

These trends had begun to cause rapid growth in mobile phone usage. Within the UK cellular phones grew as a percentage of the market by value and volume (see Tables 11.1 and 11.2).

Cellular telephony accounts for much of the growth in overall tele-communications revenue in this period, increasing from 6 per cent in 1993 to 14.2 per cent in 1994, 18.7 per cent in 1995 and 22.6 per cent in 1996. In volume terms, the total market grew by 31.8 per cent. The higher value growth rate reflects an increase in premium rate and value-added services. Cellular phones achieved a growth rate of 288 per cent between 1993 and 1996.

Table 11.1 UK telecommunications by sector (% of total revenue)

	1993	1994	1995	1996
Fixed telephones	52.67	47.95	42.93	39.7
Exchange Lines	19.20	17.79	18.04	17.47
Cellular Telephony	6.04	14.16	18.66	22.62
Public Payphones	2.44	2.32	2.11	1.91
Private Payphones	0.61	0.54	0.46	0.36
Telex	0.16	0.11	0.10	0.07
Revenue from terminating calls	10.03	9.14	10.03	10.43
Total	100	100	100	100

Source: Keynote Reports 'Telecommunications', November 1997

Table 11.2 The UK telecoms market by volume (million call minutes) 1993–96

	1993	*1994*	*1995*	*1996*
Fixed Telephones	98,320	105,417	114,560	125,818
Cellular phones	2,579	3,271	5,122	7,433
Telex	394	360	326	277
Total	101,293	109,048	120,008	133,528
Index	100	107.6	118.5	131.8

Source: Keynote Reports 'Telecommunications', November 1997

The major impetus behind the growth of mobile phones in the UK was the entry into the market of additional operators. In 1993, Mercury One-2-One targeted the consumer market with slightly higher subscription costs but low usage charges. They also made a great play of free weekend calls at launch. This had a dramatic impact on the cost of owning a mobile phone:

> 'At the start of 1993, the business user had to pay 33p a minute for daytime calls in the London region. By the year-end that had dropped to 20p for those on the new London tariff packages.'
>
> Adonis, 1994

Mobile phones were coming within the reach of the broader business market and, more significantly, of consumer markets.

However, Mercury One-2-One were so keen to take advantage of the new market opportunity ahead of potential rivals that they launched with only 30 per cent coverage of the UK market. This meant that the Mercury mobile phone was regionally focused on customers within the M25. A major opportunity existed for someone to combine this pricing with more extensive market coverage. Moreover, there was an opportunity to capitalize on the move toward the digital technology of the future. Hutchison Telecom, 65 per cent owned by Hong Kong conglomerate Hutchison Whampoa Ltd, 30 per cent by British Aerospace and 5 per cent by Barclays Bank, seized this opportunity by launching Orange mobile phones into the UK market in April 1994.

The launch of Orange

Hutchison had been operating in the UK telecommunications market since the 1980s, both with pagers and as a mobile phone service provider acting as an airtime reseller for Vodafone and Cellnet, who were prevented from selling directly to end customers by telecoms legislation. Hutchison's experience of the telecommunications market had been increased by the unsuccessful launch of the Rabbit telepoint service in 1993/4. This had reinforced their belief in the importance of getting the service offer right.

Hutchison had been researching and planning their launch into the mobile phone market for five years. Research showed the mobile phone market to be large, but hugely confusing. However, the impetus for change towards digital technology presented opportunities for new market entrants:

> 'Henceforth cellular phones can probably be expected to penetrate both the business and consumer sectors in parallel, the one reinforcing the other against a backdrop of progressively – but not precipitately – falling prices. Price reductions will owe something to technological advance; something to competition between operators; and something to cultural attitudes, which at some point are bound to make the mobile phone as essential as the fridge. That time may come fairly soon, if the progress of the UK market over the past year is any guide.'
>
> Adonis, 1994

Although at that point there were only two firms providing mobile phone services, they were selling via a number of different airtime resellers. On the high street, these airtime resellers were competing to offer attractive deals, mainly on handsets. Call rates were high, at around 40–50p per minute. In addition to confusion, research also showed customer perceptions of being 'ripped off' by the big firms. Price propositions were felt to be unattractive. They were dissatisfied with old analogue technology. Before the launch of Mercury's One-2-One there was an absence of strong brands, so customers had little with which they could identify. Most importantly, customers were very concerned to have an appropriate level of market coverage.

It was clear to Hutchison that a successful launch into the mobile phone market could only be achieved with a strong service offering:

> 'Hans Snook . . . the 48 year old managing director of Orange, the UK mobile phone group, . . . is one of a new breed of telecoms manager, more concerned with what customers want from a telephone service than with the technical detail necessary to make it work.'
>
> Cane, 1996

When Mercury launched One-2-One in September 1993, Hutchison was close to launching Orange. However, research had showed 50 per cent coverage of the UK population to be the minimum level acceptable to customers. Whilst Mercury had a strong proposition, with new phones and cheaper calls, their 30 per cent coverage of the UK market was not enough to shake the big operators, although it eroded their rate of connections. After the launch of One-2-One, both Vodafone and Cellnet initially resisted calls to cut their prices:

'Vodafone, the UK mobile communications group, said it expected to make no cuts in mobile phone tariffs this year and dared its rivals to cut theirs. At yesterday's results meeting Mr Gerry Whent, chief executive said: "They dare not cut another single penny, otherwise they will never see profit." Cellnet, Vodafone's main rival in the mobile cellular market, immediately responded that it was "happy that Vodafone shares our view that no price cuts are needed."'

Adonis, 1994

The following week, Mercury cut its prices still further:

'Mercury One-2-One, the mobile phone operator in the London region, yesterday announced a sharp cut in its business tariff. The move comes a week after Vodafone, the largest cellular operator, said that tariffs would be unchanged for the rest of the year ... The move will put pressure on Vodafone and Cellnet, the second largest operator, to cut their tariffs, although both operators said their networks did not need to be price competitive with One-2-One because they offered national coverage.'

Adonnis, 1994

It was this last weakness in the One-2-One proposition which caused Hutchison to make the difficult decision to delay the launch of Orange. Although Mercury gained considerable positive press and attention from challenging the two big firms first, Hutchison felt that it was important to have a minimum 50 per cent coverage on entry into the UK market and to press ahead aggressively with plans achieve over 90 per cent coverage. This commitment has required considerable capital outlay by Hutchison:

'Orange has become the largest single investment in telecommunications for the Hong Kong group. Mr Hans Snook, group managing director for Hutchison Telecom (UK), said investment to the end of [1994] when the service would reach 70 per cent of the population, would be £450 million. Some 900 base stations, filing cabinet-sized pieces of equipment to receive and transmit calls, were in place and a further 550 sites had been bought. He said the peak funding requirement, including all capital expenditure, operating expenditure and operational losses would be about £700 million.'

Cane, 1996

Commitment of capital outlay on this scale made the challenge of Orange to Vodaphone and Cellnet of a different order to that of Mercury. It allowed Orange to take the process of change in the mobile telephone market forward, although Mercury had been the catalyst for this change:

> ' ... the Orange network looks attractive. Since it will cover the
> main UK metropolitan areas and the connecting motorways at
> launch, it has a significant advantage over its rival Mercury
> One-2-One. Its expansion will also be more rapid. Orange will
> cover 70 per cent of the population by the end of the year and 90
> per cent by mid 1995. One-2-One will only have around 30 per
> cent by the year end. Coverage is wide enough to make Orange a
> realistic alternative to Vodafone and Cellnet ... the old networks'
> profitability is critically dependent on their business tariffs. Those fat
> margins could be undermined if business users drift to Orange in
> significant numbers. Wide coverage and lower handset prices are
> also a threat to One-2-One. It may suffer from its decision to
> constrain capital spending and roll its network out slowly.'
>
> *Financial Times,* 1994

Orange was designed to incorporate more benefits than One-2-One, greater coverage, Nokia handsets which doubled as radio pagers and had screens which could display voicemail and caller ID, and, most importantly, a total service proposition which would cut through the confusion and offer clear value for money to customers.

The target market for the Orange mobile phone is described by head of product marketing, Graeme Oxby, as:

> 'Not those right at the top of the corporate market, but the
> remaining 90 per cent of the populace. Business customers were
> initially the principle target. Predominantly middle managers and
> small business owners. Largely ABC1 customers and predominantly
> younger age groups attracted by the possibilities of digital
> technology and an attractive price and service offer.'

These customers wanted access to mobile telephony in a value for money way and would not be satisfied with analogue technology.

The Orange brand

The values which Orange wished to encapsulate within the brand image for their mobile phone were those of:

- simplicity
- integrity
- friendliness
- innovation
- optimism

Orange head of product marketing, Graeme Oxby, described the process of creating the brand identity as follows. Identity consultants Wolff Olins worked together with Hutchison to determine that these values were all incorporated in Orange. Orange was a word for which no one could find any negative connotations. Moreover the associations which people make with Orange were: 'distinctive, dynamic, open, positive, ... simple, friendly and approachable' (*Financial Times*, 1994).

However, it was important that the name Orange was associated with the colour, not the fruit. Although the fruit also has positive associations for a majority, it does not convey the right values for a high technology company. Accordingly, the Orange logo is designed as a square (see Figure 11.1) to remove this connotation.

Figure 11.1 The Orange company logo

The images used in conjunction with the logo are black and white, to provide maximum contrast with Orange. These images are designed to attract attention by being very stark, very striking and very odd to convey simplicity and innovation (see Figure 11.2). They often depict children (see Figures 11.3 and 11.4) who are intended as a symbol of the future. A future, which Orange

Figure 11.2

Figure 11.3

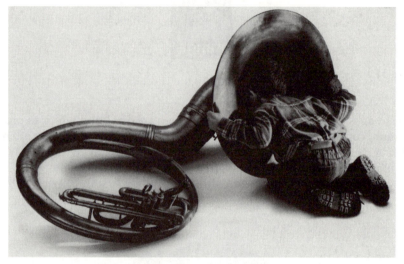

Figure 11.4

believes will be 'wire free'. The Orange strapline: 'The Future is Bright – The Future is Orange' conveys the Orange values and the vision of mobile phones replacing traditional landlines.

The service offer

As Graeme Oxby says, the Orange brand values can only be reinforced to customers 'if they are supported by what you do.' Accordingly, only simplification of the service offer could reduce customer confusion. First,

Orange set up a one-point-of-contact call centre to handle customer queries. This can be reached via widely publicized Free Call telephone numbers. The package to which a customer subscribes with Orange comprises a number of elements. First, there is the mobile phone. Second, a connection charge. Third, a set of call charges. Finally, insurance for the mobile handset.

Much of the confusion about mobile phones comes from the first of these elements, the handset itself. When it first entered the mobile market Orange priced the Nokia handsets at between £200 and £300 compared to £50 to £100 for analogue handsets. However, this proved counter to its aim to open up mobile communications to the mass market. Customers considered the price premium prohibitive as they were unsure of the value of a mobile telephone. Consequently, Orange took the step of gradually lowering the handset price to the point at which it is now fully competitive with Vodafone and Cellnet, ranging from £10 to £149.

Graeme Oxby justifies this move as follows:

> 'Most customers overestimate how expensive a mobile phone will be. They often begin by saying that they will only use it for emergency purposes and are reluctant to pay a large amount for the handset. We overcome this barrier by offering the handset at a reasonable price, and by offering free insurance and 24 hour replacement. We also offer bundled minutes, so the customer has a number of free minutes in with the monthly charge. For a while the customer only uses these. Then they exceed these and realise that the calls are not as expensive as they expected. Gradually the customer uses the mobile telephone more.'

The idea of an inclusive package overcomes barriers to entry and builds a long-term relationship with the customer. Other operators have subsequently made similar sacrifice of connection revenues to attract new entrants into the mobile phone market. Market research shows revenue within the mobile phone sector is currently gained more from rental and call charges than from connection (see Table 11.3).

Table 11.3 Cellular telephone revenues from customers 1994–97 (£ million)

	1994	1995	1996
Connections	32	60	48
Rentals and calls	1,134	1,619	2,241
Total	1,166	1,679	2,289

Source: OFTEL cited in Keynote Reports 'Telecommunications', November 1997

Table 11.4 UK cellular telephone tariffs (excluding 17.5% VAT)

Type of service	Connection (£s)	Monthly rental (£s)	Call charge (p)	
			Peak	Off peak
Vodaphone				
Business	50	25	25	10
Low Call	25	12.8	43	17
Capitalcall	50	20	20/50	10
EuroDigital	50	25	25	10
MetroDigital	50	20	20/25/50	10
Cellnet				
Primetime	50	25	25	10
Lifetime	25	12.8	43	17
Citytime	50	20	20/50	10
GSM	50	25	25	10
Mercury One-2-One				
Business Call	20	20	16	8
Personal Call	20	12.5	25	free/10
Orange				
Talk 15**	30	15	25	12.5
Talk 60**	30	25	20	10
Talk 200**	30	50	18	9
Talk 360**	30	75	16	8
Talk 540**	30	100	14	7

** Includes the number of free minutes in name
Source: FT Newsletter – Mobile Communications, *Financial Times*, May 5th 1994

Pricing

Both Mercury and Orange are lower both in connection charges and monthly fees than Cellnet and Vodafone. Orange offers the advantage of free minutes and call charges thereafter which are broadly comparable with those of Mercury. Orange was also the first of the mobile phone companies to introduce per second billing.

Analysts believe that Orange's pricing strategy is innovative. Such has been the popularity of bundling guaranteed airtime and charging by the second that Vodafone introduced similar price offers to digital subscribers from March 1997 (Price and Cane, 1996).

Distribution

As Hutchison already had experience of the telecommunications market with their pager systems, they were able to build upon existing links with retailers to distribute their mobile phones. In addition to distribution through channel intermediaries, Orange has also supplied direct to customers from the outset. This provides them with greater control over the service which is offered to customers compared to rivals who make use of intermediaries:

> 'Service providers, such as Talkland and People's Phone sell airtime to dealers and customers, arranging their own tariff structures, discounts and special offers. Crucially it is the service providers who own the customers, not the network operators. "We are responsible for customers from end to end" says Mr Graham Howe, Finance Director of Hutchison Telecom UK, Orange's parent company. "Because of this, we are able to build a relationship, be responsive and offer a consistency of service." Orange emphasises this by offering a wine club and lifestyle magazine to subscribers in addition to telecommunications services.'
>
> Price and Cane, 1996

Promotion

The campaigns manager for Orange, Adrian Fedyk, summarizes the communication aims as simplicity and clarity. These are used as benchmarks for all promotional activity. When deciding on advertising or below-the-line promotional activity, Orange employees always question how these activities fit with the promotional aims. These aims are exemplified by television advertising designed by agency WCRS which uses the starkness and simplicity, identified above under brand image, to build awareness of Orange as an innovative and dynamic company looking to the future. Launch advertising was designed to tease potential customers. An initial poster campaign conveyed the fact that Orange was something new, but did not reveal the full message of what it stood for until one to two weeks later.

In addition to this corporate level awareness building, successful promotion for Orange involves taking this activity down a level to incentivize channel partners and to help them to communicate with potential customers. Orange have a broad range of factual sales promotional material to describe the features of their different Talk Plans. These are designed to be simple and easily understood (see Figure 11.5).

There is a close relationship between Orange and its advertising agency. Robin Wright, partner in WCRS works closely with Orange chief executive, Hans Snook, and is frequently invited to top-level executive meetings where the strategy for Orange is decided.

choose your
group talk plan

There are two Group Talk Plans available - Group Talk 60 and Group Talk 200 - allowing you to choose the amount of inclusive minutes you'll be able to share. Of course, you can connect any of our promotional twin packs to the Group Talk Plan which suits you best.

One-off connection charge £30.00 (ex VAT)

talk plan	monthly charge	standard talk time included	standard call charges (per minute)		Orange to Orange call charges (per minute)	standard and Orange to Orange weekend call charges
			peak	off-peak		
group talk 60	£37.50	60 minutes	20p	10p	10p	5p
group talk 200	£62.50	200 minutes	18p	9p	9p	5p

Note: All prices exclude VAT. Peak times are from 7.00am to 7.00pm Monday to Friday. Off-peak is at all other times including Bank Holidays. Weekend call charges apply to standard rated calls only, from midnight Friday to midnight Sunday. Weekend calls are not taken from your inclusive minutes. Standard rated calls include most UK national calls and those between Orange phones but exclude those to other mobile or premium rate services.

Figure 11.5

Measures of success

By early 1996, Orange had gained 7 per cent of the total UK cellular market. More significantly, they had achieved 26 per cent of the digital phone market, equal to Vodafone and ahead of Cellnet and Mercury.

In March 1995, in a share offer, which was ten times over-subscribed, Orange floated on the UK stock market. This raised £624 million to finance further expansion of the network. Moreover, it showed the level of customer confidence in a firm of whom the FT writes:

> 'Even rivals admit grudging admiration for the group's chutzpah. Innovative pricing, esoteric advertising (with a clever emphasis on 'bright' and 'the future') and a determination to treat Orange customers as sophisticated individuals who understand the cost and value of mobile telephony have all contributed to a campaign which has resulted in Orange attracting 410,000 subscribers since its launch in April 1994.'
>
> Cane, 1996

Orange reached the 1 million subscriber mark in July 1997. By August 1997, Orange had spent £829 million in developing its network infrastructure and anticipates spending a further £800 million in the next two years. Such has been the commitment of capital that Orange anticipates that it will first achieve pre-tax profits by the end of 1997. This is earlier than its original forecast of 1999 (Key Note Report, 1997). Table 11.5 shows the turnover data for the major mobile phone suppliers in the UK. 1996/7 figures are based on first half estimates. Financial data are not reported separately for Mercury One-2-One, the smallest of the four UK cellular phone operators, now 50 per cent owned by Telewest. However, One-2-One arranged an eight-year syndicated credit arrangement for £1.2 billion in order to accelerate its network development (Key Note Report, 1997).

Table 11.5 Turnover of major cellular operators 1993–97 (£000's)

	1993/4	1994/5	1995/6	1996/7	1997/8 (estimated)
Vodafone	850,000	1,152,600	1,402,200	1,749,000	
Cellnet	462,545	685,303	919,290	–	
Orange Personal Telecoms	23,493	118,527	–	572,180[1]	854,000[2]

[1]Estimate based on first half figures 1996/7
[2]Estimate based on first half figures 1997/8
Source: ICC Database cited in Keynote Reports 'Telecommunications', November 1997: Table 26

Other measures of success include 'churn', the number of customers who leave the network. Orange have a churn of around 19.9 per cent against an industry average of 30 per cent (Key Note Report, 1997). In addition, Orange has gained positive accolades for its service quality. A survey by the Consumers' Association showed that Orange has far higher satisfaction rates than its rivals.

the
talkshare
offer

2 phones on
1 talk plan

share the benefits

Figure 11.6

Creating sustainable advantage

One of Orange's principle aims is to build long-lasting relationships with its customers. This has resulted in innovative marketing mix decisions such as that of lowering the price of handsets and including free minutes in the initial deal. The concept of the lifetime value of the customer has been extended to look at the ways in which the firm can introduce a broader range of customers to its network. The way in which Orange aims to do this is by developing the 'Orange Community'. The concept of the 'Orange Community' is founded on the belief that the one mobile phone user within a household may influence a partner or children to have phones. The development of Talk Share packages reduces the barriers for the use of two or more handsets. Importantly, whilst these group packages are aimed at small businesses, in targeting whole family usage of Orange phones, they are aimed at penetrating the consumer as well as business markets. Recent promotional activity has built on images of groups and multiple usage (see Figure 11.6).

Orange were the first of the mobile phone companies to tackle the issue of how to tap the massive potential consumer market. Introducing the next generation to mobile phones at an early age may be a significant step in making this process easier in the future. Moreover, building lifetime relationships with these customers should provide an income stream well into the twenty-first century. In March 1997, Orange began on the next stage of its development when it announced plans to offer cellular telephone services with multinational and transatlantic use capabilities. This development may ultimately allow Orange to access other international mobile phone markets.

References

Adonis, A. (1994) Survey of Telecommunications in Business (2): Enhanced Services on the Way, *Financial Times*, 15 June.

Anonymous (1994) The Lex Column: Mobile Phones, *Financial Times*, 9 March, p. 20.

Cane, A. (1996) People: Snook hopes Orange stays sweet, *Financial Times*, 2 September, p. 22.

Key Note Reports (1997) Telecommunications, November.

Price, C. and Cane, A. (1996) Orange pips its rivals with sparkling debut: Despite gloom in the mobile telephony sector, analysts expect the flotation to succeed, *Financial Times*, p. 7

Chapter 12

Psion: the Organiser

Jonathan Freeman

'Success is a lousy teacher.'

Bill Gates

Genesis

Seed corn

Psion was founded in 1980 by David Potter, a lecturer in mathematical physics at Imperial College, London. Dr Potter used the funds he had generated from an investment in a duvet manufacturing company having astutely anticipated the growth of demand for duvets.

Dr Potter was joined in 1981 by Dr Charles Davies, a graduate student who had worked with him at Imperial, and Colly Myers, an experienced computer program developer, who both worked on software and hardware design and development. Andy Clegg joined the firm in 1982 and took responsibility for managing manufacturing, while Peter Norman joined in 1983 as director of marketing.

Vision

From their inception in the 1940s onwards, the physical size of computers was being reduced, and their computational power and functionality was being increased. In conjunction with the increasing power of computers was the rapid growth in the volume of electronic data. By the early 1980s David Potter had come to the view that small yet powerful hand-held computing devices would become possible, and would be needed to handle the vast volume of electronic data which he anticipated would be ubiquitous. He believed that developing such tools was where Psion's future lay.

The development of personal computers, (PCs), in the mid-1970s (Campbell-Kelly and Aspray, 1996) had given support to this belief, as the PC represented a significantly different computer design from that of its predecessors, bulky mainframe and minicomputers. The architecture of a PC offered unprecedented flexibility to users by providing:

- off-line data storage – enabling data to be transported from one machine to another;
- off-line software – which could therefore be added to at a later date;
- a programming language – giving a PC the capability to learn (unlike a calculator).

In 1980 the design of PCs had taken a further leap forward in convenience, speed and improved storage with the development of rigid disk drives. These enabled data to be stored within the PC and increased its speed of operation. Rigid drives were initially used in 'desktop' PCs and then, when smaller drives were developed, these were used in portable 'laptop' PCs, (1983) and, later, even smaller 'notebook' PCs.

Well before portable PCs were developed Potter's vision was that the desirable qualities of PC architecture which generated this flexibility could be provided in a device far smaller than anything then available. However, this degree of miniaturization would also require a radically innovative computer design, something quite different from the standard PC design and he firmly believed that technological developments would occur to make such miniaturization possible. Potter's vision thus depended on the development of various necessary 'enabling' technologies. However, before Psion was in a position to develop a radical design it had some testing times to go through.

Embryonic services and core skills: contract software development

Initially the company earned its income as a sub-contract software designer for UK computer makers such as Sinclair, which had pioneered and grown with the home computer boom in the early 1980s. The early home computer market started with the Sinclair Spectrum and early software had an educational orientation but this rapidly began to shift towards entertainment and games. Though Psion's early software products included games, the company developed a reputation for quality and intellectual software; they developed versions of flight simulator and chess rather than violent 'shoot 'em up' games.

A key skill requirement, which they refined at this time, was the ability to write 'lean and mean' programs, which took the minimum of memory. To do this, programmers trained themselves to write using Assembler, a 'low-level' language. Higher-level languages enabled programs to be written more quickly but required more capacity and were therefore less efficient in their use of memory. The difference between levels can be considered in terms of modularity: low-level languages can be regarded as component parts, while higher-level languages can be considered as consisting of ready-assembled modules of such components. Skill with low-level languages and the ability to write compact programs is considered one of Psion's core skills.

Though the early home computer market initially provided support for the new company there was a concern that it had grown too rapidly and that the growth bubble would soon burst. In addition the new games products which the home computer market wanted did not fit well with Psion's culture. As a result Psion's software development for games atrophied.

Instead Psion contracted to develop a suite of applications including a word processor and a spreadsheet for a new computer which Sinclair was going to produce, to be known as Quantum Leap (QL). Unfortunately, when this machine was launched its sales were poor, and Psion's expected sales did not materialize. Psion thus rapidly moved to developing its own commercialized products, the first of which was an adaptation of the QL suite called the PC4.

However, soon after Psion's launch of the PC4 suite Lotus launched the spreadsheet application Lotus 1-2-3. which out-performed the spreadsheet in Psion's suite and this devastated sales of PC4. The company had failed to understand the manner in which end-users evaluated software. They prefered to buy one excellent spreadsheet rather than an inferior spreadsheet even if bundled with a suite of other applications. Thus again Psion was forced to react quickly when the market for their applications did not materialize.

First generation architecture and early products

By 1998 Psion had become famous in the UK as the pioneer of the 'Organiser' market. In the late 1980s and early 1990s electronic organizers were seen as an essential tool for the 'upwardly mobile' business person, replacing pen and paper based Filofaxes which were used by many to record appointments, contacts' names and telephone numbers, keep expense records and to make occasional notes. Production of organizers had meant a significant shift in the activities of the firm as they represented a movement from writing software programs to both writing software and designing and manufacturing the hardware on which it would run. As with Psion's earlier software production experiences, the path to success was not straightforward, and many lessons had to be learnt on the way

Organiser I

The idea for the first Organiser had come from observing the weaknesses of a database product for the Sinclair ZX81, called 'Vu-file'. Though this program allowed the user to enter hundreds of records and retrieve them using a search clue, it operated slowly – it took five minutes to load the program and a further five minutes to load the data. The idea and challenge was to create a battery-powered, hand-held machine to do this kind of database work. The result was the Organiser I, launched in August 1984, a hand-held device which allowed data entry, manipulation and transfer.

Once developed the Organiser was launched with a full-page advertisement in a national paper, but initial sales were disappointing, perhaps because no clear target market had been identified for the product. However, an executive for UK retailers Marks & Spencer saw the advert and, following negotiation, bought 30,000 Organisers to use as a specialist inventory management tool.

Organiser II

Learning from this initial brush with failure, Psion redesigned the Organiser and in 1986 launched Organiser II, which met with much greater success and with it the 'organizer market' was born. Though the core benefit proposition was much the same for both versions – an electronic address book, calculator and diary – the Organiser II delivered more of it.

The Organiser II was a portrait shaped device with a screen at the top, below which was a grid of keys (referred to as an ABC keyboard as the layout was in alphabetical order, unlike that of a typewriter). It was designed to be held in one hand while the keys were tapped with the other. It incorporated four basic functions: diary, address book, a calculator and a clock. One of the radical design features, which represented a breakthrough in miniaturization, was the way in which the Organiser II stored data. Unlike a PC, it had no rigid disk drive. Rather it used a special electronic memory chip (electronic programmable memory – EPROM), which had the advantage of being much smaller than a rigid disk drive, though it had to be constantly powered to retain the data. Though considered a radical move, in the sense that no manufacturer had ever used EPROM in this way before, doing so enabled the designers to provide both removable storage and a sensible battery life for a portable machine.

The Organiser II also included its own programming language, to enable users to develop their own applications for it. Though originally intended for the consumer market, most buyers turned out to be business people and the programmability enabled it to be used for industrial purposes.

However there were a number of marketing barriers to be overcome. Gaining distribution was difficult. For example, Psion approached Dixons, a major UK retail outlet for household electrical goods, but were initially rejected. As the product didn't fall into a readily recognized category Dixons had no identifiable buyer to deal with Psion. In addition, being a British company was seen to be a liability; a British electronic product was not thought likely to be as reliable as a Japanese product. Even today some users assume that Psion is a Japanese firm.

In the early days another major task was to increase awareness of what the product could do. Initially low-cost marketing tools like public relations and word-of-mouth were very effective in reaching people. The visibility of the product, e.g. when entering data, combined with the enthusiasm of users, made word-of-mouth a particularly powerful communications tool. Each usage occasion became a potential demonstration of the product to others who were likely to be in the potential market for the product.

Psion constantly sought to improve product features and functionality. The Organiser I had had a one line by 16 character display. Organiser II provided two lines and was followed in 1988 by the Organiser LZ, which provided a screen with four lines. This was seen as the company's best product to date, but up to this time there had been no competition.

At the end of the 1980s, Sharp, a Japanese computer manufacturer, produced the first Wizards. The screens on these machines were in some ways more advanced than the text-based screens of Psion's Organisers. The Wizard's screens provided graphics and used liquid crystal displays to show them. Though small, these machines enabled users to do more than they could with their Organisers.

The Psion engineers examined Sharp's product and realized that though superior in some respects, particularly the hardware, the Japanese machine was weak in its software design, the area Psion considered its main strength. For instance though the product did have a screen which could show graphics, it was only used to produce bigger digits. To the Psion engineers the Japanese approach to adding functionality seemed to boil down to adding keys and enlarging the keyboard whenever an additional function was required. This flew in the face of the Psion design ethos. The Psion team had gone to a lot of trouble to create a simple looking machine with as few buttons as possible in the belief that looking complex was not an advantage when most potential users did not know what an electronic organizer did or was for.

The next generation: SIBO

The success of Psion with the Organiser II and its improved versions had engendered a feeling of immense confidence within the company. Programmers and engineers felt that there was virtually nothing they could not now achieve if they set their minds to it.

In 1987, anticipating the limited life of the Organiser II, Psion thus set about developing the next generation of machines. This was to be based on a new architecture using a more powerful, 16-bit processor. Instead of simply showing text characters the screen would show graphics. The design would also have to be capable of running powerful applications like a word-processor and a spreadsheet.

Psion's aim was to produce a small computer, which would be seen as capable of running major productivity applications. It saw its core skill to lie in writing tight software code and believed that this would give it an inherent advantage over other manufacturers, all of whom were trying to shrink their existing DOS-based software programs down to fit into smaller machines. Software applications for PCs were designed to work with Microsoft's DOS which was the PC standard operating system software, but they had grown so large that they were sometimes referred to as 'bloatware' and were far too large to be stored on the EPROMs used by Psion. Thus to achieve its aims the software program at the heart of the new machine, the operating system, would have to be designed again from scratch.

This ambitious sixteen bit operating system, (SIBO), architecture was to be the basis of not one product, but was, in fact, to form the platform for a whole line of new products to include a new mobile computer (MC), a new 'palmtop' computer (Series 3) to replace the Organiser II, both of which were targeted at the consumer market, and a hand-held computer (HC) targeted at the industrial market. The MC represented Psion's attempt to be seen in the eyes of consumers as a computer manufacturer, rather than a maker of organizers. The MC design was to result in a machine smaller than any portable 'laptop' computer then on the market.

Despite the number of systems and products which were to be designed from scratch, the original intent was to develop the MC and Series 3 in parallel and to equip both with the same software, thus enabling the user to easily transfer information between them. However, after initiating this parallel development process it was realized that the company didn't have sufficient resources to develop both products at once. Given that the Organiser LZ was still selling well it was thus decided to develop the MC first.

Development was under the leadership of Colly Myers and Charles Davies. Colly's team was responsible for developing the operating systems and graphical user interface (GUI; a GUI enables users to run applications by using the cursor to point at and click on icons which appear on the screen, rather than typing instructional code words), while Charles' team were to develop the applications. Both team leaders were also directors of the company.

The development of this next generation of machines had depended on the advancement of technologies underlying the products of Psion's suppliers. For instance, though 16-bit processors were already widely in use in desktop and laptop PCs, they had not been suitable for a small battery-powered, hand-held device and for which power consumption was at a premium. The use of the greater processing capability of a 16-bit architecture depended on the development of a low-power 16-bit chip, which only became available around this time.

The decision to use this chip was also influenced by the fact that chips of that general type were widely used in PCs. This wide distribution meant that software development tools were already available and that many more compatible development tools were likely to become available for PCs which would therefore also be available for the Psion developers. The lack of such tools had hampered Psion's development of the software for the Organisers.

Three core concepts underlay the design: powerful desktop applications were to be put into a piece of hardware you can put in your pocket, reasonable battery life was to be provided – measured in weeks and months rather than hours – and removable storage was to be provided.

The MC series: another step into the unknown

The mobile computer was an ambitious project, aiming to create a small, portable computer using a new architecture. Because the operating system was different from the widely established Microsoft DOS, which was the standard for PCs, all the applications to run on it, including the word processor and the spreadsheet, were also to be newly developed. However, to the Psion developers the year allowed for the work seemed an incredibly long time. Beyond this estimate little was done to plan the work or what it might require.

The new MC design would enable extraordinary improvements in battery life. Laptop PCs then on the market averaged about three or, at best, four hours of use on one set of batteries. The MC would achieve over 60 hours. In addition Apple Corp. had recently launched the Macintosh desktop PC which used a GUI, and to many in the computer industry it was clear that a graphics-based interface would become the standard. The MC would have a GUI. Using their six years' experience gained in the hand-held market, the engineers decided to include many of the productivity tools, like a built-in agenda and a notebook, which had been included in the Organiser. They also decided that once the product was launched a word processor and a spreadsheet would then be developed which users could later add to their machines.

On launch, even though the MC range was competitively priced from around £500 to £1500, the market's verdict was that this was not what they wanted. Psion had repeated the mistake they had made earlier with their PC4 software. The market wanted spreadsheet and word processing applications and the productivity applications of a hand-held organizer, such as a notepad, a GUI, long battery life, small size and a reasonable price did not compensate for their lack.

As before with the PC4, Psion also discovered that competitors could ensure that the window of opportunity for their new product launch was very narrow. Soon after Psion launched the MC, competitors, such as the Japanese based Nippon Electric Corporation (NEC), launched DOS-based 'notebook' machines using newly developed, small, magnetic disk drives, capable of providing sufficient storage capacity for the large DOS-based applications programs. Because of their ubiquity, DOS-based word-processing and spreadsheet applications could be quickly offered with these machines, and it was these applications with which customers were familiar with and wanted, in spite of the fact that the MC outperformed these machines in battery life.

As a result, the MC was a dead duck almost as soon as it was first shipped in the second quarter of 1989. Psion was left holding cripplingly large inventories of hardware including thousands of expensive screens. The only way to clear the inventory was to complete the development of the word processing and spreadsheet applications, which was done some eight months later. Once the machines were offered with the desired applications they sold and the backlog was cleared, and even a DOS compatible machine was offered. However, by then further-improved DOS-based machines had entered the market, and Psion, the pioneer of the notebook computer, withdrew.

The MC failure, combined with competition and a recession which was threatening the organizer market, along with the drain of Dacom, a specialist modem manufacturer acquired in January 1989, had a disastrous effect on both performance and morale. In 1990 turnover growth halted and profits shrank (see Table 12.1). In an interim announcement the blame for this was laid at the door of Dacom and on the costs of expanding and supporting the MC range. The following year the company made a £2 million loss, staff were sacked, and many of these were from the MC development team.

Though development had also been in progress on products for the industrial market, and these were launched in due course, their sales were lacklustre. The newly emerged competition to the organizer, the firm's core product, had made it imperative that a replacement product was launched as a matter of urgency.

Table 12.1 Profitability and sales for Psion plc 1982–96

Year	Turnover (£m)	% Change	Pre-tax profit (£m)	Cumulative PT profit
1982	1.727		0.613	1.613
1983	4.808	178.40	1.593	3.206
1984	4.594	−4.45	−1.37	1.836
1985	4.174	−9.14	0.441	2.277
1986	5.029	20.48	0.383	2.66
1987	11.811	134.86	1.863	4.523
1988	19.226	62.78	2.758	7.281
1989	31.435	63.50	3.345	10.626
1990	31.396	−0.12	0.546	11.172
1991	21.333	−32.05	−2.197	8.975
1992	35.088	64.48	1.42	10.395
1993	41.159	17.30	3.03	13.425
1994	61.291	48.91	6.545	19.97
1995	90.546	47.73	11.654	31.624
1996	124.178	37.14	16.036	47.66

The Series 3: one step backwards, two steps forward

The use of a new architecture enabled the Psion designers to reconsider basic features of the new organizer's design. For instance decisions had to be made about whether the machine should be portrait or landscape shaped. Though the Organiser had been portrait-shaped, a landscape shape meant that the new design could have a standard QWERTY keyboard. The designers had thought that it was important for users to hold the machine in one hand and tap keys with the other but when the Sharp Wizard came out with QWERTY versions they began to question this. They did some tests internally and found that if the user wasn't a touch-typist, performance wasn't adversely affected by having an ABC grid. However, the tests also suggested that whatever their skill level, people think they perform better with a QWERTY design.

Such internal testing was indicative of the focus of market research in the company at this time. The developers believed that they were the prototypical users of the product. As Colly Myers described it:

> 'The target lead-users are to be found in this organisation. Every one of us is an avowed user and fanatic of the product, the most sophisticated IT and technology people and knowledge workers imaginable ... Much of our success is based on the fact that we are our own users of the product ... the development group has done most of the marketing, defining the product.'

Nevertheless, an extensive database of suggestions from users had been collected, and was examined in the development of the Series 3 machine.

In addition, learning from the development of the MC was consolidated. The enormity of the task Psion had undertaken in producing the MC should not be underestimated. The company had decided to develop three completely original aspects of a computer's architecture: the operating system, the GUI and the applications. Any one of these would have been considered a major undertaking by specialist software firms. For a relatively small company to do all three was positively heroic especially considering that despite their software experience they had few skills in GUI development.

Development of the Series 3 was managed by a small, informal development committee consisting of David Potter, the managing director and company chairman, Colly Myers, Charles Davies, the two directors of product development, Peter Norman, the marketing and sales director, and Andy Clegg the director of manufacturing. Though all would meet on a frequent basis in intensive discussions of progress, Charles' team had initially concentrated on the MC applications. Thus Series 3 development was initially under the leadership of Colly Myers whose team was working on the operating system and the hardware design. Unlike the development of the Organiser, where specification writing had been limited, the company was now able to go to the other extreme. As a result the developers held lengthy, detailed and intensive discussions into all aspects of the embryonic product and detailed specifications were written and frequently revised. This intense analysis enabled a high degree of coordination of the look and feel of the product. Of paramount importance was to make the Series 3 easy to use. Associated issues were also discussed such as the design of the hardware, what development language to include, whether to add tones of grey to the screen, whether to include a word processor and so on. Charles' applications team joined the development process and he suggested that rather than including the notepad, which was being planned, the Series 3 should include the word processor, which had been developed for the MC. Doing so, it was argued, would enable the product to offer a unique selling proposition, a distinct point of differentiation. Even more than this, such a product would provide 'enchantment' to the user – significantly exceeding his or her expectations. The early experience of competing with Lotus 1-2-3 and the subsequent MC failure had taught Psion the need for depth of functionality and the inclusion of a word processor was accepted. This was a significant decision. The word processor underpins the entire information system of the Series 3 because text handling is ubiquitous throughout its design. The decision to include the word processor was a brave one, as by doing so the development time for the product was considerably increased.

The developers reviewed the list of things which users would like in a machine. To the developers, the priorities were data management and the agenda. They decided to concentrate on the agenda feature and four people spent nine months developing the specifications for it, equivalent to the time usually devoted to actually writing such a program.

The Series 3 was launched in September 1991, one year after the development process had begun. The development team itself was amazed at how good it was; even better than they had imagined. Fortunately, the market thought so too.

Advertising for the product attempted to position it as a 'pocket computer' with all the flexibility and power which that might imply, rather than as an improved Organiser. In part this was due to encroaching competition from cheaper, dedicated 'organizer' type machines, which provided some similar functions in terms of clocks, address books and calendars to those of the earlier Organiser II, but did not have its data management capabilities. However customer perceptions proved difficult to change. Because of the initial, limited built-in functions of the Organiser, many users defined the product category in terms of them. However, the fundamental design of the machine, along with its programmability, essentially meant that Psion had created the world's smallest, mass-market computer. Later in the development of the market, when the functionality of Psion's core product had been increased immensely to include word-processing and spreadsheets, it was still being referred to as an Organiser. Though Psion tried to change consumers' perceptions of and term for the product, e.g. in advertisements the product is continually referred to as a computer, they still stubbornly continued to refer to it as an Organiser.

Two years later, in September 1993, an improved version, the Series 3a, was launched, priced from £269.95 to £329.95. However, the lack of competition to that point appeared to be coming to an end, when, shortly after this launch, Apple Corporation announced their Newton Personal Digital Assistant (PDA). This small, hand-held computer dispensed with the keyboard and used a built-in pen along with handwriting recognition software. Competitors such as Sharp, Casio, Tandy, Compaq, Microsoft, AT&T, Motorola, Sony and General Magic all soon announced their own versions. Overnight, the keyboard was to be made obsolete and industry analysts forecast that Psion would be wiped out.

However, Psion had been monitoring the development of pen-based computing and concluded that the technology was as yet too embryonic to work well. In the event they were absolutely right, and the Newton and other similar PDAs were 'an overhyped and underpowered flop' (*Business Week*, 1996). However, Apple and other companies including the Japanese have continued to invest in this keyboardless approach. The same issue of *Business Week* reported on the success of Sharp's Zaurus product, a hand-held device with which one could surf the Internet and which could read handwriting – though only Japanese at that time.

Further developments

The tremendous recovery of the company from the failed launch of the MC and the success of the Series 3 became the basis for its further growth. Forrester Research estimated that in 1995 Psion accounted for almost one third of the one million units sold in the hand-held computer market (Taylor, 1996). By 1996 the company had also become strong enough to consider major acquisitions and in that same year negotiated with Amstrad to take over that company's computer manufacturing division. Though these negotiations were not successful, the company remained financially strong and interested in other acquisition targets. In June 1997 Psion launched another new generation architecture around a 32-bit chip, which was to become the platform for a new range of products, including the latest palmtop, the Series 5. Though this launch was met with strong demand, partly cannibalizing demand for the Series 3, the problem this time was a failure to gear up manufacturing to meet it. These manufacturing problems led to lost sales, and Peter Norman, the managing director, left the company in that year.

However, the nature of the marketing game which currently faces Psion has changed significantly since the days in which it pioneered a product category. Today there are many more competitors offering lower-cost products, which have some similarity to the Series 3. Furthermore computing and communications technologies are merging, yielding the opportunity for the development of new devices. As a result new competitors like Nokia, the Finnish manufacturers of mobile phones, have launched products which offer both communications and computing functions.

Though Psion takes a broader view of its product than simply 'palmtop computers' or even 'hand-held devices', it faces increasing competition there too. In June 1996 *The Sunday Times* reported that Psion 'is to license its software for use in rival miniature computers ... in a bid to make its system an international standard.' (Lloyd, 1996). Psion see their software operating system as having a potentially huge market, as such software could be adapted for use in a multitude of intelligent machines and household appliances. However in the autumn of 1996 the software giant, Microsoft, launched its version of palmtop computer software, Windows CE (Consumer Electronics), which rapidly established itself in the marketplace and in nine months had gained a 20 per cent share of the hand-held market (*BusinessWeek*, 1998). Microsoft has a reputation as a formidable competitor, which if it fails to push its way into new markets – and Windows CE is its third attempt – has the financial muscle to buy its way in.

In many senses therefore the competitive challenge may have only just begun for Psion. It may be for this reason that Psion reorganized itself in 1996, splitting its software development and hardware manufacturing into separate divisions.

Conclusions

Psion undertook the high-risk strategy of product-market pioneering which required immense effort both in innovative product development as well as in developing market acceptance. One of the main problems facing market pioneers is market uncertainty, both in terms of the level of demand and in terms of customer requirements. The company used little formal marketing research and was guided in its understanding of market requirements by the developers' own needs. The radicality of the Organiser product concept meant that the then current users of computers would have been hard-pressed to provide useful insights into user requirements, and the Psion developers were themselves leading-edge users of the product. However, this did not apply to the MC, which was an attempt to establish an extension of an established product category. The lack of market testing and analysis for the MC and the project development control difficulties which led to changes in product development priorities, led to the damaging launch of an inadequate product.

This experience led to salutary project management lessons being learned and although the company still jealously guards its informal culture, some more bureaucratic project management and control procedures have been introduced. These inevitably became necessary as the company grew and identified increasing numbers of new product development opportunities. These new systems and procedures include the establishment of a committee of directors and developers, which now vets project proposals and allocates resources to them, as well as much tighter project management timetabling and control.

As a young company entering the uncharted territory of a radical new product, Psion was both challenged by and liberated by its ignorance.

Challenges came in the form of the immense uncertainty of where to invest scarce resources and the firm thus had to make commitments well in advance of knowing their value. For instance, when in 1987 they started to design the new SIBO architecture they were doing so two years ahead of the expected decline in sales of their main revenue-earning product, the Organiser II. As Colly Myers observed:

> 'In the early days of the Organiser and of the company there was
> only a general understanding of the development problems that
> were going to be faced. The development team knew in a broad
> sense that they would face problems but they didn't know the kinds
> of problems they would have. However, in retrospect they didn't
> know what really counted in doing world-class product designs at
> that time. This knowledge came from trying solutions and
> understanding what worked.'

Liberation came in the sense that the young company hadn't yet learned what were the bounds of sensible practice and dictums. As one manager expressed it, 'We didn't know what we couldn't do.' Psion's reach may in its earlier years have exceeded its grasp, but it is only through trying that its understanding of its limitations has developed.

The period described here is one in which the company largely faced limited competition. Rather the challenge it faced was to develop market acceptance for a new product category. It was helped in this by the enthusiastic support of its customers, who act as salespeople almost every time they use the product. However, the window of opportunity represented by the new market appears to be closing and the competitive environment is becoming crowded. The company now operates in a highly turbulent and more competitive environment in which innovation and new product development are essential for survival.

For Psion, long-term success thus rests on being capable of developing a stream of innovations, not just one. Psion's design efforts have been at the level of the 'architecture' from which a number of different products can be produced, and it was this which provided it with the flexibility to recover from an otherwise fatal market entry. Computer manufacturers are not alone in doing this. For instance automobile manufacturers have also produced a range of cars based on one common 'platform'.

Finally, it is clear from the Psion case that being innovative is not enough. This lesson has been exemplified by the experiences of many innovative UK manufacturers, including Sinclair, Psion's early client. Psion had the skills to produce an innovative new product, which met a suspected need. Their earliest versions were not very successful and they had to have the resources to continually refine and improve them. They required further resources to build customer acceptance and grow the market. In addition they had great faith in their understanding of the market's needs, in part because these were difficult to identify. In pioneering the handheld, or 'palmtop', computer market through their development of the Organiser, Psion may well have been right in focusing their 'market' research internally – the product was so radical that potential buyers may have been unable to provide any useful information. However, it was an error to continue this focus when entering a market closer to established users' experience. In this case conventional market research may have yielded some valuable information.

References

BusinessWeek (1996) 25 November.

BusinessWeek (1998) 19 January.

Campbell-Kelly, M. and Aspray, W. (1996) *Computer: A History of the Information Age*, Basic Books.

Lloyd, C. (1996) 'Psion opens up its software system to rivals', Section 3, *Sunday Times*, 30 June.

Taylor, P. (1996) 'The appliance of science', *Financial Times*, 6 April.

Chapter 13

Le BonBon plc

Peter Doyle

'Business is going great – I wish I knew why' laughed Paul Bevin, joint managing director of Le BonBon a leading manufacturer and retailer of high quality confectionery. Certainly his good humour appeared justified, while the competitive retail situation in the United Kingdom was causing most retailers to show little volume growth and declining margins, four months into the financial year, Le BonBon's sales from their 148 shops were 4 per cent up on budget and profits were even further ahead.

Nevertheless there were many decisions that needed to be taken on how to move the business forward. In particular, it was not obvious how many new stores the company should aim to open, whether franchising offered an effective method of long term growth, or whether the company should seek to manufacture confectionery for a broader range of retailers at home and overseas. Further, while the current situation looked satisfactory, in the recent past it had appeared much less rosy and the directors felt that major mistakes had been made on pricing policy, advertising and overhead cost control which has significantly curtailed profit performance. The board of directors, in discussing these issues, had identified the need for a corporate strategy to provide a longer term perspective than that of the annual budget. Mr Paul, as he was known in the company, had agreed and had offered to present a paper for the next meeting outlining his ideas about the strategic direction for the business.

Company background

The company was founded in 1921 by A.B. Bevin, who began making hard-boiled sweets in a coke stove in the basement of his shop in Liverpool. His sons Archie and Oliver soon joined him. In the years that followed the company opened more shops and gradually extended its product range. In 1935 the company's Special Toffee was developed which is still the shops' best selling

Table 13.1 Some general UK economic indicators 1986–96

	Retail sales	Sales of CTN's[1]	Company profits[2]	Cost of living index
1986	100	100	100	100
1987	108	105	120	103
1988	119	115	130	108
1989	127	125	134	113
1990	136	133	125	122
1991	142	139	111	133
1992	147	133	116	141
1993	155	136	139	146
1994	162	137	163	152
1995	168	135	174	158
1996	174	135	183	163

[1]Retail sales of confectioners, tobacconists and newspaper shops.
[2]Before providing for depreciation and stock appreciation.
Source: UK Annual Abstract Statistics

product. Another milestone was Archie and Oliver's decision to develop a really high quality range of chocolates. During a continental holiday in 1964 the brothers visited the Berne School for Swiss Chocolatiers and recruited one of the top students. The result was the Bevin range of Continental Chocolates which now sells 600 tons annually. In 1964 the company changed its name to Le BonBon with the aim of giving the shops 'a continental feel'. By 1997 the company had grown to over 1000 employees, two factories and 148 shops.

The company had always emphasized certain features. Most important was the commitment to product freshness and quality. Unwillingness to hazard the business's hard won reputation in these areas accounted for management's long reluctance to sell confectionery outside their own shops, despite many requests from interested retailers. This philosophy together with the desire to develop a distinctive specialist confectioner image also made them increasingly reluctant to buy products for their shops other than those produced from their factories. Bought-in goods (mainly greeting cards) now account for only 5 per cent of shop turnover. A consequence was that the shops continued with a narrow range of products – three basic lines: chocolate, toffee and hard-boiled sweets account for over 90 per cent of sales.

The company has continued to emphasize traditional values. The shops have changed relatively little over the years and there has been no major product introduction since the range of Continental Chocolates over 30 years earlier. Advertising made much of the products being 'all made in the good old-fashioned way'. Finally, it remained very much a family business; all the shareholders and all eight members of the board including president, chairman, the two managing directors and the company secretary were Bevins.

Table 13.2 Le BonBon Ltd: selected performance data

Financial year	Sales £000 (ex VAT)	Gross profit	Pre-tax net profit	Total assets	Stockholders' funds	No. of shops
1986	13,762	7,544	1,442	7,399	4,914	107
1987	14,588	7,727	1,773	8,581	5,819	110
1988	15,964	8,702	1,927	8,629	5,988	122
1989	17,340	9,364	2,726	9,475	6,202	126
1990	19,818	10,556	2,697	11,010	6,904	130
1991	22,845	11,323	2,328	11,836	7,006	128
1992	25,046	13,507	2,504	12,099	7,072	130
1993	26,423	13,344	1,653	13,278	6,962	130
1994	27,249	13,846	1,774	11,899	6,667	132
1995	28,074	14,696	2,071	13,562	5,653	138
1996	31,102	16,720	1,336	15,025	6,223	148

Source: Annual Reports

Hence the practice within the company of calling the directors Mr Ted, Mr Paul etc., was not just quaint, it was necessary.

After the mid 1970s, Mr Archie's three sons Ted, Paul and James, together with Mr Oliver's son Mark, took an increasingly large part in running the business. In 1995 Paul and James became joint managing directors when Ted moved up from managing director to chairman. Previously both Paul and James had shared responsibility for the manufacturing side of the business. Under the new structure Paul's main sphere of responsibility covered marketing and retail, and James looked after manufacturing and product development.

Until 1990 the company had seen almost uninterrupted progress (see Table 13.2). Probably the peak year was in 1989 when the company earned a pre-tax margin of 16 per cent and a return on shareholder funds of 44 per cent. Then, like many other smaller retailers, business got more difficult as the slow growth of consumer expenditure and increasing competition from the multiples hit margins and cash flow.

Retailing in the United Kingdom

The 1970s and '80s saw substantial changes in the pattern of retailing in the UK. A number of forces created the stimuli for change. Car ownership grew substantially, so that by 1997, 70 per cent of households had at least one car. This trend both increased mobility of shoppers and enabled them to carry more goods in one trip. A second feature was the dispersal of population from major towns. While the drift to the suburbs was less dramatic than in the US, it did result in a notable shift in retail buying power from the inner urban areas to the outer suburbs. A third factor was the rise in female employment, which increased the pressure for longer shop opening hours and for facilities for shopping with the family. Finally the period was marked by a continued rise in real disposable incomes.

The most important responses to these stimuli were:

- The growth of self-service across many sectors of retailing. Self-service offered savings both to the retailer and the shopper. In food, for example, supermarkets dramatically increased their share of spending.
- A trend towards fewer, larger shops. The total number of food shops fell during the period, but the development of self-service in particular meant that on average the newer shops had much larger floor space.
- Economies of scale in buying and marketing led to increased concentration in retailing. The major multiples, notably Tesco, Sainsbury, Asda and Safeway, increased their share of trade at the expense of independent shops in all sectors of retailing.
- A consequence of this greater retailing concentration was increased bargaining power over manufacturers. Manufacturers' margins were squeezed as the larger retailers demanded their own private label brands and larger discounts.
- The extension of intertype retailing competition or 'scrambled merchandise'. Retailers sought to strengthen their margins by broadening their merchandise assortment. Food retailers diversified into non-foods and non-food businesses added on food lines.
- The development of out-of-town retailing and growth of new types of shops such as superstores, hypermarkets, discount stores and catalogue showrooms. Many innovations took place during this period and grew rapidly at the expense of retailers that had reached the maturity stage of the institutional life cycle.
- Working wives, greater car ownership and new types of mass merchandising encouraged the trend towards once weekly, one-stop shopping, increasingly at the large suburban superstore with ample parking. High street shops, particularly those specializing in grocery and commodity items, found it increasingly difficult to survive.

The confectionery market

British confectionery consumption per capita at 25 kg per annum is the highest in the world. The British eat twice as much as the Americans and French and four times as much as the Italians and Japanese. Retail sales in 1996 stood at £5000 million and amounted to over 750,000 tons (in 1997 £1 = US$1.64). Two-thirds of this by tonnage was chocolate, the rest being sugar confectionery. In value the chocolate sector was worth about £3000 million and sugar just over £1000 million. Over recent years the volume of the chocolate market had been growing marginally, sugar slowly declining. A more detailed breakdown is given in Table 13.3.

Confectionery manufacturing is fairly concentrated; five companies account for 60 per cent of sales, strongly biased towards chocolate, while over 100 companies fight for the remaining 48 per cent biased towards sugar. Cadbury, Nestlé and Mars are the three leading groups. Competition is fierce in advertising and brand development, especially in the filled chocolate bar/countline segment, the most buoyant and valuable sector of the whole confectionery market in recent years. Around £130 million was spent on in 1996 making confectionery the most highly advertised of all product groups. There are many brands – the top 40 account for about 40 per cent of the market. Other

Table 13.3 UK confectionery tonnage by product group 1988–96[1]

CHOCOLATE	Thousands of tons		
	1988	*1993*	*1996*
Milk chocolate bars with fruit,nuts etc	25	24	29
Plain chocolate bars	60	68	73
Count lines[2]	277	283	290
Chocolate assortments (inc. boxes)*	56	54	53
Straight lines*	12	13	13
Easter eggs/novelties*	40	43	44
Total	470	485	502
SUGAR			
Hard boiled*	58	54	52
Toffee, caramel and fudge*	31	31	28
Gums, jellies, pastilles*	51	51	54
Liquorice	21	20	21
Chewing gum	14	19	19
Medicated	8	10	9
Other	87	79	76
Total	270	265	259

[1]UK sales by UK manufacturers only. Approximately an additional 50,000 tons of confectionery were imported in 1996.
[2]Countlines are items sold for individual consumption rather than by weight or quantity. Well-known examples are KitKat and Mars Bars, each with annual sales of almost £100m.
*Main sectors in which Le BonBon competes.

than Le BonBon (which ranks about twelfth) no major manufacturer is integrated forward into retailing.

Distribution of confectionery is extremely wide through a great variety of retailing outlets. The main channel now is the supermarket groups (e.g. Tesco, Sainsbury and Asda) which expanded their share of confectionery from 30 per cent in 1987 to 37 per cent in 1997. The next most important channel is the mass of largely independent small confectioner/tobacconist/newsagents (CTNs). Around 40,000 of these account for 30 per cent of confectionery sales, down from 33 per cent in 1987. Other important outlets are Co-ops, filling stations, off licenses and cinemas.

Women are the main purchasers of confectionery, although children are the largest per capita consumers, especially in sugar. Women buy about 67 per cent, men 20 per cent and children 13 per cent. Half of purchases are made on Fridays and Saturdays. The average amount spent on each purchase occasion was about 75p in 1997. The gift market is very important, especially for Christmas, Easter and Mother's Day. About 40 per cent of spending is for gifts, mainly women for children and secondly men for women. A recent survey shows that among adult 'heavy users' of confectionery women consume more than men and that they are predominantly in the lower (C2D) income groups. Survey researchers classify households and adults by social class. Broadly, A refers to upper middle class households (3 per cent of all households), B middle class (13 per cent), C1 lower middle (22 per cent), C2 skilled working class (33 per cent), D working class (21 per cent) and E lowest level of income (8 per cent).

Le BonBon channels and products

The company now had 148 shops controlled by a sales manager supervising 16 area manageresses. While in recent years shops had been opened in Scotland and the south of England, the majority of them were in the Midlands and north of England. Virtually all shops were in the town centre shopping areas. Most of the shops were very small, the majority having less than 300 square feet of selling space although the company had tried to open somewhat larger units in recent years. The shops were not self service and queuing was a significant problem at peak periods. In 1996 the average turnover per shop was £200,000, though some of the better shops were achieving two or three times this figure.

After 1991 under Mr Ted's lead the company began to sell its confectionery through other shops. The real stimulus for this change in direction was the alarming rise in high street shop rents, which, if continued, threatened to make many of Le BonBon's shops unprofitable. The most significant move was the decision to allow other shops (generally small CTNs) to sell Le BonBon confectionery as part of their range on a franchise basis. In return for a small fee, franchisees could buy Le BonBon at 25 per cent off retail price. During its first five years franchising showed considerable growth (see Table 13.4).

Table 13.4 Le BonBon Ltd: sales by selected channels of distribution (£000)

Financial year	Le BonBon shops	Franchise	Marks & Spencer	Other chains	Export
1991	22,814	4	9	9	9
1992	24,090	181	502	252	21
1993	24,203	725	1,200	270	25
1994	23,740	2,010	1,105	274	120
1995	24,090	2,620	890	310	164
1996	26,598	2,518	1,524	310	152

Currently there were 45 shops with a Le BonBon franchise. The second important development was the request by Marks & Spencer, Britain's most successful variety store group, to sell Le BonBon's chocolate under its own private label. Currently this exceeded £1.5 million in sales. Besides franchising and Marks & Spencer, small amounts were sold to a few other UK multiples and some £150,000 worth was exported to distributors in 14 countries overseas.

Le BonBon was represented in product groups representing only about one-third of the chocolate market (mainly assortments, straight lines and Easter eggs, etc.) and about two-thirds of the sugar market (boiled, toffee and jellies, etc.). In particular, they were not represented in 'countlines' and chocolate bars, which made up the most valuable segment of the chocolate market. Besides confectionery the shops sold small amounts of bought-in greetings cards (£1 million in 1996) and ice cream (£400,000). Percentage value added averaged 60 per cent for sugar confectionery, 57 per cent for chocolate, 50 per cent for cards and 30 per cent for ice cream.

The Le BonBon consumer

When Mr Paul took over responsibility for the marketing operation in 1995 his lack of experience was balanced by an enthusiasm to get the business moving ahead again. He was critical that many important decisions had been neglected in the past due to differences of opinion and priorities on the board. In an early memorandum he said that product standards had dropped, production convenience was taking precedence over marketing needs, shortages at peak times were losing business, and shop display, hygiene and stock control standards were all declining due to insufficient investment in shop-fitting and management.

Paul inherited Tucker Advertising, a Manchester advertising agency appointed by Mr Ted some months earlier. The agency convinced Paul of the need to undertake some research into Le BonBon's consumers and the confectionery market before a marketing strategy could be developed. Until then the company had undertaken little market research. But from Tucker's research, and that conducted by the two agencies succeeding it, a fairly complete picture had been developed.

The main research findings were:

- In socioeconomic terms the Le BonBon shopper profile was close to the average profile of confectionery buyers: AB 15 per cent, C1 26 per cent, C2 38 per cent, D18 per cent, E3 per cent.
- In areas where Le BonBon has shops, 71 per cent of confectionery eaters shop at Le BonBon, at least occasionally. The average expenditure per shopper was £2.00 in October 1996, rather higher for the AB socioeconomic groups.
- Le BonBon's shoppers have very positive attitudes to the shops. A sample of 544 Le BonBon shoppers found 42 per cent mentioning product quality as the most attractive feature, 21 per cent good service and 11 per cent window displays. Only 20 per cent of respondents could think of anything unattractive about the shops. Of the negative responses 'too small' and 'queuing' were most frequently mentioned.
- Price did not appear a problem. Respondents thought generally that Le BonBon were a little more expensive but they believed the products to be of higher quality and good value for money. This was especially true of chocolate, but boiled sweets were seen as neither more expensive nor of better quality than elsewhere. Chocolate and toffee were seen as of very good value by over 90 per cent of Le BonBon shoppers.
- Most Le BonBon customers buy more confectionery from other outlets than they do from Le BonBon. As the agency noted, this is not surprising, 'However good the product and reputation, however conveniently located the outlets, Le BonBon account for a tiny proportion of confectionery distribution. When heavily advertised, well-established products are available at the checkout of a supermarket that Le BonBon's customers have to visit to buy groceries, it is not surprising that they purchase competitive brands. Customers typically buy a wide range of confectionery from a variety of outlets'. Le BonBon's 148 shops compete with 127,000 other outlets selling confectionery!
- Non-Le BonBon customers appeared to be much younger, to be often heavy confectionery eaters, especially of countlines (i.e. market leaders like Mars Bars, Kit-Kat, Yorkie) and to be more down market. Le BonBon products appeared to appeal to older consumers, especially women.
- Gift purchasing is very important in confectionery, especially for boxes of chocolates. The majority of boxed chocolates are bought for family or friends. Self-consumption is more frequently the purchase motive for loose chocolates, toffee and boiled sweets. Toffees and boiled sweets are the most favoured purchases for children.

The advertising agencies came up with various proposals from their research findings. Tucker Advertising recommended targeting on C1, C2 and D housewives aged over 25, focusing on increasing awareness of Le BonBon's traditional product quality. Penelope Keith, a well-known television comedy actress was used in humorous TV and radio commercials to communicate the product benefits. Beaumont, Robock and King (BRK), a leading London agency which won the account early in 1995, defined the primary target as the 'heavy confectionery purchaser' who was female, aged 16–34, in the C2DE groups with two to three children and whose life style might be summarized as 'laugh and grow fat'. Their creative approach was again humorous and traditional, based around singing confectionery workers at Le BonBon's factory. The creative proposition was aimed at expressing Le BonBon's shop as a 'treasure trove' of high quality confectionery and 'a family firm making your family favourites'. The Cundiff Partnership, a small London agency which gained the account in mid-1996, decided to target on 'medium' confectionery buyers who were younger and more up-market – ABC1C2 rather than the typical Le BonBon consumer. Creatively they concentrated on telling straightforward product quality stories about the brands and linking with main gift giving occasions such as Christmas and Easter.

Le BonBon's marketing organization

In 1995 Mr Ted asked Dr John Riley, a professor of business administration at a local university, to take an overall look at the company's operation. In his report he showed that profitability had significantly declined since 1989. He argued that this was due mainly to external factors: little market growth; the changing pattern of retailing and tough competition eroding margins. But he also suggested the problem had been worsened by management cutting back on marketing investments, falling shop volume and a switch in the product mix towards less profitable items. On the positive side he noted the remarkable growth of franchising, the success of Continental Chocolates, good cost control and the margin protection the shops offered ('unlike other manufacturers Le BonBon are not easily squeezed by the buying power of the major retail groups').

Mr Paul accepted most of the points in the Riley report and was intent to attack these problems quickly. One difficulty he faced immediately was the lack of retail experience of his two senior managers, Joe Royston, the marketing manager and Len Andrews, the sales manager. After much exasperation with his inability to get information and implementation from his marketing and sales people he hired a retail manager, Colin Shaw, in June 1996. The new man was not a retailer but Paul felt that he was young and bright and that his experience in brand management would be very valuable. Andrews resigned around the same time and Paul was hoping to find an experienced successor quickly.

Dr Riley also drew attention to the need to improve the management information and planning procedures. Paul agreed that most of the information the directors receive is still production-oriented. A vast amount of information was available on manufacturing costs and standards but it was not easy to determine sales and profit performance trends of the products, channels of distribution and shops. Evaluating price and promotional changes on different parts of the business was virtually impossible. One of the problems he felt was forcing the accounting department to give a greater priority to providing better information.

Le BonBon had never undertaken formal longer term planning. In recent years, however, the accountant had developed a useful annual budget for them, although it often did not appear until a few months into the financial year (beginning 1 June). Another problem was that sales appeared as residual rather than an output from a marketing forecast. Generally overhead costs for the forthcoming year were taken as 'given', target net and gross profits were then agreed by the board, and turnover was subsequently defined as that level needed to balance these assumptions. It was perhaps not surprising that the sales volume figures generally proved too optimistic. In the 1996 financial year this budgeting procedure had, however, produced more serious consequences (see Table 13.5). Overhead costs in the budget had been allowed to escalate by

Table 13.5 Le BonBon Ltd: income statement and budget, 1997 (£000)

	Actual 1995	*Actual 1996*	*Budget 1997*
Sales (ex. VAT)	28,074	31,102	36,500
Direct costs	13,378	14,382	17,520
Gross Profit	14,696	16,720	18,980
Wages and Salaries	6,451	8,309	9,331
Pension scheme	206	232	261
Distribution	583	642	720
Repairs	770	810	910
Rent and rates	1,369	1,442	1,619
Post, telephone, travel	364	400	449
Power	493	538	604
Legal and financial charges	530	574	645
Advertising	335	1,051	526
Display	105	104	117
Miscellaneous	197	194	218
Depreciation	1,113	1,106	1,246
Total trading overheads	12,516	15,402	16,646
Trading profit	2,180	1,318	2,334
Non-trading net income (expense)	(109)	18	(52)
Pre-Tax profit	2,071	1,336	2,282

a heavy commitment to advertising and a decision to introduce a new layer of management to strengthen the manufacturing team, but the level of sales needed to meet these costs proved to be much too high and net profit suffered severely. The directors were determined not to let this mistake be repeated and in future they were sure that budgeted cost increases would be checked by realistic or even pessimistic budget sales forecasts.

Marketing policy

In thinking about the longer term, Paul felt that there were a number of areas where fundamental decisions needed to be made. Getting these choices right would determine whether the business would have a successful future or not.

Shop policy

This was perhaps the area where the most crucial decisions were needed. There were a number of obvious questions. Should Le BonBon continue to see the shops as providing the vast majority of sales and profits? How many shops should they have? Where should the shops be located? What 'image' should the shops aim to present to the public? Paul initially concluded that their own shops should be the dominant form of growth rather than outside sales. He argued, 'in this age of the superstore and self-service with impersonal indifference there is a demand for a specialist with a unique proposition. We are in a position to fill this role with our unique business. We have a fine manufacturing plant, involved people, high street sites and quality products to build on'. He argued for opening as many shops as the company could afford, probably 10–20 a year.

Another area of concern was the shop image. Several observers believed that the stores were not right and that their appearance was confusing, lacking in impact and old fashioned. Over the years the board had experimented with various piecemeal modifications to layout and window display but there had been no real fundamental changes for many years. Worse, many of the older shops were now much in need of refitting and modernization. Paul, influenced by the successful remodelling ventures of a number of leading British retailers, became convinced that Le BonBon's shops needed a comprehensive repositioning guided by experts. After interviewing all the top retail designers he commissioned Fitch and Company, the largest and most experienced of these organizations, to develop a complete shop redesign and corporate identity programme for the group. Fitch's past clients included many of Britain's largest and most successful retail organizations. In October 1996, Fitch produced their models which proposed to completely redesign the shops, merchandising methods, packaging and company image. A programme for implementing these changes at a cost of about £85,000 per shop was also defined in detail.

During the following six months, experience and changed circumstances led to some rethinking. One problem was that sales and profit were less buoyant than expected. Another was that rising costs of rents and staff, and the failure of the advertising campaign to boost shop volume made the race to open new ones look very risky. In particular, the shops opened in new types of off-centre locations – at the Tesco, Sainsbury and Safeway hypermarket complexes for example, proved highly disappointing. Finally, there was the view on the board that while the Fitch proposals contained some good ideas, the complete shop redesign they proposed was really not the type of atmosphere that would appeal to Le BonBon's traditional customers.

Franchise

Both Ted and Paul were less than enthusiastic about the Le BonBon franchise operation and in 1994 they agreed to halt further growth despite many requests for franchises. All the franchisees were independent CTN shops, which sold Le BonBon lines as part of their general range of tobacco, newspapers, other confectionery and miscellaneous merchandise. Thus the shops retained their own names and trading formats, only agreeing to give a portion of their selling space (averaging 20–40 per cent) over to the Le BonBon range. In general Paul believed that the profit potential was insufficient to attract people to devote their entire shop to the Le BonBon range. Paul recognized that a Le BonBon franchise could never offer anything like the level of profits of a McDonald's or Bodyshop franchise. The limited commitment which resulted from these partial franchises left Le BonBon unhappy with the franchise business. The board felt these outlets generally failed to display the products properly and kept stock too long, so threatening the Le BonBon quality image as well as losing its exclusivity. Finally, franchised confectionery offered a lower gross margin than sales through its own shops.

But both felt that now this attitude should be reconsidered. Average shop volume was slipping marginally nearly every year. Further Dr Riley had pointed out that while the gross margin was higher from throughput in their own shops, when average shop operating costs were allowed for, the margin on

Table 13.6 Estimated profit margins at Le BonBon

	Gross margin (%)	Trading profit (%)
Le Bonbon	55	6
Franchise Sales	45	14
Marks & Spencer	37	7
Other Home Sales	35	3
Export Sales	33	−6

franchise sales appeared to be at least as good. A report the directors had received the previous week from Mr Mark and the company accountant supported this analysis. Their analysis estimated the gross and net trading margins as shown in Table 13.6. The report did emphasize, however, that the allocation of overhead costs was very subjective.

Two other points also counted. First, their franchise operation had developed too fast and without proper understanding of the problems involved. The directors felt they now had the experience to develop a much better control system, which would overcome many of the past weaknesses. Second, with only 45 franchises there was undoubtedly vast sales growth potential.

Marks & Spencer

With 290 stores in the UK and a turnover of around £7000 million, Marks & Spencer is generally regarded as one of Britain's best managed retailers. Since 1992 its business had become very important to Le BonBon. M&S merchandising policy was based on developing very close, durable relationships with a small number of high quality British manufacturers in each product field. Manufacturers produced to M&S's exacting quality standards exclusive products sold under the 'St Michael' brand name. In 1996 M&S purchased around £1.5m of Le BonBon's boxed chocolates and was also beginning to take Special Toffee and fudge on a trial basis.

Ted and Paul had always been hesitant about the M&S business. One reason was that the mark-up M&S required, exceeding 25 per cent, meant it was a lower gross margin business for Le BonBon. Profitability of the whole business was affected too, they believed, because M&S were reluctant to accept price increases not justified by corresponding manufacturers' cost increases. This was making it difficult to increase margins and since Le BonBon were not willing to be undercut in prices by M&S, the whole of Le BonBon's margin was held back. There were also strategic issues. M&S offered such large potential that Le BonBon might risk becoming too dependent upon them in the future. In addition, the directors asked what is the differential advantage of a Le BonBon shop if the customer can buy its confectionery at Marks & Spencer? M&S also interfered with Le BonBon's flexibility in other directions. They were unwilling to allow it to sell the products M&S bought to competitive retailers, severely limiting diversification options, although it was possible this objection could be overcome by introducing product differences which could differentiate the M&S range. Finally M&S made life difficult for the factory: they could cancel or significantly increase orders with little notice. For example, in 1995 M&S purchases dropped substantially when for tax reasons they ceased to supply their Canadian stores with Le BonBon confectionery. Finally, M&S orders were generally at peak times when capacity was already fully stretched. Nevertheless, in 1997 M&S orders were expected to top £3 million.

Export and other commercial sales

The board believed there were many other exciting growth opportunities. In 1995 they exported some £169,000 of products to 14 countries mainly through overseas distributors. While the volume was small, with sufficient management attention they felt it was possible to achieve major expansion, perhaps through overseas franchising. Le BonBon toffee and chocolate had gained much favourable comment, many enquiries from interested buyers, and a number of prizes for quality at international confectionery exhibitions over the years. The board felt in many overseas markets Le BonBon confectionery could offer a unique combination of very high quality at prices which were affordable by the average consumer.

At home too, a large number of enquiries continually came into Le BonBon from large department stores, supermarket groups and other retailers interested in the lines. In recent years a small amount of business had been built up with a few retail groups, the largest being the Waitrose supermarket group which in the last year had bought £100,000 of fudge and chocolates for sale under the Waitrose label. The Marks & Spencer constraint and the board's doubts about whether this was the right direction had restricted growth in this area. Finally in the last year, mainly under the enthusiastic direction of Joe Royston, Le BonBon had begun selling by mail order, sales reaching around £18,000 over the period.

Product policy

On reflection Paul admitted that what Le BonBon sold was largely based on tradition ('what we have always sold') and what the factory people thought they could produce, rather than on much consideration of market opportunities. But even without a changed strategy the market was shifting the nature of Le BonBon's business. In recent years it had become much more a chocolate and gift retailer. Volume sales of chocolate had increased by 70 per cent since 1990 while sugar confectionery had dropped by nearly 20 per cent. The highest growth was in boxed chocolates, which had almost doubled over the decade; the weakest area was the traditional boiled sweet which had almost halved (Table 13.7). Chocolate now represented 57 per cent of Le BonBon volume and over 67 per cent of sterling value.

This change had not helped profits. Hard-boiled sweets in particular had high profit margins and a relatively low cost of sales. Further new growth areas that had compensated (i.e. chocolate boxes) had required additional investment, which adversely affected return on assets and net profit. But there was probably little that could be done since Le BonBon's hard boiled, unlike its chocolate, had few distinctive features and the factory could not compete in unit cost with the large modern facilities of the major competitors.

Ted and Paul spent considerable time thinking about what products the shops should carry and 'what business are we in'. But defining the customer

Table 13.7 Le BonBon shops: confectionery tonnage by product group 1990–96[1] (tons)

	1990	1993	1995	1996
CHOCOLATE				
Continental and other boxed chocs.	523	566	704	773
Continental – loose	241	250	282	279
Other chocolate – loose	567	458	489	491
Easter eggs, novelties	79	74	94	127
Mis-shapes	124	159	99	78
Total	1,534	1,507	1,668	1,748
Average price per ton	£6,575	£7,862	£8,550	£9,550
SUGAR				
Hard boiled	620	529	421	409
Toffee	1,619	1,481	1,551	1,396
Fudge	185	190	219	179
Jellies	92	75	67	80
Total	2,516	2,275	2,268	2,064
Average Price per ton	£3,868	£4,187	£4,306	£4,784

[1] Le BonBon shops only. Sales through other outlets amounted to 927 tons in 1996 (Table 13.8).

Table 13.8 Summary: sales by product and channel, 1996

	Tons				
	Shops	Franchise	M & S	Other	Export
Chocolates					
boxed	773	145	183	25	28
other	975	115	50	15	16
Hard boiled	409	80	0	16	13
Toffee and misc.	1,655	127	70	24	20

'need' or 'want' Le BonBon served in operational terms was not easy. The shops had sold at various times cigarettes, lemonade and more recently greetings cards and ice cream. But the current view was that such extensions were inconsistent with the image of a unique specialist that Le BonBon wished to create. However, they did not rule out certain complementary lines (e.g. cakes) in the future. Another possibility was broadening the confectionery lines carried by adding bought-in ranges to complement their own products. This had not been done in the past, Paul said, partly because there was a tendency in the company for the shops to be seen as an outlet for the factory.

Mr James Bevin had a committee, which met on a regular basis, to consider new product development in the factory. Le BonBon's past advertising agencies had been eager to push the company into producing a countline or filled chocolate bar like Yorkie or Cadbury's Fruit and Nut to compete in those sectors representing up to 75 per cent of the chocolate market and where Le BonBon were unrepresented. But Le BonBon felt this was unrealistic since these often massively advertised products relied for their sales on virtually universal distribution and impulse purchasing. However, Le BonBon were thinking about new lines. Additions and replacement items to the basic ranges of boiled sweets, toffee and chocolates were being made continually. Up to 12 different centres or flavours might be introduced in a year. Four years ago 'Traditional Assortment' had been introduced on a trial basis. This was a new range of super quality, hand-finished chocolates selling at almost twice the price per pound of the Continental range. This was now in some 40 shops and generated a turnover in 1996 of around £200,000. Other items on trial included additions to the children's confectionery lines and a small range of confectionery for diabetics.

Price policy

Like other retailers, Le BonBon's margins had been affected by price competition and raw material cost increases. But now they believed margins were under much better control. Paul said pricing strategy was based on the recognition that Le BonBon were high priced shops (e.g. a half pound box of Continental was around 20 per cent more expensive than a box of best selling Cadbury's Dairy Milk) but that the consumer recognized their superior quality and this allowed them to be perceived as good value for money. On the other hand, he believed that where their products were not unique they must be priced competitively. Recent experience he believed had proved this view. Continentals had been unaffected by fairly steep price increases whereas boiled sweets had shown impressive volume gains after a price cut. However, he admitted that fudge had not shown a similar increase after the same policy had been applied.

Advertising and promotion

During his first 12 months as managing director, Paul had spent an enormous amount of time with the advertising agency attempting to formulate a decisive marketing and advertising campaign. Between 1990 and 1995, Le BonBon had tried to hold up net profit margins by restricting the growth of advertising and promotional expenditures. On taking over, Paul had felt this lack of investment had been a material cause of Le BonBon's recent sluggish performance. In 1995

Paul appointed BRK, a large London advertising agency, to handle the account. The advertising budget was trebled to over £1 million and BRK developed a campaign employing television and a wide range of media to boost Le BonBon's image as a traditional and special type of confectionery shop. But the results were disappointing and net profit was severely affected. In 1997 Paul began a serious reconsideration of advertising's role in the business.

He felt that a business of Le BonBon's size could not compete in advertising terms with Cadbury's or Nestlé which spend over £2 million supporting an individual brand. He also felt that broad 'image' advertising for Le BonBon was not the way. Instead he believed that advertising should be tailored to support Le BonBon's brands with the strongest identity – Special Toffee and Continental Chocolates – and to help build new ones.

A new agency, the Cundiff Partnership, was appointed in mid-1997 with a much reduced budget. Local radio was chosen as the prime medium on cost efficiency grounds with local press as a 'top up'. Advertising was targeted around the main gift seasons – Christmas, St Valentine's Day, Mother's Day and Easter. In addition a Special Toffee promotion was scheduled for October 1997 to restimulate volume.

With his new retail manager Colin Shaw, Paul was also seeking to strengthen Le BonBon's public relations. They had retained the services of a local PR consultant at a reasonable fee and they were also considering retaining Harry Jones' new PR consultancy in London. Mr Jones had worked for 30 years as head of PR at Marks & Spencer and had recently resigned to start his own business. Paul felt that they were not on the right track as far as advertising and PR were concerned.

Marketing and organization

The directors were fairly happy with the current situation. Important decisions were being taken and there were some favourable features in the environment. For example, while in the mid 1990s they had been squeezed by rising commodity prices, cocoa was now trading at record lows. This year the price had dropped by £400 a ton and since Le BonBon was buying 1000 tons annually this was having a significant effect on profitability.

Besides changes in marketing strategy, Ted and Paul knew that changes in marketing organization were also needed. Currently, Colin Shaw was retail manager looking after advertising and promotion, Joe Royston was now responsible for exports, Marks & Spencer, franchise and other home sales, and a new sales manager responsible for the shops was to be appointed. The last was felt to be particularly important since there was much to do in the area of sales control and supervision. Training was poor and the manuals detailing expected behaviour from retail staff were now out of date and not used. Paul knew from experience that strategy would never be implemented properly without the right people and organization.

Chapter 14

NIS Invotec: a totally innovative business

Stuart Chambers

Introduction

'The business was like a runaway train, heading steadily towards a cliff edge ... the end of the rails was in sight, but we hadn't a plan in place to change direction! We knew we had to change radically to survive, but we were still unprepared for the magnitude and extent of what we would have to do. We were traditional capital plant manufacturers, with a fine new production building, but full of old technology plant, much of it thirty to forty years old. We did have a workforce with exceptional engineering craft and design skills; but we were highly dependent on a declining demand for nuclear processing equipment, our main market category. Worst of all we were losing money, with around 10 per cent losses on our £7 million turnover, leading to a sense of desperation all round the company. We were facing a crisis, and knew that we had to create a widespread awareness of the urgent need for change and innovation. Failure to do so could only be terminal ... liquidation! It certainly was a challenge, but here we are today, less than ten years later, a profitable innovator in several new markets, aggressively exporting high quality goods and services; a completely refinanced, re-equipped and re-skilled business. We now serve global markets with confidence and pride, delivering high quality solutions very fast. We have changed everything we do, and the way we do it ... innovation has become a way of life here!'

Phil Robson, a director of NIS Ltd, was describing the nine year transition of the company from a small, ailing capital plant manufacturing business in 1988 to a rapidly-growing, profitable £23m turnover group of companies, employing 350 people, and now supplying technical and business consultancy, site services, speciality chemicals, and large-scale specialist capital plant design and manufacturing. To understand the nature and magnitude of these changes, one must first consider the recent history of the business.

Background

The company is part of what used to be a group of five companies known as the B&R Taylor Group. This specialized in the design, project management, manufacturing, and installation of capital plant, mainly for the nuclear industry; and more recently of purpose-built coating lines for production of cathode ray tubes for leading global electronics companies including Philips, Sony and Thomson.

The deep recession in the early 1980s resulted in a severely reduced order book, and high interest rates led to inevitable financial difficulties. In 1983 its UK bankers decided to liquidate the company, largely because of its unacceptably high gearing. SAC Group, a large company specializing in design, systems development, and project management, acquired the non-manufacturing part, comprising four of the companies. This acquisition continued to be managed and developed under the management of Phil Robson (deputy MD) and Liam Ferguson (financial director). By 1987, turnover was £10 million, and approximately 350 people were employed in the company, known then as SAC Hitec, now Ricardo Hitec Ltd.

The one remaining company, the manufacturing arm of the B&R Taylor Group (B&R Engineering), was rescued by Lancashire Enterprises, a local authority organization, which took ownership along with the brand new factory building and seven-acre site at Chorley, Lancashire. Their objective was to allow an important local manufacturing business to continue to trade and recover until it could be 'adopted', and so their strategy was to avoid long-term capital investment. The business was therefore run primarily to ensure sound cashflow. In 1987, Liam Ferguson left SAC to run this manufacturing company, but he soon found his opportunities to pursue the major changes he recognized the company needed were severely limited by the local authority. Namely, he was unable to develop a new non-nuclear business, re-equip the factory with CAD design and CNC machine tools, retrain the workforce, and provide the long-term financial resources needed for these developments. Meanwhile, Phil Robson also left SAC, and joined PA Consulting at Cambridge, as director of manufacturing systems engineering.

Liam Ferguson knew that his top priority had to be refinancing the business, and given his unhappy experiences with the UK bankers, decided to take a trip to the Far East, and to explore opportunities with banks there, which had a reputation for longer-term perspectives towards industrial development. Although some good opportunities were identified, he headed back for the UK without any specific agreements. On the return flight, by chance he got talking to a man in the next seat who expressed interest in Liam's reason for having visited the region. In the discussion which followed, this man introduced himself as Dr Chen, entrepreneur and owner of Wan Hai Lines, one of the world's top ten container transport fleets. Dr Chen became interested in the business and within weeks agreed to invest in the business, acquiring 90 per cent of the shares from Lancashire Enterprises in a debt for equity swap. Dr Chen's explicit objectives were long term capital growth, in contrast to the short-term profitability demanded by the UK banks and venture capitalists. Shortly afterwards, Phil Robson left PA and also joined the company (by then known as NIS Ltd), as managing director. Both directors bought shares in the company. They were now in a position to create a long-term plan, free from the pressures of short-term dividend growth, that would give long-term capital growth; profits being reinvested rather than distributed. Liam and Phil were also ready to repeat the type of growth that they had achieved with SAC Hitec. Phil summed up his views on financing the business:

> 'As a UK engineering company, making the sort of returns required by large UK stakeholders is virtually impossible ... they would have wanted around 15 per cent compound dividend growth per annum. Then we could not have put in the capital investment needed for what we knew the company must retain to innovate and grow ... to continue product and process development.'

Managing change

The first step on the road of successful change is recognizing that change is actually required. Thus it was vital that a catalyst for change was identified – to make things happen, to take the business forward with new innovative strategies. Then the change process had to be controlled, as unfettered change can be both a destructive and often chaotic force.

In the first instance Liam and Phil conducted a SWOT (strengths, weaknesses, opportunities and threats) analysis that examined the outlook for NIS. Their analysis highlighted a number of key issues:

- Whilst capital expenditure in the nuclear industry was steadily falling, the dependence of the company on nuclear-related work remained alarmingly high. The removal of trade barriers across Europe, and the increasing importance of the economic union, along with new government policies allowing free trade in the nuclear industry was leading to an influx of new EU competition, competing with the company in its key home market.

- Company personnel demonstrated a poor age profile. As a forward-thinking organization, NIS could no longer afford to rely only on its more mature and experienced (though certainly valuable) personnel, but would need to look at additional resources to face a rapidly changing industrial environment.
- Recognizing the need to reduce the alarming dependence on the nuclear industry was a most vital step in the successful change process. Given the economic pressures, a rapid move into new markets was clearly required, but it was recognized that NIS would face an unknown 'mixed bag' of competitors; price levels would have to be benchmarked in each new sector.

New markets: new horizons

To enter new markets, one of the first tasks was to assess where the company's strengths lay, and of equal importance, where weaknesses were apparent. The SWOT analysis was critical in focusing the analysis at this stage.

NIS was found to be dangerously dependent on one nuclear customer (BNFL), whilst at the same time it lacked the necessary selling skills that would rectify this position. As a 'Jack-of-all-trades' NIS would be unable to compete on price alone, whilst at the same time it employed a high level of indirect staff. Contract and project management was weak.

The organizational structure was traditional and very departmentalized, formal training was scant, and communications tended to be ad-hoc and unstructured. Project teams appeared to be more re-active than pro-active, lacking forward thinkers, and were product rather than process driven.

Despite the many apparent weaknesses identified during the SWOT analysis everything was not necessarily 'doom and gloom'. NIS had developed a proven track record as being technically able, providing a totally comprehensive package of services.

Apparent frailties in some areas were balanced by strengths in others. The NIS management team was found to work well under pressure (perhaps through necessity!) and loyalty and commitment were high. The experienced team at NIS demonstrated versatile shop floor skills, a willingness to improve, and in general a professional outlook. The SWOT analysis had helped management to clearly identify strengths and to assess how best these might be applied to other markets, but with very little track record outside the nuclear sector, the broadening of NIS activities was not to be taken lightly!

During the early years of developing what became the NIS Group, Phil also worked two days a week as the SME (small and medium sized enterprise) Representative on the Innovation Unit set up by the Department of Trade and Industry (DTI), along with secondees from Rover, TI, Unilever and 3i. That is when he really began to understand that innovation should be treated as a business process. The unit looked in depth at 100 companies, and went below the glossy skin to discover that only about one in ten exhibited truly holistic

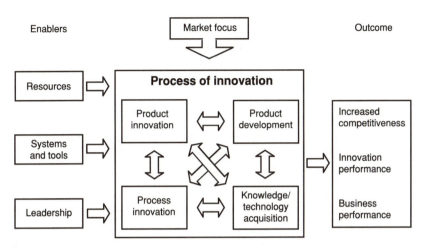

Figure 14.1 The innovation business process model

innovation processes (involving finance, treasury, marketing, human resource management, operations, etc.). This experience enabled Phil to clarify his thoughts about innovation, and to bring back to NIS the best ideas on how this could be achieved in their very conventional manufacturing business.

For example, by exploiting its understanding of the innovation business process model (Figure 14.1) the company could cultivate and encourage innovative thinking and attitudes within the manufacturing environment. NIS might then be able to gain a 'foot in the door' of new customers in new sectors.

The new strategy

Liam and Phil decided that the way forward for NIS had to be through a new strategy and a major change programme, to take the existing people and business and turn them into a new entity, which would add much more value. After much careful planning and preparation, the resulting initiative came to be called SPRINT:

S   Sales-led business
P   Partnerships
R   Rapid response
I   Innovation
N   New resources
T   Total quality and training

All elements of SPRINT were to be pursued in parallel (the order did not suggest any priority) and can be summarized as follows:

Sales-led business

This would involve becoming much more market-orientated, looking for new opportunities, and not simply waiting for packs of drawings to arrive, as had often been the case up to then.

Partnerships

These were seen as the way to acquire or share resources for the business that would otherwise be unaffordable. The company had the first example of this already in the vital area of the finance from Dr Chen!

Rapid response

Lead-time was important in new markets, and could be used to differentiate NIS from competitors. NIS wished to halve existing lead times. For example, cathode ray coating lines formerly took most manufacturers around twelve months to design and build, but this was often on the critical path of new factory projects, so there would be real competitive advantage in being able to supply much faster, say in six months. To do this would require simultaneous engineering, project management skills, and much better use of sub-contractors.

Innovation and consultancy

NIS was already good at designing innovative solutions to customers' needs, but this competence in design alone would not be enough to ensure future success. Innovation had to become the pervasive business process under-pinning all the changes that were to be done. The newly acquired skills in the process of innovation might also be mobilized and sold as consultancy, separated into a specialist division.

New resources

Much of the key production equipment was over thirty years old, so output had been kept in tolerance by the skill of the operator, but productivity and quality capability were poor in comparison to what could be achieved with the latest technologies. Design would also have to be upgraded to CAD, and ideally this would be linked to CAM in the production departments. New technology would require retrained people and perhaps some new skills bought in from outside, for example to support CNC machine tools.

Total quality management and training

Phil knew that despite the high skills of the operators, and the apparently modern appearance of the factory building, many processes and working practices were far from ideal, resulting in avoidable quality problems and costs. For example, although the open-plan building facilitated crane movements of large assemblies throughout the plant, dust from the welding and fabrication areas was affecting cleanliness in the machine shop and final assembly areas. Investment would be needed in new air moving equipment and filters to keep the new CNC machine shop and the assembly areas clean. As well as tangible improvements to the plant, continuous improvement to all processes would be needed, initiated and sustained by TQM and appropriate training. The company set a target of implementing TQM practice within nine months, led by Liam and quality teams. This plan would involve all staff.

There were a series of initiatives identified under each of these SPRINT headings. The rate of implementation planned for each varied, depending on priority and the level of resources to be applied. SPRINT was presented to all the employees in 1990, shortly after completion of the financing agreements with Dr Chen. Promises were made to the existing 150 employees that the company would:

- invest in a new CNC machine shop (around ten machines for prismatic and turned parts);
- build and equip a design centre with CAD, and linked to the CNC ('CAD-CAM');
- improve the fabrication facility;
- bring in high skills where needed;
- retrain existing staff in the use of new technology, and in TQM;
- develop teams to pursue continuous improvement.

Salaries would have to be frozen until the company returned to profit. This plan was well received and widely supported by the staff.

Telling the world

Once the SPRINT initiative had been finalized and was ready for full implementation, the potential markets needed to be informed of the changes at NIS. To unveil the new and improved company a suitably grand venue had to be used – the Grosvenor Hotel in London.

Present at the press conference were representatives of all the major industrial publications, including *The Engineer, Engineering,* and *The Financial Times*. The aim of this event was to publicize the changes at NIS and the applicability of its expertise across a number of industrial sectors. The conference was a success, with a number of articles appearing in the leading journals over the next few months.

The growth in awareness of NIS and its capabilities led a number of multinational blue-chip companies to approach NIS. From these initial contacts a number of prestigious contracts were awarded to the company. This exercise had not only succeeded in increasing the client base, but it had also enabled NIS to enter new markets – thereby reducing its reliance on the UK nuclear industry. The directors were confident that once a company had sampled the skills of NIS they would remain a customer and would place repeat business in the future.

At this time there was a revamp of the corporate image and marketing materials. The current NIS logo was adopted and a new brochure was produced. This formed the basis of the range of a dozen 'family style' brochures currently used by the four group companies.

The plan unrolls

The arrangements with Dr Chen gave the business the financial resources and stability to tackle much of the SPRINT plan, but the team felt that use of expensive CNC machines might be obtained by a partnership agreement rather than by the conventional route of outright purchase. The plan was to search for users of suitable CNC machines who, because of low utilization or the wish to exit metal machining, might wish to form some sort of a partnership, where NIS managed the equipment on their behalf and used the spare capacity for NIS production. After a false start with an aerospace company, Phil and Liam agreed a deal with Kratos in Manchester, which involved relocating the plant and workers to the NIS plant in Chorley, continuing to produce their parts at an agreed favourable rate to both parties, and providing the much required capacity for NIS. The equipment was almost a perfect match to their needs. This approach has been a great success with the output from the machine shop exceeding initial expectations, and it is now a valuable part of the NIS manufacturing capability.

Dr Chen appointed a chairman, Ian Meffan, with whom he had worked over many years in South East Asia. The board now set about thinking through what innovation really meant in NIS. Phil and Liam knew that they and the business were capable of successfully tackling and commercializing new but complex opportunities. This had been an every-day part of the business of making special plant for the nuclear and cathode ray tube markets, but had rarely been extended beyond these boundaries.

> 'We began to recognise an important part of the business output as being knowledge, which had previously been undervalued. We had expertise, but the only way it was sold was inside capital projects. This went out as low added value attached to hardware – at about a third of the price that you would pay for a motor mechanic to repair your car! So we broke this out into a new company, NIS Invotec.'

From these simple beginnings, NIS Invotec has grown to be a £1 million turnover consultancy company. Its teams, comprising existing and newly recruited staff, can be configured to tackle any process design or improvement projects, in a wide range of industries. The core competence is the mix of knowledge and experience to improve clients' processes, or even to create new ones based on the clients' R&D. Clients place great value on this expertise which, in some cases, allows the group to get 'a foot in the door' for design-and-build contracts. Early contracts have been in the food, fine chemicals, and pharmaceutical sectors, and have frequently resulted in spin-off projects for NIS Ltd to design and make the process plant.

One early NIS Invotec product was a series of 'Masterclasses in Innovation' based on Phil Robson's experience on the DTI Innovations Unit. This resulted in a contact with a multinational food supplier. To begin with, Invotec completed a consultancy project for them, which then turned into a design-and-build contract to build processing lines that cooked, coated and dried cereal products. Once these had been installed, the client company contracted with NIS as their 'supplier partner' for a number of these processing lines for their factories worldwide.

The unique selling point of NIS Invotec is the ability to offer design and build capabilities to compliment the consultancy skills, something very few consultancies can offer. This simple fact differentiates Invotec from the vast majority of manufacturing consultancies. Its business is all about helping large customers to innovate ('the business process of innovation'). Usually this involves bringing a holistic approach to projects, integrating their research and development, product and process engineering, and operations functions under a market-focused initiative.

Acquisitions

Since the launch of SPRINT, three strategic acquisitions have reinforced the group's capabilities, in each case connected with the existing capital plant manufacturing and/or consultancy competencies. These widened the group's opportunities for growth, because of the synergies with the core businesses, which could bring these more sales opportunities, and vice versa, as outlined below:

The acquisition of Phosphor Technology Ltd: speciality chemicals (in 1990)

'We used to be in the client's hands when it came to the complexities of putting phosphor on glass, in the cathode ray tube (CRT) industry. Phosphors and their treatment appeared to be black magic that our clients held, so we simply had to design plant to their instructions. We needed an understanding of this science that they seem to guard so tightly, so we acquired Phosphor

Technologies Ltd, a small group of technologists and chemists, that now helps us sell to the CRT industry. We don't do the high volume phosphors used on TV tubes, but small quantities for R&D and low volume production in specialised applications (e.g. Radar, which has very technical requirements). We are now Europe's largest suppliers of a phosphor pigment in ceramic false teeth, which matches UV response of natural teeth! This is particularly important for young people who socialise under UV light, as in discos, where ordinary ceramic false teeth look black. We also make trace phosphors used in security printing inks (used for printing bonds and other valuable documents) and special phosphors for well-known artists' signatures on paintings. We make clever things for large companies in small quantities, with high added value. There is no doubt that this expertise is now allowing us to innovate in one of our core areas of capital plant, the CRT coating lines, but it also is a good, profitable business in its own right.'

The acquisition of NSG Environmental

NIS Ltd was already indirectly involved in nuclear power and land remediation through the design and manufacture of mobile encapsulation plants for radionucleide-contaminated waste. But it did not have the ability to locate and evaluate this contamination, or the skilled operatives to undertake this type of work.

In 1993 NIS bought a small company, NSG Environmental, which although it had made simple equipment for its own use, was largely operational; providing teams of well trained, and appropriately monitored workers to undertake surveys, to evaluate radioactive contamination, and to subsequently decontaminate sites. They also had the knowledge of procedures for the disposal of the various grades of waste, and to package and consign them to the appropriate depositories.

'We saw this as an opportunity to get a direct involvement in the rapidly growing decommissioning and decontamination industries. Many nuclear facilities are approaching the end of their useful lives, and the resulting global opportunities must be on a scale similar to that of the original development of the plants. With our existing competencies in design and fabrication to the demanding standards of the industry, we felt that we should pursue this new opportunity, through NSG Environmental.'

One natural extension of this business is to build up similar experience in handling other toxins and hydrocarbons on contaminated sites. At the same time, by owning, understanding, and operating radionucleide decontamination equipment, the group expects to be able to improve the product and hence sell more plants abroad, which will in turn benefit NIS Ltd.

Moves into food plant manufacturing

The initial success of the migration from a value analysis consultancy project into full scale repeated manufacture of food processing plant highlighted both the commercial validity of the innovation process itself, and also the considerable design and manufacturing competencies of the business. Nuclear work requires outstanding capabilities in welding and other fabrication details, along with fine surface finishes, all to avoid 'traps' where material can catch up and accumulate. These features, and especially the absence of bacteriological traps, were also found to be valued by food manufacturers to assist in hygiene assurance. Both industries use fabrications of stainless steel, and both often require innovative solutions to their problems. It appeared that competitors in this industry were slow to innovate, providing 'standard' solutions across whole sectors, and generally offered long lead-times of about 26 weeks for major processing lines. Large, multinational customers needed novel, customized solutions to help create their sustainable operational advantages, and NIS demonstrated that it could deliver this in much shorter lead times.

Another acquisition has added to the logic of building a portfolio of capabilities in the food sector. Petrie Technologies Ltd was acquired in 1995, and had considerable expertise in microwave and radio frequency heating technology. This has been applied to a wide range of food processing tasks, including defrosting of two tonne per hour of frozen chicken in meat processing plants. This early experience has allowed NIS to become a significant player in this sector, and much of the output is exported via another partnership with EA Technology. The current expanded range of equipment includes several new specialities; toasting equipment, pressure cookers, coating lines, process dryers and microwave process cookers.

Into robotics through partnerships

Customised automation and robotics applications technology were key aspects of NIS's engineering activity, but the company lacked a 'standard' product range. Careful market research highlighted two international companies offering complementary product ranges: Par Systems Inc. of Minnesota, US; and Cimcorp OY of Pori, Finland. Partnerships with them have not only broadened NIS's capabilities, but also provided opportunities for selling complete processing plant in these new territories.

Latest innovations

Design and production facilities

The design office is fully networked for CAD use and is constantly being updated to keep pace with customer requirements and the latest developments in hardware and CAD software. With the advent of the CAD system came a purpose built facility to house it. An extension to the existing NIS offices opened in 1993 and has proved to be a valuable extra space. With a large contract in early 1997 came the need to build a high bay extension to the factory building to house the project. This new structure covers 8000ft^2 and can accommodate structures up to 50ft high. The growth of Invotec in its first two years has necessitated its recent change of premises. The original offices, designed to accommodate about twelve people, quickly proved to be too small. In late summer of 1997 Invotec moved to its new offices – a seventeenth century coach house, sited in the beautiful grounds of Duxbury Park Golf Course at Chorley.

Information technology

All the group companies have recently been linked together with a management information system (MIS). This now enables all the companies to have access to the latest accounts, which will give better control of invoicing and purchasing.

There is extensive use of information technology throughout the group. All companies have Internet access and E-mail accounts, and the use of computers in everyday life is prevalent. NIS Invotec's IT resources have grown as the company has grown. The company has moved from initially owning only two PCs running Windows 3.1, connected to a single laser printer via a print share box, to an environment that is fully networked, using a Windows NT 4 Server (Pentium Pro 200), with 17 PCs (three of which are CAD/multimedia PCs). The standardized software is Office 97 running on a Windows 95 platform. The office suite is supplemented with Publisher, AutoCAD 14 and other utility software. The office has an ISDN connection, which has enabled, with the integration of an ISDN router, each PC to have access to the Internet and for every staff member to have a personal E-mail account. The ISDN line is also used for the video conferencing facility; this was originally purchased to help with a specific project but has since proved useful for all aspects of the business. The latest piece of hardware to be added to this growing list is a Gestetner digital photocopier that initially scans and then prints the image, providing a cheaper and more accurate service. This machine does more than copy. Through its networking capabilities it can be used as a printer, and when connected to a telephone line can also be used for faxing. The telephone system is a fully integrated ISDN system that enables internal paging, voice mail and direct dialling. The system also has a self-diagnostic feature that may be activated remotely from the system suppliers.

NIS Invotec has designed and built its own website as a marketing tool. Once the strategy for the site had been prepared, various agencies quoted for its design. However, with the large graduate skills base, the decision was made to keep the project in-house. The results can be seen at www.nisinvotec.com. The site continues to be updated with all the changes at Invotec.

Communications

As well as the extensive brochures, the group has recently launched its corporate newsletter Insight. The aim of this is to keep customers informed of the projects recently completed across the group. Customers in, for example, the food industry are able to discover the work completed in the nuclear industry, and vice versa. As Petrie and NSG cover diverse industries, food and waste management respectively, their customers may be unaware that both companies are in the same group and share some of the design and manufacturing facilities. The newsletter helps the group to keep such a diverse range of customers informed. Recently NIS Invotec has started to produce its own in-house newsletter. This means that everyone in the organization can keep abreast of the latest developments on the various ongoing and proposed projects and any other important events over the previous weeks.

Networking

A major part of how NIS does business is through its network of contacts. These cover a number of areas, including:

- The Department of Trade and Industry (DTI)
- Local government
- Government agencies (e.g. GONW, Business Links, TECs)
- Academia
- Blue chip companies

Synergy and innovation

The examples above have illustrated some of the interactions between the increasingly diverse parts of the business. Market entry has sometimes been gained through the consultancy practice of NIS Invotec, but has then been pursued by the design and manufacturing capabilities of NIS Ltd. Each part of the group is not only responsible for its own profitability and growth, but also for its contribution to the development of the group. There are a number of organizational and cultural mechanisms which reinforce these objectives:

Firstly, each of the five directors of the group has responsibility for one of the businesses, but each has several other roles. For example, Phil Robson is managing director of NIS Invotec, chairman of NSG Environmental, business development director for the group, a non-executive director of Phosphor Technology, and marketing advisor to the managing director of Petrie Technologies. In this way, each business has its own management team, but close working contact with the other businesses.

A second approach, which reinforces the synergy between the companies is the monthly meeting of the five directors in a local pub! In a relaxed and informal way, they put aside the time to discuss opportunities and visions; in effect a form of macro-brainstorming, allowing innovations to be discussed and screened.

Because the directors must spend more time on the development of the group and on large opportunities that arise, they have had to free up their time to undertake these larger tasks. This has been achieved by a strategy of recruiting graduates in a personal assistant role. Phil explained:

> 'The old business hardly ever employed graduates, because they did not bring the immediately required technical skills to the design or production departments. We now recognise a much wider range of skills needed for the development of the business, so we now employ graduates of economics, manufacturing systems engineering, information technology, and even a few MBAs. We identify people with the potential for senior management; but above all, people who are prepared to work in a dynamic, changing environment: adaptable and creative people who will be the drivers of innovation in the future.

> 'We are also looking to get closer to a number of universities. In particular, we are interested in acquisition of, or partnership in, new technologies. Many important projects can be helped by an injection of cash or equipment at appropriate stages in the development, such as building a prototype. In the long run, involvement must be mutually beneficial to the researchers, their universities, and to our businesses. Invention has not been the problem here, it's the entire development and commercialisation of the ideas where financial and business help is needed. We have established an innovation budget to cover this type of development.'

Innovative trade services

One of NIS Invotec's philosophies is that it would supply consultancy not only to manufacturers. Phil had already worked for the DTI and recognized that the company's skills could equally be of use in the public sector, banks and other services where there was already a growing understanding of the need for help in such areas as value analysis and business process re-engineering.

Local manufacturing businesses in the north west of England already had access to a huge amount of government-supported advice, including the services of fourteen Training and Enterprise Councils (TECs). However, Phil and his team felt that these were not always adequately focused on getting local companies more work, particularly from overseas! Perhaps the new linkages with Japan through Dr Chen and Wan Hai Lines could be exploited to set up a marketing network in Japan for north west manufacturing businesses, to take advantage of the relatively low costs and high skills of the engineering products and component companies in the region.

Accordingly, with its explicit mission of innovation, NIS Invotec designed a scheme to provide this service, and successfully went for EC funding of around £1 million for a project to set up a professional sales/marketing organization in Japan. Experienced, early-retired Japanese executives were recruited to work from bases in the Wan Hai Lines offices in six cities, and already after only one year, this scheme (known as 'Iriguchi') has brought in many valued enquiries and orders for many quality-assured north west-based suppliers. The partnership with Dr Chen and his company has been invaluable, since this brought with it a portfolio of existing Japanese manufacturing business customers, as well as an understanding of the way to do business there. Having accredited, quality-assured suppliers removed the need for Japanese customers to undertake the usual expensive evaluation visits and audits. Iriguchi earns a small percentage commission on all the contracted supplies through the scheme, and the contacts made give potential opportunities for the other NIS group businesses. Phil summed up his perception of the project:

> 'Although this was quite an unusual thing to get involved with, we had not abandoned our existing competencies. Yet again we were examining how we could exploit new opportunities, and we were learning to make new business. This success has inspired us to look at some other ideas, which exploit our competences, our creativity, and our partnerships. Some very big ideas are in the pipeline. Dr Chen is an innovator, and the success of Iriguchi has demonstrated to him that we are too!

> 'NIS is Dr Chen's only technology asset: he encourages us and supports our culture and aspirations. I am certain that without such enthusiastic and patient top-level support no business could sustain the pace of innovation that is needed to keep ahead in this very competitive world.'

Evidence of success

The benefits that were accrued from the successful application of the SPRINT initiative enabled NIS to build on its own core competencies. By developing partnerships with businesses such as Par Inc (a US manufacturer of advanced robotics systems) the company was able to gain market entry into new sectors such as aerospace, chemicals and food where the skills demonstrated by NIS were equally applicable. Over the last three years the food equipment market share was up by 200 per cent. There was a 50 per cent increase in the number of new clients; profits were up by 40 per cent and turnover by 60 per cent.

Sectors served:

- 1987   Nuclear, CRT

- 1997   Nuclear, CRT, food, chemical, pharmaceutical, glass,
          explosives, manufacturing industries (e.g. plastics, electronics)

Clients:

- 1987   BNFL, AEA, Thomson Polkolor, AWE

- 1997   BNFL, AEA, Thomson Polkolor, Sony, Pilkington Glass, ICI,
          Ciba, Kelloggs, Mars Group, Danone, Sun Valley, Philips,
          Nokia, Zeneca, Ilford

Figure 14.2 NIS: 1987 to 1997 comparisons

In the case of TV coating lines, where lead times once stood at 52 weeks, the same task has been halved to only 26 weeks – a mark that competitors found impossible to match. Similarly, in the case of food lines, lead times were also reduced from 26 weeks to only 16 weeks.

An important measure of any project's success is the Customer Satisfaction Monitor. Completed at the end of each project this report aims to improve the company's reaction to client needs, whilst allowing the company to see how it in turn is perceived.

Conclusions

NIS Ltd is an example of a company which has used a wide range of innovative practices to overcome severe and potentially terminal problems resulting from changes in its markets and economic environment. The case illustrates the holistic nature of its process of innovation, incorporating all business functions in the changed strategies and practices. Several important lessons can be learned from the approach adopted:

First, there has been a strong market focus throughout the business, with an emphasis on commitment to a deep understanding of the customers' changing needs. For example, in the cathode ray tube market, NIS invested (by acquisition) in an understanding the science of phosphors. In its traditional market of nuclear processing equipment, the company recognized the increasing importance of decontamination and waste disposal, and built up expertise initially through manufacturing specially designed equipment, and then through acquisition of an operating decontamination contractor. In every case, identifying potential work for other parts of the group became normal practice for the companies, reinforced by good communications, IT, and a supportive managerial structure.

A second lesson to be drawn from the case is that innovation itself can be managed as a business process, and therefore has to be planned, controlled, and invested in like any other part of the business. It crosses functional boundaries, and works best when all parts of the company are well co-ordinated and support an integrated strategy and implementation plan. This, in turn, may require a new recruitment and training strategy to ensure that the appropriate human resources are available when needed.

A third important aspect is that a culture of company-wide innovation must be seen to be critical for success. Change should be perceived as positive and of widespread long-term benefit to the business and its employees. In this company, great emphasis has been placed on communication and involvement to achieve a positive outlook on opportunities as and where they arise.

Chapter 15

LINX Printing Technologies plc: a 'high-tech' start-up

Gordon Murray

No money, no product, no customers – but a great idea

In 1986, two mechanical engineers, Mike Keeling and Hillar Weinberg, with over thirty years technical consultancy and industrial design experience between them, came to a key decision. Instead of continuing to use their internationally acknowledged expertise in the design of continuous inkjet printing (CIJ) for the benefit of established manufacturers, they would form their own UK based manufacturing company. They believed that their pre-eminent knowledge of the sophisticated technologies, customer needs and market requirements of industrial print users could be translated into producing a family of advanced continuous inkjet printers of a functionality, reliability and ease of use materially better than any existing product currently available on the international market.

A little over one decade later, their creation, LINX Printing Technologies plc, is a £21 million turnover, publicly quoted business with sales in 45 countries and an 11 per cent share of the world market for continuous inkjet printers. The company is presently the No. 2 manufacturer of CIJ printers in the UK and No. 3 in Europe by market share. The founders' stated ambition is to grow LINX, through both internal growth and acquisition, into a world class business in its chosen areas of industrial printing by the year 2000.

New technology based firms

Attractiveness

LINX is one of a generation of new technology based firms (NTBFs) which are becoming of increasing economic importance and, accordingly, of considerable interest to government. The outstanding performance of American start-up firms in several areas of leading-edge technologies, and their consequent economic contribution, has made the genesis and encouragement of NTBFs a major new focus of policy for the governments of virtually all developed economies. NTBFs are seen of being of particular importance given their contribution to four cardinal areas of economic advantage: (quality) job creation, technological and commercial innovation, export growth and industrial competitiveness.

Uncertainty and risk

However, while successful NTBFs potentially offer significant advantages to the economic prosperity of a nation, their genesis and early years are fraught with extremely high levels of uncertainty and risk in virtually all areas of activity, including financing, technology and marketing. For the individual NTBF, an exceptional technological offering is a necessary but not sufficient condition for economic success. Their entrepreneurial founders have also to manage continued organizational and product/market demands in both internal and external environments which are characterized by their complexity and rapid rate of change. The experiences of LINX demonstrate clearly the nature of the advantages of NTBFs and the challenges, which they will invariably face.

Small innovative businesses are different from large companies

There is a substantial body of evidence that NTBFs are often considerably more productive at creating and exploiting innovation than their larger corporate counterparts. Reasons posited for their comparative efficiency have included culture, organizational flexibility, efficient internal communication and closeness to market issues where the smaller entrepreneurial firm may exploit (small) size advantages. However, small scale also has significant threats for the entrepreneurial business. Less than half of all European and US firm start-ups survive to their tenth year. Frequently, their first mistake or misjudgement is their last. Formal and rigorous product/market appraisal is often largely replaced by intuition, experience and the founder(s) being prepared to bet the future of the company on the success of one key innovative idea. Only a tiny minority of these survivors go on to create significantly sized businesses. In comparison to entrenched competitors, their resources are minimal. Rapid innovation and focused product/market positioning is often used to avoid or attenuate the threat of large firm competitive reprisals. Until the new entrant has gained critical experience and mass, its ambition is to be invisible or perceived as irrelevant by its established competitors while rapidly forging close links with new customers.

Continuous inkjet printing – the technology

Continuous inkjet printing is a method of 'non-contact' printing at high speed. This is achieved by producing a high-pressure jet of ink and stimulating it with ultrasound to break up the flow into a stream of uniform droplets. These droplets are produced at rates of up to 120,000 a second. They are given an electrical charge and then deflected as they pass through an electrostatic field. Computer software controls the droplet charge via the voltage applied to form a desired pattern of characters on the surface of a product as it passes the print head. CIJ technology has to apply a complex combination of physics, chemistry, electrostatics and fluid dynamics in order to achieve consistent high quality results, in what are often hostile factory environments. This technical complexity has to be coupled with high reliability in continuous, high volume production situations because any breakdown will result in expensive downtime to the industrial users of the technology.

Product marking and coding can be achieved by a number of methods, but continuous inkjet printers have significant advantages to commercial users, as shown in Table 15.1.

Table 15.1

High speed	The fastest printers can run at 2500 characters per second
Non-contact	Because the drops are propelled through the air it is possible to print onto uneven or delicate surfaces and at much higher speeds than conventional contact printing processes
Flexibility	The software based control of the droplet charging enables patterns, or continuously varied text and number characters of varying dimensions, to be printed

Continuous inkjet printing – the market

Continuous inkjet printers enable manufacturers to identify and code their products with fixed or variable data. These printers can be used effectively in all manner of production environments almost regardless of the surface or shape of the product and without affecting the pace of production flows.

Industrial applications of CIJ printers

Food and beverages

Continuous inkkjet printing achieves finished product coding and marking in the food, dairy, soft and alcoholic drinks industries – necessary due to legislation requiring 'use by' and 'best before' dates to be printed on packaging. Initially, the food and beverage industries were the two largest sectors using this labelling/identification technology.

Pharmaceutical, household goods, toiletries and cosmetics

CIJ printers are able to satisfy manufacturers' requirements for clear and flexible coding and labelling. Such products often require high quality and detailed marking with characters sized down to 1.0 mm.

Industrial and other products

Continuous inkkjet printing is of importance in batch and parts coding for production and inventory control purposes, particularly in the electronics, aerospace and automotive industries. The non-contact nature of CIJ printing makes it ideal for marking delicate materials without affecting structural integrity. It allows the printing of complex codes on a wide range of materials including products with irregular surfaces.

The above users are commonly characterized by very high volume production lines. A canning or bottling plant producing beer or soft drink products may well run multiple production lines, each of which is capable of operating at in excess of 2000 units per minute. Similar flows are also commonplace for pharmaceutical product packers. Under these conditions, contact printing technologies are unacceptably slow. Thus, there have been, to date, no substitute technologies to CIJ printers for large volume users. However, this scale of volume places considerable demands for printer robustness and reliability on CIJ manufacturers.

Market size

At the time of LINX's formation, the company's founders estimated the total international market size to be approximately £130 million per annum. No direct information was available on the CIJ printer market as company statistics were not released by competitors and industrial manufacturing statistics were too aggregated to be of value. It was estimated by LINX that the total market was growing at about 10 per cent per annum in 1986. This estimate was derived from statistical forecasts of the growth of, primarily, food and beverage manufacturing which was the largest market for CIJ products.

Environmental factors influencing customer demand

Since the mid-1980s, three mutually reinforcing trends have each impacted to increase the important of product identification, labelling and coding and, thus, the derived demand for CIJ printers.

Legislative requirements

Particularly within perishable foodstuffs and medical drug markets where product quality can or does degrade over time, individual countries have imposed legislation requiring manufacturers to clearly display 'use by' and 'best before' dates on their products. Parallel legislation was also imposed by the European Commission as part of the harmonization of European commercial law leading up to the 1992 integrated market objective. Given many small firms' unawareness of the requirements and implications of this legislation until months before the date of legal compliance, 1992 saw a major increase in the demand for CIJ printers with market growth rates reaching in excess of 25 per cent per annum. This legislation had a continued 'knock-on effect' post 1992 as importers into the European Union also came to appreciate that they would similarly have to meet the product coding legislation demanded of domestic European firms.

Traceability and product security requirements

For companies selling products in consumer markets, the spectre of quality defects, which can potentially harm their users or consumers, is a critical issue. Again, this concern is particularly acute for producers of medical supplies or food processing companies. Well-publicized cases of bottled mineral water contamination and the criminal adulteration of food stuffs have made it imperative for companies to be able to quickly and efficiently trace suspect batches of product throughout the distribution chain. In extremis, the future of company brand reputations and consumer goodwill valued at tens of millions of pounds can be placed at risk. Effective and durable product coding and labelling is a central element of a manufacturers' or retailers' product security system.

Inventory control systems

The increasing use of sophisticated computer-based, inventory control and component tracking systems in factories, warehouses and retail outlets has more recently produced a further increase in demand for equipment which can transfer complex coding details often onto irregular product, component or packaging surfaces and/or delicate materials. Non-contact marking is particularly useful in such applications. The CIJ industry and its ink suppliers have developed an innovative portfolio of inks and solvents for use on highly specific materials (e.g. acrylic, glass, polycarbonate, aluminium, etc.) under a wide range of demanding conditions (e.g. heat sensitive, alkali resistant, fast drying, ultra-violet readable, etc.).

Competitors

In 1986, five companies dominated the international CIJ printing industry (see Table 15.2).

The US company Videojet Systems International was the largest manufacturer in the industry, although its sales were largely confined to the USA. Videojet Systems International was also the technology supplier to Hitachi, which, in common with many Japanese firms' first involvement in a new product/market area, had chosen to license overseas (US) technology. Domino Printing Sciences plc was the biggest UK supplier and a direct competitor to LINX.

Table 15.2 Established CIJ suppliers and their market shares, 1986

Company	Country	Estimated sales	Nearest £ million
Videojet Systems International	US	$150,000,000	£100
Domino Printing Sciences PLC	UK	£13,670,000	£14
Imaje S.A.	France	FFr 77,320,000	£10
Willett International Ltd	UK	£7,175,000	£7
Hitachi Ltd	Japan	n/a	

Total estimated value = £131 million

Conversion US$ @ $1.50 = £1 Sterling
Conversion FFr @ FFr 8.02 = £1 Sterling

The company – LINX Printing Technologies Plc

Genesis – 'If they can do it, so can we!'

Both Michael Keeling and Hillar Weinberg had worked in the Inkjet Printing Group of Cambridge Consultants in the mid-1970s. As senior technical consultants, they had been responsible for developing advanced CIJ printer designs, which were now incorporated in the products sold by three of the main industry manufacturers. Both men had been involved in the development of the first commercial inkjet printer in the UK, which was later marketed by Domino. They had also worked together for Willett Technologies, which had been established by Keeling for Willett International, an industrial group in the packaging industry. Willett was in 1986 the number two CIJ manufacturer in the UK after Domino.

Thus, they had seen the fruits of their technical expertise result in innovative new printing applications but not at a significant economic gain to themselves. Keeling and Weinberg's decision to start their own CIJ printing company was first translated into a business plan, which articulated and quantified their commercial ambitions. This document was an essential requirement in order to interest external investors. They estimated that a total of £950,000 would be needed to undertake the necessary technical development, and to translate their technical plans into a small but viable, initial manufacturing and marketing operation.

While the founders believed that it would have been possible to start and 'boot strap' a new enterprise without recourse to external finance, such an action would not have allowed them to launch an international company from day one. Thus, substantial external finance was essential if the scale of their longer-term plans was to be realized. This level of funding was not available from banks which were not prepared to advance more than a few thousand pounds of loans given the lack of substantial collateral of the founders. The entrepreneurs had no real option but to seek equity finance from the venture capital industry.

The first marketing hurdle – selling the concept to professional investors

The difficulties of raising initial finance for a new and untried technology-based business is one of the most enduring findings of research into technology entrepreneurship. Institutional investors in Europe have traditionally been extremely wary of backing NTBFs. In many cases, the technology entrepreneurs have not inspired confidence in either venture capital organizations or bank lenders. Providers of both equity and debt commonly cite the very limited commercial experience or track record of technical entrepreneurs. Their concern is compounded by the entrepreneurs often negligible understanding and experience of even rudimentary business practice, particularly marketing expertise and financial controls.

Keeling and Weinberg experienced similar reactions as they laboriously went through the British Venture Capital Association members' handbook to identify and approach prospective financial backers. The investors' typical reaction could be summarized as: 'You have no money, no product, no market, no commercial experience. Yet you want us to invest a million pounds?'

The two technical founders' reactions to wholesale disbelief that they could create a company with planned sales of nearly £7 million in the first five years was two-fold. First, they invited a professional marketing manager, John Shead, to join the founding team. The executive chosen had worked in a marketing role for major companies in the printing industry, including Xerox. He also had an MBA qualification. Second, the three founders invited an experienced senior manager, Derek Harris, to become the fourth co-founder and to assume the role of non-executive chairman of LINX. This senior manager had been a main board director of a major UK company. He was also a chartered engineer and could understand both the technical and commercial concepts and complexities of the CIJ business.

Keeling and Weinberg correctly surmised from their earlier and unsuccessful efforts to raise external finance that professional investors would be much more inclined to take their proposal seriously if the company included an experienced marketing professional and was headed by an established senior manager. Shead with an employment record in a number of highly successful corporations and Harris with a history of board appointments in manufacturing, new product development and international sales and marketing, each lent a commercial credibility to the founders' plans which could not have been achieved by the technical entrepreneurs alone.

> 'The first things we look at are the product, its technology, the business and the people, and, if we are satisfied, we will then see whether the financial numbers make sense.'
>
> Dr Paul Castle, founder and chief executive,
> MTI Managers Ltd (venture capitalists)

Venture capitalists, in undertaking appraisals of new ventures in which they might invest, place very considerable importance on the venture having a 'balanced team' of professional and experienced managers. The four co-founders now could legitimately argue that their team embraced marketing, technical, manufacturing and general management skills and experience. The remodelling of the original founder management team, based on the feedback from investors which had refused finance, was a clear example of LINX management's sensitivity to capital market signals. Their perceptiveness was rewarded when MTI Managers Ltd, a venture capital firm specializing in early-stage technology investments, agreed to support the new venture. MTI with a French co-investor, Banque Paribas, agreed to invest £870,000 or 91.2 per cent of the total finances for an initial equity stake of 80 per cent. (An incentivizing 'ratchet' arrangement was negotiated by which the founders' equity participation would increase from 20 per cent to 50 per cent if, on the realization of the investment by the venture capitalists, the company was worth £30 million.) With a contribution from the founders of £83,750, LINX started life with £953,750 of shareholders' funds. With strong guidance and support from MTI Managers, particularly related to issues of financial control, they now had coverage of all key functional management areas prior to the establishment of the business.

The innovative concept – 'just like an office copier'

In order to intervene in an established market, LINX had to create an offering to customers which was materially better than that provided by incumbent suppliers. Keeling and Weinberg were convinced that they could provide innovative products based on the enhancement of existing technologies. Three of the five international competitors were supplying CIJ machines, which were still largely based on technological advances that the founders themselves had designed nearly ten years ago. In developing the original technology, the two engineers had spent a considerable time in the manufacturing facilities of the customers for CIJ printers. LINX's innovative processes and the new company's positioning in an established market was, and had to be, driven by their deep understanding of the needs of industrial customers for CIJ technology. In their view, which was articulated in their business plan, LINX had to offer substantive improvements in three critical areas of functionality:

- print quality, detail and accuracy
- ease of operation
- robustness of use, including rapid servicing and repair

> 'Our objective was to make it just like an office copier. You just
> pressed the button and the printer did the rest.'
>   Mike Keeling, MD of LINX Printing Technologies

Thus, over several years, the founders had developed a detailed understanding of customers' needs and how LINX's products could add value. Their first commercial CIJ printer, the 5000 Series, produced by LINX some nine months after the initial funding, embodied significant advances over competitors' products in each of the three key areas of functionality.

Print quality

Existing printers could only produce two lines of print in 1988. Customers for LINX 5000 Series CIJ printers could specify advanced facilities, which could produce up to four lines of print. The software and mechanical advances could also allow the printing of bar codes, up until then a notoriously difficult challenge for CIJ printers.

Ease of operation

Given the complexities of setting up a CIJ printer for labelling/coding on a production line, it was common for users to be obliged to provide a dedicated and trained operative to run the equipment. By incorporating advanced software in the operational design, a considerable element of the complexity was 'designed out' of the system thereby allowing the machine to be operated by regular line staff. The software also allowed for the rapid change of printed code marks or labels at the control console without complicated and time consuming line stoppages during a production run.

Robustness of use

A major innovation introduced by LINX was the 'modularization' of the key components on all their CIJ printer models. A faulty or worn part could now rapidly and easily be replaced by a line maintenance engineer. This had very significant savings in both unplanned downtime and regular maintenance. The incorporation of continuous cleaning of the sensitive nozzles at the end of the printing cycle or at operation shutdown also reduced a common source of downtime due to dirty or blocked jets.

Users were ensured of accuracy of print marking over long production runs, and the reduction of downtime to a minimum. Given that the efficiency of production runs in high volume manufacturing plants remains conditional on the reliability and robustness of the 'end of line' printing/coding operation, the innovations introduced by LINX represented a material improvement to existing CIJ printers of significant benefit to customers.

LINX – product and market positioning

A new business is highly vulnerable to competitor reaction during its first introduction of new products or services to an established market. Existing companies are able to challenge the new entrant in a number of ways. They may rapidly attempt to upgrade their own product offerings, mount specific promotions targeted at key or vulnerable customer accounts, change marketing variables particularly price, or seek to deny the new company access to channels of sale and distribution. These reactions can be fatal for a new business without the substantial backing of a large corporate parent prepared to weather hostile and protracted competitive responses.

> 'One of the reasons that we had chosen to develop a machine with such a high specification was that we would not have to compete with the existing manufacturers directly. As a result, they did not see us as a direct threat at the time.'
>
> Mike Keeling, MD of LINX Printing Technologies

Despite their very strong technical competencies, the founding management team was highly sensitive to and aware of the importance of an effective marketing strategy. They fully appreciated that innovative advantages were insufficient to ensure the success of the new enterprise. Accordingly, the first CIJ printer models from LINX were deliberately positioned at the high end of the market. While product variants were available that were direct substitutes for competitors' products, the emphasis of their new offerings to the market was on highly sophisticated printers for demanding, and less price sensitive users. The founders employed a classic 'niche strategy' in common with many NTBFs. LINX's most popular models were priced, on average, 10–15 per cent above those of their competitors' products. This pricing policy gave two important signals. To the customers for CIJ printers, the company's clear belief in the benefits of their innovative, new product features was clearly signalled to prospective users. Conversely, competitors could infer that LINX did not appear to intend to attack their core product/market areas.

Lucky break I

At the time of LINX's first product launch in early 1988, the market for CIJ printers had started to accelerate. The legislative demands for product coding were beginning to impact on manufacturers, who realized that they would have to install more sophisticated printing facilities. By 1992, LINX estimated that the international growth in total sales of CIJ printers had accelerated to approximately 25 per cent per annum. LINX's original business plan was structured on an estimate of total international sales demand of 6,000 printers per year. This was later revised by the marketing director to 16,000 units and still proved to be an under-estimate of total demand.

In this situation, established printer manufacturers were increasingly hard pushed to meet existing demands for their products. Keeling observed that, at this time, customers were just happy to get any CIJ printer, and that they were frequently obliged to wait until one was available from their supplier. A growing market with incumbent producers unable to meet existing demand was a highly fortuitous beginning for LINX. Competitors appeared not to concern themselves overly with a small and unproven start-up, although the expertise of the two founders was well recognized by the industry. In addition, the robustness of demand during this period meant that competitors did not see the urgent need to continue to upgrade existing product offerings. The benign market conditions had, arguably, made the incumbent manufacturers complacent. They had forgotten the strategic truism that in technologically innovative markets it is always better to ensure that your own internal innovative efforts make your existing products obsolete before competitors do it for you. The outcome of this peculiar operating environment was that LINX was allowed to establish the company for approximately two years before competitors fully realized the nature and seriousness of the threat posed by LINX's advanced and highly innovative CIJ printers.

LINX – internationalization

From its inception, the founders of LINX realized that in order for their company to be successful they would have to rapidly establish overseas sales. The UK market accounted for only approximately 17 per cent of world wide demand. Given the ambitions to create a company valued at £30 million within five years, it was imperative that international sales provided the majority of revenue and profit. The sales projections in the original business plan were for a £7 million turnover within five years. This target, if constrained solely to domestic customers, would have required LINX to capture approximately one third of the existing UK market for CIJ printers. Keeling believed that the realization of such a goal would be very vigorously resisted by their competitors, and would threaten the viability of the young company. Thus, the establishment of an overseas distribution network was a major priority of LINX from its inception.

Lucky break 2

At the time of LINX's formation, one of its major European competitors was the French company, Imaje S.A., with international sales of around £10 million per annum. The founders of this French manufacturer had been a client of the engineering design consultancy for which Keeling and Weinberg had previously worked. The founders' earlier designs were still in evidence in the current product range of Imaje's CIJ printers.

For reasons which are still not fully clear to the founders of LINX, in 1988 Imaje decided to change fundamentally its distribution strategy moving from a distributor network to a direct sales activity world wide. This unforeseen development had profound consequences for both LINX and Imaje. The French company's erstwhile country distributors were left without a CIJ product range in a market, which from all indications was growing rapidly. The distributors needed product and LINX needed an international distributor network. Within six months of Imaje's change of direction, LINX had recruited its former distributors in France, Germany, Belgium/the Netherlands and Switzerland. The first CIJ printer sale ever made by LINX was via the Belgian distributor.

The internationalization focus established in the business plan continues to dominate LINX's current sales activity. Over 80 per cent of the company's total sales of machines are exported to customers in 45 country markets including both the North America and Pacific Rim regions. LINX was awarded The Queen's Award for Exports in 1992. The Prince of Wales' Award for Innovation was also received the same year.

Performance

The operating results of LINX demonstrate clearly the potential attractiveness of NTBFs and their economic contribution to both the local and national economy (see Tables 15.3 and 15.4 for profit and loss and balance sheet information). LINX was legally constituted as a business in December 1986. Its first sales of CIJ printers were made in 1988 after the technical ambitions of Keeling and Weinberg were initially translated into prototypes and then into the first production models. The Series 5000 CIJ printers were first exhibited in November 1987. Two years later, the lower priced 4000 Series was launched. Linxnet, a proprietary software programme allowing LINX machines to be networked was launched the same year. A further two years of development produced their most advanced printers to date, the 6000 Series, which was launched at the end of 1991. By 1997, LINX, now a public limited company, recorded annual printer, spares and consumable sales of £21.3 million. This represented a profit before taxation of £2.63 million (see Figure 15.1).

Table 15.3 Profit and loss account (£000's)

Date of accounts	30/6/97	30/06/96	30/06/95	30/06/94	30/06/93	30/06/92
Turnover	21,302	17,337	15,339	10,923	11,940	10,470
Exports	16,890	13,513	12,050	7,819	9,362	7,421
Cost of goods sold	12,565	10,287	9,366	N/A	N/A	N/A
Gross profit	8,737	7,050	5,973	N/A	N/A	N/A
Number of employees	222	197	182	162	176	151
Operating profit	2,362	1,576	1,288	303	1,400	1,647
Non-trading income	243	217	180	101	136	124
Pre-tax profit	2,605	1,793	1,424	332	1,429	1,640
Taxation	979	620	480	83	440	577
Profit after tax	1,626	1,173	944	249	989	1,063
Dividends payable	590	412	307	146	302	29
Retained profits	1,036	761	637	103	687	1,034

Table 15.4 Balance sheet (£000's)

Date of accounts	30/6/97	30/06/96	30/06/95	30/06/94	30/06/93	30/06/92
Fixed assets	3,262	2,985	2,801	2,238	2,449	2,263
Stock	2,434	1,547	1,448	1,065	1,627	1,176
Debtors	3,313	2,294	2,195	2,223	2,590	1,588
Cash	4,093	3,630	2,699	2,441	2,061	1,609
Misc. current assets	0	256	329	141	119	264
Other current assets		3,886	3,028	2,582	2,180	1,873
Total current assets	9,840	7,727	6,671	5,870	6,397	4,637
Total assets	13,102	10,770	9,523	8,135	8,919	6,910
Total current liabilities	5,347	4,274	3,830	2,156	3,034	2,945
Total assets *less* current liabilities	7,761	6,496	5,693	5,979	5,885	3,965
Long term loans	0	0	0	943	990	1,037
Other long term liabilities	364	334	294	284	254	218
Total liabilities	5,705	4,608	4,124	3,383	4,278	4,200
Called-up share capital	738	735	734	730	725	417
P & L account reserve	5,065	3,855	3,094	2,457	2,354	1,667
Sundry reserve	1,594	1,572	1,571	1,565	1,562	626
Shareholder funds	7,397	6,162	5,399	4,752	4,641	2,710

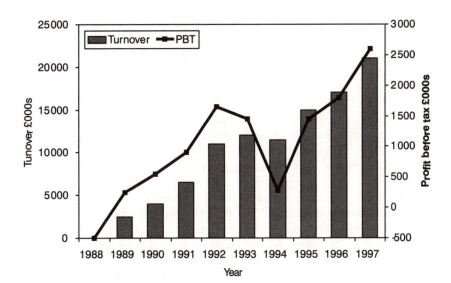

Figure 15.1

Flotation on the London stock market – the 'upside'

The sales and profitability figures indicate that, despite the successes of the company to date, the growth of LINX has not been without its problems. In 1992, LINX had an Initial Public Offering on the main London stock market. Despite the difficulties of a UK economy in recession, LINX raised £2 million from public investors, thereby allowing its venture capital partners to realize the majority of their original investment. The flotation valued the total company at £18.7 million. On the incentive structure agreed at the time of the initial financing, the management founders of LINX owned 40 per cent of the equity of the company at flotation – their initial investment of £83,750 was now worth £7.5 million. The two venture capital companies controlled 60 per cent of the equity worth £11.2 million. This represented an internal rate of return on their original £870,000 investment of 68 per cent per annum over the six year period. LINX had become a 'star' investment.

Flotation on the London stock market – the 'downside'

Keeling acknowledged that the process of preparing for a market listing was extremely onerous on a small and management extensive business during a time of rapid growth and evolution. From the period in December 1986 up until 1992, the company had been highly successful in their innovative efforts in a very conducive and receptive market place. By its own efforts, and with the help of a couple of lucky breaks, LINX had demonstrated very significant growth. The company was 'on a roll' and management had not yet been 'tempered' by any major difficulties or setbacks. This progress was to be checked in 1992.

In that year LINX successfully completed an initial public offering of their stock. However, for six months, senior management had to divert their attentions from the company and its customers to persuading market makers and institutional investors that LINX was an attractive and rewarding business in which to commit their funds. At around the same time, LINX and its founders also came up against a growth-related barrier, which many young companies never succeed in surmounting. Keeling was running the company as managing director. Yet, by his own acknowledgement, Keeling was not a professional manager. What he was, and wished to continue to be, was a very gifted engineer. As the business grew larger and more complex, the absence of a professional manager in charge of company-wide administration began to tell on the company's performance. Keeling and his co-directors recognized the shortcomings of the present senior management team and, in 1994, an operations director was recruited to assume day-to-day responsibility for the running of the business. Keeling, while remaining managing director, was able to redirected his energies to areas of marketing and technological innovation where his skills and experience could be best exploited.

The consequences of the considerable demands of the flotation process coupled with the lack of professional executive management control each took their toll. Within months of going public, LINX's share price had more than halved from the original offer price of 130 pence. The shares eventually started to recover in early 1994 and continue on a sustained upward trend. Similarly, earnings per share dropped from a figure of 8.2 pence in 1992 to a bottom of 1.7 pence in 1994 before returning to 11.1 pence in 1997. It has taken over two years to address fully the managerial problems first identified in 1992. LINX had weathered successfully a period when senior management, by their own confession, had started to believe that they had the 'Midas touch'. This was a dangerous illusion further supported by the public recognition accorded to LINX of prestigious awards for exporting and innovation.

Continued and dominant export focus

Despite the problems of the period following the 1992 public offering, LINX has continued to remain predominantly an export-based organization. Initial sales via European distributors were added to with distributor arrangements in key markets including the United States and Japan. Since the company's inception, domestic sales have never been greater than 30 per cent of total sales and, in 1997, stood at 22 per cent.

Sales into the US and Japanese market were made on the basis of an increasingly established European base. LINX was the first company to market a fully customized CIJ printer in Japan with a full Kanji character set on the keyboard and software controls. Up until that date, products on the Japanese market were essentially slightly modified US models. As a result, LINX rapidly gained market share to become No. 2 with approximately 60 per cent of the sales of the incumbent Japanese multinational manufacturer.

The basis of LINX's internationalization efforts depends heavily on a close and reciprocal relationship with key distributors. It is company policy that LINX sales should not represent more than 40 per cent of the total sales of a selected country distributor. A higher level of sales would represent an unacceptable vulnerability for both parties. Given the relatively low labour content in their products and their high unit value, LINX has no present ambitions to invest in manufacturing facilities overseas in the near future. However, a future ambition is to increase its existing 'foot hold' presence in the burgeoning Chinese market for CIJ printers.

Commitment to innovation

Expenditure on producing the next generation of product and process innovations is the lifeblood of NTBFs in highly competitive, technology based markets with limited technology and product life cycles. With a current workforce of over 200 people, LINX has a specialist engineering group of some forty staff of which two-thirds are educated to at least first degree level in related engineering, electronics and software disciplines. In addition, special projects groups are regularly created to address specific technical challenges. Technical service support staff who work in close collaboration with existing and new customers are similarly viewed as a key stimulus for future product development. R&D as a percentage of sales has averaged 9 per cent over the last four years. Given the use of technical and support staff within the innovative process, this statistic likely underestimates the total commitment of LINX to investing in future innovation.

Employment growth and company culture

In 1986, LINX started with three founder employees. By the time of flotation in 1992, the company employed 155 persons at its Cambridgeshire offices and manufacturing site. In 1997, with 214 employees, the company is one of the largest employers in the area. Importantly, a significant number of the staff have technical and commercial qualifications. NTBFs are rarely major employers of unskilled casual staff. Their futures are very largely predicated on the quality, innovativeness and commitment of key 'knowledge workers'. Accordingly, incentive systems, including both profits share and share option schemes, attempt to ensure that staff benefit directly from the commercial success of the company. At the time of the flotation, over 40 per cent of the existing staff elected to purchase ordinary shares in the company (see Figure 15.2).

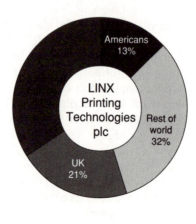

Figure 15.2

Keeling is confident that the relatively small size of the company, its focused product range and the tradition of customer driven, technological innovation will enable younger staff increasingly to assume the mantle of innovative responsibility initiated by Weinberg, himself and the original team. The culture of the company extols and rewards creative solutions believing that it has no choice but to create meritocracies by all possible means.

> 'LINX is committed to developing individual initiative at all levels within the company, to create a culture where each person takes responsibility for their own work and improving the way in which it is performed.'
>
> LINX policy statement

Present and future innovation

The history of LINX has been the continued incremental development of an established technology. Technological developments have made CIJ printers faster, more versatile regarding the materials to be marked, more able to print accurately, easier to programme multiple codes/labels, and more robust in operation. In achieving and furthering these customer-demanded attributes, LINX has adopted several innovations.

Current machines are programmed in a Windows-based operating environment allowing a network of up to 32 printers to be controlled from a remote PC. Up to 100 pre-recorded codes, bar codes, logos and other graphics can automatically be stored. The print format can incorporate a wide diversity of

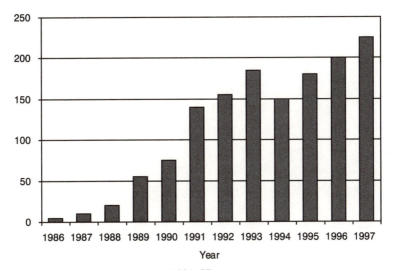

Figure 15.3 LINX employment growth 1986–97

designs, including sequential numbers and text, in a character height range from 0.8 to 25 mm. Printers can be connected to in-line weighers and counters in the production flow and automatically mark the product accordingly. The company has also developed, in house, a comprehensive range of specialist inks and solvents to meet the specialist needs of demanding users in the food, beverages, toiletries and pharmaceutical industries.

In 1997, a laser beam print system was introduced into the LINX product line. Lasers remain preferable to CIJ printers in some very precise applications. Laser technology until recently has been too expensive in relation to inkjet printing. However, while a laser is still of an order of twice the cost of a CIJ unit, the ability to use this technology to etch a mark at an accuracy of an order higher than an inkjet represents an important contemporary development. Fortuitously, the software control systems developed by LINX, which currently direct and focus the inkjet flow can readily be adapted to guide a laser beam.

Index